Mike's uplift has been a real bles
the prayer he has composed hour
I need to share and verbalize to the Lord that very same day.
prayer is unique, but they all are choice, intimate words that connect
us to our Creator God.

> Rev. Dr. Mike James
> Pastor

Having read and prayed Dr. Mike Powers's prayers almost daily for
several years, I am truly amazed how often they are on point with
what my heart has been feeling and what my voice has been unable
to articulate. Mike is gifted from the Holy Spirit with the ability to
sense what his fellow "pilgrims" feel, desire, and have experienced
(in spite of the fact that he has most likely never had most of those
exact needs and struggles himself), and also includes powerful prayers
of inspiration and challenge for the church universal. He is able to
humbly express these prayers and praises from his heart and they
touch my own heart with uncanny timing on a regular basis.

> Ms. Katherine Patat Crook
> Banker

We are not alone in these anxious times we are living. Dr. Mike
Powers's timely daily prayers came on time to inspire me and uplift
my inner being. At times, I felt as if he knew what I was going through.
You will find this book as a fresh rain in the early spring. Breathe
deeply! Listen to the soothing voice of God's healing hand. May each
prayer propel you to God's divine destiny today!

> Rev. Dr. Eliseo Mejia-Leiva
> Pastor

Mike's daily prayers are truly a gift. Christ is always at the heart of
what he writes. And as a result, those prayers take us straight to him—
with a fresh, clear call to enter into a deeper commitment and a more
meaningful walk with Jesus.

> Dr. Nevil Speer
> Beef Industry Consultant

I so greatly appreciate Mike Powers for the daily Pastor's Uplifts. They are a wonderful start to my day. In the midst of what is often a very busy and chaotic schedule, these Pastor's Uplifts help me to slow down, catch my breath, recalibrate my spirit to God's Word, and confidently launch into my day! So very relevant, insightful, and encouraging!

> Rev. Charles Young
> Spirit Anew Ministries

Dr. Powers's ability to articulate prayers is so evident. He captures our moments in life, prepares us as we approach his throne, and plunges our souls into the very depths of God's heart.

> Rev. Dr. Quentin Scholtz
> Pastor

I have read Mike's Pastor's Uplifts from the very beginning. Mike and I were in youth group together as teens. His Uplifts are a blessing in my daily walk.

> Ms. Sue Holtzclaw Coyle
> Elementary School Teacher

There is a yearning in all of us for a deeper connection with Father, Son, and Holy Spirit. I experience that deeper connection in the prayers that Mike shares so humbly in love. It allows me to pause and reconnect into that depth of love that only Father, Son, and Holy Spirit can bring to the souls that seek and share.

> Rev. Jerri Williams
> Pastor

I have looked forward to this book for a long time! Mike's prayers acknowledge many of the prayer concerns of my heart and guide me to think more deeply about them, to feel that hunger for a closer relationship with God, and to always include praise and thanksgiving in prayer. Somehow Mike's daily scriptures and prayers are always relevant to my situation and often are exactly what I needed for that day! Mike has always taught us not just with words but by example, and his humble servant heart comes through in these prayers. This book of prayers will be a blessing for anyone seeking a stronger relationship with God.

Dr. Ruth Ann Shepherd
Neonatal-Perinatal Medicine

The most exciting thought for me about the Rev. Dr. Mike Powers's book is it is the work of a shepherd. In all ages, our shepherd's words carry us to the safest place in eternity.

Dr. Ron Smith
President, Francis Asbury Society

Pastor Powers's wonderful devotionals prompt moments of quiet and reflection in my noisy and busy day. They offer impactful and eloquent reminders of what matters most: God's eternal love. I come away feeling humbled, encouraged, and with a renewed sense of purpose.

Dr. Sevan Terzian
Professor, University of Florida

These prayers have become an important part of my devotional life. Though Mike's prayers are deeply personal, they are both timeless, in that they are built on a solid theological foundation, and timely as they share a Spirit-filled faith in the midst of these troubled times.

Rev. Mark B. Girard
Pastor

PRAYERS
for the
JOURNEY

MIKE POWERS

PRAYERS
for the
JOURNEY

MIKE POWERS

Francis Asbury Press
Wilmore, Kentucky

Cover design by D. Curtis Hale.

Prayers for the Journey by Mike Powers
Published by The Francis Asbury Society
ISBN 978-0-915143-40-5
Printed in the United States of America

To order this book, go to www.francisasburysociety.com or contact:
PO Box 7
Wilmore, KY 40390-0007
859-858-4222
800-530-5673
fas@francisasburysociety.com

To Audrey and Elizabeth:

*So you can pray with Mimi and
Papa all along your journey*

FORWARD

I have been blessed to be one of Mike Powers's friends on our journey of faith. Over the years his prayers have been a daily part of my life, prompting me to stop and pray with him. His faithful ministry of prayer has enriched my life and called me to engage in this paramount discipline of Christian living.

Prayer is a means of grace. While not a sacrament, prayer is, along with Scripture and fasting, what we Wesleyans call an instituted means of grace commanded by Christ.

John Wesley discussed the importance of prayer in his sermon, "The Means of Grace," by quoting Matthew 7:7–8, "Ask and it will be given you; seek and you will find; knock and the door will be opened to you. For everyone who asks receives; the one who seeks finds; and to the one who knocks, the door will be opened."

Wesley was convinced that prayer was a critical part of an ongoing relationship between the believer and God. Without the relationship, the words are hollow. Prayer is communication where the one praying is often transformed. These prayers by Mike Powers open the door for us to stop, reflect, and change as we seek to be formed by Christ.

In his sermon, "Upon our Lord's Sermon on the Mount," Wesley said:

> So that the end of your praying is not to inform God, as though he knew not your wants already; but rather to inform yourselves, to fix the sense of your continual dependence on him who only is able to supply all your wants. It is not so much to move God—who is always more ready to give than you to ask—as to move yourselves, that you may be willing and ready to receive the good things he has prepared for you.

Wesley considered prayer as central to our spiritual lives as breathing is to our physical lives. We are all indebted to Mike Powers for helping us to breathe deeply in our relationship with God.

Bishop G. Lindsey Davis
United Methodist Church

INTRODUCTION

Traditionally, the Divine Office is a focus on daily services of morning prayer and evening prayer, usually following some kind of guided liturgical formulary like *The Book of Common Prayer*. Thus, the "office of prayer" is the practice of committing the day to prayer, orienting all of the activities of the day in and through prayer.

In March 2015, a small group in our church participated in a study of Peter Scazzero's book, *Emotionally Healthy Spirituality*. Included in our weekly discussions of emotional health and contemplative spirituality was "The Daily Office," a prayer guide that offered a structure for two offices of prayer per day from Monday to Friday. Most in our class were not familiar with the term "office" regarding prayer. However, at the conclusion of our eight-week study, class members found these prayers to be very helpful in establishing a regular prayer time each day. They asked if I would continue providing daily prayers for them, and so began a weekday prayer ministry I entitled "Pastor's Uplift." Over the past six years, friends and colleagues have requested and received these prayers through email and Facebook.

The purpose of these prayers is simply to create a moment each day for pilgrims on the journey to spiritual wholeness to experience God's presence. Many have commented that they read and pray these prayers first thing every morning. Others prefer to pray at the end of the day. Pastor friends have shared how they have found these prayers helpful as they prepare and offer the pastoral prayer in worship services. Seekers also are thoughtfully reading these prayers as a regular conversation with God. Others often ask permission to share these in a variety of ways, and my standard answer is that once these prayers leave my computer, they belong to everyone. We are on this journey together.

One of the clearest patterns of spiritual journey is found in the Old Testament story of the Exodus. God provided a cloud during the day to guide the Hebrew people and a pillar of fire at night to give them light so they could travel day or night through the Sinai desert and finally into the Promised Land of Canaan. Along their way, God intervened in moments of miraculous deliverance and provision, but it was in crisis moments that God demanded them to walk by faith in obedience. Deuteronomy 6:23, "He brought us out from there [Egypt] to bring us in [to Canaan]...." They were People of the Way on a spiritual Journey.

The journey of the Jewish people 3,400 years ago is not just interesting biblical history. It is a picture of the Christian life. It is not just *their* story, it is *my* story and *your* story, *your* journey and *my* journey. *Their* journey helps us to understand *our* journeys.

Prayers for the Journey is a book of prayers to help Christian pilgrims understand, embrace, and enjoy the blessings of spiritual wholeness amid the challenges and complexities that confront followers of Jesus on the Way. Every prayer is not for everyone, but some prayers the reader may want to share with others. Like the Psalms, we will pray the prayers of others and for others, hoping that others likewise are praying our prayers with us and for us. Generally, each week of prayers is designed to begin with praise and preparation, followed by personal petition and confession, intercession and supplication, and then miscellaneous prayers at the end of the week. Scripture references are provided not to "pray scripture" (which is a wonderful approach to prayer) but to anchor the prayer of each day firmly in the bedrock of God's Word.

I am indebted to many who inspired, encouraged, and coached me in developing this book of prayers. My wife, Sherry, has listened to my thoughts, offered valuable insights into the text and context of these prayers, and tolerated my use of the kitchen table as my writing desk. My colleague Stan Key introduced me to the "map of salvation" as a metaphor of journey in our Christian experience of walking humbly with God (Micah 6:8). The recipients of these daily prayers over the years often have responded with commentary and helpful suggestions. I also am indebted to classic and contemporary Christian leaders whose written prayers were the model and inspiration of assisting other pilgrims to practice a daily office of prayer. The careful reader will recognize the influence and insights of several of my personal instructors in the school of prayer including Augustine, Thomas Aquinas, St. Francis, John Wesley, John Baillie, Oswald Chambers, John Killinger, Rueben P. Job, Kenneth G. Phifer, and the Book of Common Prayer. I gained a deeper understanding and appreciation of written prayers as a means of praying with others, learning how to pray through the prayers of others, and the value of preserving prayers for future generations (Revelation 8:3–4).

My prayer is that this book of prayers will be a daily "uplift" as a helpful companion as you walk with God on your journey to spiritual wholeness. "And your ears shall hear a word behind you, saying, 'This is the way; walk in it,' when you turn to the right or when your turn to the left" (Isaiah 30:21 ESV).

Mike Powers
June 2021
Lexington, Kentucky

WEEK ONE

DAY 1

The LORD had said to Abram, "Go from your country, your people and your father's household to the land I will show you. I will make you a great nation, and I will bless you; I will make your name great, and you will be a blessing. I will bless those who bless you, and whoever curses you I will curse; and all peoples on earth will be blessed through you." So Abram went as the LORD had told him.... (Genesis 12:1–4a)

We dare not miss those moments, O God, when you speak. Day by day you are unfolding your divine purpose for all eternity, and in those rare moments, you speak directly into our lives in ways we can discern, understand, and obey. The greatest regrets in our lives are when you have spoken, and we listened to voices other than yours. May we learn from your servant Abraham what you desire of us as your friends on this journey: full surrender to you and your full possession of us. Thank you that you are diligent to seek us out along the way and patient with us when we sometimes wander away. Jesus, we have heard your call: "Follow me." May we be diligent in our obedience to your voice and patient as we have much to learn. So let us begin. Amen.

DAY 2

I have promised to bring you up out of your misery in Egypt into... a land flowing with milk and honey. (Exodus 3:17)

O God, we confess that the deepest cry of our hearts is to come home. You fashioned our hearts so that we are restless—homesick—until we find our rest in you. Your people could never feel at home in Egypt, a place overshadowed by pain, bondage, and fear. In the far country we are oppressed, powerless, hopeless, and desolate. Yet in your great mercy you come to us in our misery to create a desire for something more, something satisfying, something fulfilling. You speak into that dissatisfaction and hopelessness, causing every restless, homesick heart to want to leave the comfort and security of the familiar, as unsatisfying as it is, and launch out on a journey of faith toward spiritual wholeness. We will not begin that journey toward you and with you unless the pain of staying where we are becomes greater than the pain of moving where you want us to be. We don't want to stay in Egypt, Lord, continuing to be victims, enslaved by addictions, bound by unhealthy appetites, resigned to the lie that there is no hope, no way out, nothing better than this. We are ready to take the first steps toward spiritual wholeness. Show us the way, Lord. Show us the way home. Amen.

DAY 3

The LORD will fight for you; you need only to be still. (Exodus 14:14)

O God, we come to faith and choose to follow you on this journey in various ways and different timetables. For all of us, it all begins with a decisive step forward at a specific moment in time. But like the Hebrews, enslaved in Egypt, it takes more than good intentions for us to get out of bondage. You first must do for us what we cannot do for ourselves. By grace, your Word came to the people and Pharaoh through Moses. By grace, you saved your people through the blood of the Passover Lamb. By grace, the children of Israel were delivered from the hand of Pharaoh through the waters of the Red Sea. By grace, where there was no way you made a way. In the fullness of time, you sent your Son, Jesus, into our world of space and time, taking on our flesh and blood, suffering our pain and bearing our sin as the Lamb of God so that through his atoning sacrifice we might experience your saving, redeeming grace. Against all odds, with no way out, Jesus made the way forward for us. And so, we step forward obediently and thankfully, believing that your grace is sufficient for our salvation. Amen.

Day 4

See, I am doing a new thing! Now it springs up; do you
not perceive it? I am making a way in the wilderness
and streams in the wasteland. (Isaiah 43:19)

O Lord, we know all too well that wilderness experiences are
included on our spiritual itinerary. Clearly, you led the children of
Israel out of Egypt and into the "University of the Desert" where they
learned to trust you for daily provisions. You gave them the Law to
teach and transform them into the unique witness of your character to
all the world. But it also was where they were tested, tried, and tempted
to resist, rebel, and reject your way out of fear and unbelief. Even after
experiencing your mighty salvation at the Red Sea and daily provision
of their needs, many hardened their hearts, doubted your goodness
and wandered aimlessly in the desert for thirty-eight more years.
Their story is our story. We are learning that desert experiences are
necessary on our journey to spiritual wholeness. Having experienced
the great joy and hope in the redeeming grace of Jesus Christ, we, too,
encounter bumps in the road, detours, delays, and disappointments.
We, too, are tempted to lose heart and consider that old life before
Christ was better than this. The desert is inevitable on the journey, but
that is where you shape us into a people worthy of your holy name.
Come what may, Lord, I choose you and the better way. Amen.

Day 5

Therefore, since the promise of entering his rest still stands, let us let us be
careful that none of you be found to have fallen short of it. (Hebrews 4:1)

F aithful and loving God, you delivered your people out of bondage
in Egypt and from the armies of Pharaoh through the Red Sea.
You provided for them in the wilderness and led them to Mt. Sinai
where you gave Words to shape them into a holy nation. Your desire
was to fulfill the covenant promise given Abraham, to establish them
in their own land, where they would be blessed to be a blessing to the
entire world. At the Jordan River, where they could see the Promised

Land, flowing with milk and honey, they were faced with a decision: trust you to make a way forward or shrink back in fear and unbelief. You grieved that in that moment of truth, they refused to continue the journey. Their hard hearts revealed that although they were out of Egypt, Egypt was not out of them. You still desire fully devoted hearts that love you without rival; fully surrendered hearts to the One who not only delivers us from slavery to our sins but also is able to save us from the power of sin; fully trusting hearts that are open to the Spirit to lead and provide all that is necessary for the journey. O Lord, in this moment of truth, we choose to leave the spiritual wastelands of the desert, go forward in faith, and follow you into the Promised Land of spiritual wholeness. Amen.

Day 6

He brought us out... to bring us in.... (Deuteronomy 6:23)

Thank you, O Lord, for being our faithful Companion all along our journeys. After forty years of wandering in the desert, your children finally believed and found you faithful when they stepped into the Jordan River before the waters parted, and you made a way forward. They were ready for their inheritance in the Land of Promise, but they also realized there is more to the journey. There still were battles to be fought, crops to plant, families to be raised, cities to build, and a nation to develop. Yes, Canaan was the Promised Land, but you did not intend for Canaan to be the end of the journey; it was the beginning of a whole new life, full of purpose and promise and power. You are teaching us as well that the promise revealed in this map of salvation is the ability, by the saving and sanctifying grace of Jesus Christ, to confront the challenges and complexities of life with spiritual victory, to live a life characterized by the self-giving love of Jesus and the fruitfulness of the Holy Spirit, and to be content, spiritually at rest, abiding in the peace of Christ which passes all understanding. Thank you, Lord, for the reality of living victorious, fruitful, and restful lives as we walk with you day by day. With glad and grateful hearts for this journey to spiritual wholeness we pray in Jesus' name. Amen.

DAY 7

Therefore, my dear friends, as you have always obeyed—not only in my presence, but now much more in my absence—continue to work out your salvation with fear and trembling, for it is God who works in you to will and to act in order to fulfill his good purpose. (Philippians 2:12–13)

As we continue on this long obedience in the same direction, Lord, we pray for patience as you show us how to work out this high calling of a holy life in every detail of our lives. Responding to your invitation to follow you as disciples was a decision that began to shape every other decision in our lives. Eventually we come to that moment of truth when we realize you demand unconditional surrender, a single-minded devotion to your will and purposes in our lives. You make us sensitive to things that never concerned us. You stir a restlessness in us where we previously were complacent and rather satisfied. You deepen our love for others and matters that demand more of us than we previously were willing to give. You place within us a passion to be spiritually whole. Grant us patience, Lord, as we experience and express sanctifying grace in the everyday stuff of life. As we continue on this journey together, may Christ be fully formed in us for your sake and for the sake of your kingdom. Amen.

WEEK TWO

DAY 1

May the grace of the Lord Jesus Christ, and the love of God, and the fellowship of the Holy Spirit be with you all. (2 Corinthians 13:14)

O Lord, our Lord, how majestic is your name in the all the earth! Your greatness gives me courage. Your mercy fills me with hope. Your truth sets me free. Your glory lifts my heart. When I feel lost, uncertain, confused, and afraid, you are with me. When I feel empty, tired, beaten down, and discouraged, you raise me up. I praise you, Father, for the life we share now and the promise to spend eternity with all who love you. I praise you, Jesus, for laying down your life that we might be delivered from the power that divides our hearts, alienates us from others, and separates us from you. I praise you, Spirit, that in a world of darkness, disappointment, and death, we can live this day in the radiance of joy, the beauty of holiness, and the reality of hope. May all praise and honor and glory and blessing and power and majesty be yours, Father, Son, and Holy Spirit, now and forever. Amen.

DAY 2

You have searched me, LORD, and you know me. You know when I sit and when I rise; you perceive my thoughts from afar. You discern my going out and my lying down; you are familiar with all my ways. (Psalm 139:1–3)

O Lord, if I may be granted one answer to prayer on this spiritual journey, let it be that I may live with a greater awareness that you are nearer than the things I touch, the things I see, the voices I hear, or the people I meet. I am asking for blessed assurance that you abide in me and I in you. Your Presence in my life makes all the difference in who I am and how I live and what I become. Let me live every day in this hope so that I do not become overly anxious about things that do not matter and matters over which I have no control. Fill me, Holy Spirit. Guide me, inspire me, comfort me, and direct me to share generously with others what you have graciously given me. In the name of the One who came into our world of space and time that we might live forever in his kingdom. Amen.

DAY 3

Yet this I call to mind and therefore I have hope: Because of the LORD's great love we are not consumed, for his compassions never fail. They are new every morning; great is your faithfulness. (Lamentations 3:21–23)

Morning by morning, new mercies I see, O Lord, for great is your faithfulness. By your mercy, you have brought me to this moment in my life. I look back and thank you for all you have done, for all you have provided, and for your companionship all along my journey. I look forward to all that lies ahead, holding firm to your

Presence to be with me, your power to give me strength, and your promise that my hope in you will not be disappointed. This morning I renew my commitment to be open to your perfect will, to embrace the possibilities of grace, and to be a channel of steadfast love and faithfulness to all I meet. With hope reawakened and mercies refreshed at the dawning of this new day, I rise to give honor, glory, and praise to your holy name. Amen.

DAY 4

Even though I walk through the darkest valley, I will fear no evil, for you are with me; your rod and your staff, they comfort me. (Psalm 23:4)

Lord Jesus, I don't understand why bad things happen to good people, good things happen to ungodly people, and many sincere prayers go unanswered. I try to make sense of it all as I think of so many whose world of happiness and hope has been shattered by sudden tragedies and calamities. I grieve with every report of an abused child or a loved one dying alone. Truthfully, there are many times I have more questions than answers, more concerns than confidence. But this I know, and therefore, I have hope: You have wept with the hurting and broken-hearted. You have suffered our grief and carried our sorrows. When all the stories of earth are told, of war and famine and disease and suffering, we will live forever in the glory of your story. You have loved us from the beginning of time. You know how fragile we are. You came into our world of space and time, took on our flesh and blood, bore our sins, died our death, and were raised to new life to give us hope and a future. Your steadfast love endures forever, including this day and this season. Therefore, I choose to continue on this journey with you, pressing on through these shadows of doubt and disappointment. In spite of the contradictions, your strength is found at the point of my weakness, your love consoles me in the depth of my despair, and your peace sustains me when I do not understand. Draw near, Lord Jesus. I need you today. Amen.

DAY 5

If my people, who are called by my name, will humble
themselves and pray and seek my face and turn from their
wicked ways, then will I hear from heaven, and I will forgive
their sin and will heal their land. (2 Chronicles 7:14)

Gracious and loving God, long ago you saved your people from
bondage and delivered them into a land of freedom, hope, and
opportunity. This morning, we pray for all who are in bondage and
longing with hope to be free. We pray for mothers and fathers whose
greatest desire is a better life for their children. We pray for leaders
to have wisdom to understand, courage to embrace righteousness,
compassion to act justly, and humility to confess their sin. We pray
for the restoration of civil discourse that will create a community of
respect and enable us to speak the truth in love. We pray that the Spirit
of Truth will convict us of the hatred that divides us and convince us
to fall on our knees and seek your face and turn from our wicked ways
that perhaps you will have mercy on us and forgive our sin and heal
our land. This we pray for your sake and for the sake of all you love, in
Jesus' name. Amen.

DAY 6

That if you confess with your mouth, "Jesus is Lord," and believe in your
heart that God raised him from the dead, you will be saved. (Romans 10:9)

Lord Jesus, we confess that we do not always embrace the gospel.
We have heard the message time and again, yet we have not
responded faithfully. We know we need you, but we don't know
how much we need you. We want to turn away from empty phrases
and worn-out platitudes. You alone are Lord and Savior. Forgive us
when we have closed off our hearts instead of allowing them to break
over the things that break your heart. Forgive us when we have said
nothing in order to avoid saying the wrong thing. Forgive us when we
have deferred to the opinion of others rather than being a bold witness
of truth and grace. We need your salvation, redemption, and healing
because we have been hurt and because we have hurt others. Help us

to live into your full salvation so that we can freely share your holy love and healing grace with those who are hurt, those who have gone astray, and those who are longing for home. We choose to follow you, Jesus, for you have the words of eternal life. Amen.

DAY 7

He got up, rebuked the wind and said to the waves, "Quiet! Be still!" Then the wind died down and it was completely calm. (Mark 4:39)

O Lord, you are the calm voice in the midst of uneasy silence. You are Light when darkness is overwhelming. You are Presence when loneliness is unbearable. You are Strength when arms are too weary and knees too feeble. You are a Friend when others abandon and betray us. You are Truth when chaos and confusion rule the day. You are all of these things and much, much more. You are God, and we are not. How we must grieve your Spirit when we complain that we are clueless, that things are hopeless, that we feel abandoned, that we just can't go on, and that we are standing on sinking sand. In such moments, Lord, help us to pause to listen for that calm voice, to look for that Light, to feel such a Presence, to find such Strength, to reach out to such a Friend, to embrace the Truth that sets us free. Remind us that every hair on our heads is numbered and we need not be afraid, for you are the gracious Savior of our souls and the sovereign Lord of our lives. That is enough. Thank you, Jesus. Amen.

WEEK THREE

DAY 1

For the eyes of the LORD range throughout the earth to strengthen those whose hearts are fully committed to him. (2 Chronicles 16:9a)

Thank you, O God, for this day of awakening and renewal—for awakening my mind to your Presence and renewing your Spirit within me. I pray that throughout this day I will recognize glory moments and embrace the possibilities of your saving and sanctifying grace. I pray that I will be sensitive to your voice that I may hear words of guidance and correction, assurance and hope, comfort and peace. And I pray that your Presence and power will be evident in my words, actions, and the meditation of my heart. For the sake of your kingdom and all you love, I pray in the holy name of Jesus. Amen.

DAY 2

This, then, is how you should pray: "Our Father in heaven, hallowed be your name, your kingdom come, your will be done, on earth as it is in heaven. Give us today our daily bread. And forgive us our debts, as we also have forgiven our debtors. And lead us not into temptation, but deliver us from the evil one." (Matthew 6:9–13)

Lord Jesus, teach me to pray as you taught your disciples to pray. Help me to be still and wait on you until my heart overflows in wonder, love, and praise. May I long for your kingdom to come and your will to be done more than anything else. I want to learn to ask simply for the things I truly need, not what I think I must have. I need to pray with conviction lest I be tossed about by the tyranny of the urgent, the seduction of Siren voices, and the disruption of circumstances. Receiving mercy, I want to be merciful to all, especially to those who have offended me. And so, I pause at the first of this new day with my heart set on your kingdom, believing that you have the power to make it a reality in this world as it is in Heaven. May that glorious thought bring praise to my lips, joy to my heart, purpose in every endeavor, and a keen sense of anticipation throughout the day. For yours are the kingdom and the power and the glory, today, every day, and forever. Hallelujah and amen.

DAY 3

In him the whole building is joined together and rises to become a
holy temple in the Lord. And in him you too are being built together to
become a dwelling in which God lives by his Spirit. (Ephesians 2:21–22)

I am discovering, O Lord, that life in the Spirit frees me from the confines of my prejudices and self-centeredness and opens my mind to the possibilities of your grace. "The life I now live in the body, I live by faith in the Son of God, who loved me and gave himself for me" (Galatians 2:20). I gladly embrace such grace, and therefore I am no longer content in resisting and rejecting others, turning a blind eye to their needs, pretending not to see their pain, or closing my ears to their cries for help. I understand better that I am created for and capable of so much more than what comes naturally—I am being re-created into your handiwork for your divine purposes. Guard my heart, O Lord, that all along the journey toward spiritual wholeness I may be faithful, graceful, and fruitful as your Spirit-filled, Spirit-led servant. For your sake and for the sake of all you love, I pray in Jesus' name. Amen.

DAY 4

For the revelation awaits an appointed time; it speaks of the
end and will not prove false; Though it linger, wait for it; it
will certainly come and will not delay. (Habakkuk 2:3)

I believe with all my heart, Lord Jesus, that there will be a day when every knee will bow and every tongue confess that you alone are Lord. Between that day and today, I want to believe that there is a divine purpose unfolding and holy power is at work beyond my understanding. Forgive my moments of doubt that limit my confidence that you, the Good Shepherd who cares and provides for his flock, are leading me. Help me to trust you day by day, step by step, moment by moment, that all that is right and true and good is revealed in your perfect timing. May I leave the burdens of tomorrow with you today, my Savior and Friend. I can bear only what you expect of me each day, and I thank you, for that is enough and all you ask of me. And so, I pray that you will open my mind that I may embrace eternal truth and my heart that I may be embraced by perfect love, for the sake of your kingdom and all that you love. Amen.

DAY 5

"You will keep in perfect peace those whose minds are steadfast, because they trust in you." (Isaiah 26:3)

You hear all of our voices as we pray this morning, O God. Some of us are lonely and are longing for a friend. Many are calling out of hurt and ask for healing. Others are confused and looking for direction. Some are compassionate and are praying on behalf of others. Many are full of praise and thanksgiving, offering you their joy. Others are desperate and are not sure how to pray. Some wonder if they should bother to pray or what they should say in a time like this. I add my words to these many voices, Lord Jesus, as I come into your holy presence. My praise joins the praise of others. My prayers for healing and help are lifted along with the others. Come, Holy Spirit. Take control of our hearts and minds. Make us sensitive to others, embracing their needs and sharing their burdens. As we turn from the quiet to enter a busy day, may we hear your voice in every moment of the day. Amen.

DAY 6

How precious to me are your thoughts, God! How vast is the sum of them! Were I to count them, they would outnumber the grains of sand.... (Psalm 139:17–18a)

Lord Jesus, there are times when we feel terribly alone and forgotten. We know in our hearts that your love is stronger than a loving mother, that you promise never to leave or forsake us, that your thoughts are continuously on us, and that we will never be forgotten. Save us from believing anything less than we are your children and forever in your love. Protect us where we are so vulnerable to negativism, prone to discouragement, and susceptible to fear. Help us believe that you know our troubles, understand our need, and are willing and able to act on our behalf. For yours is the kingdom, and the power, and the glory forever and ever, and that includes all that concerns every one of us. Thank you and amen.

Day 7

But we ought always to thank God for you, brothers and sisters loved by the Lord, because from the beginning God chose you as firstfruits to be saved through the sanctifying work of the Spirit and through belief in the truth. (2 Thessalonians 2:13)

Lord Jesus, thank you for your patience and never-ending love even when we feel unworthy. Thank you for your messengers who convey such patience, standing with us when we make a mess of our lives, sitting down with us when our hearts are broken, not quitting on us even when we let them down. Thank you for your servants who reach out every day with such compassion to the spiritually lost, the desperately lonely, and the disregarded least among us. Thank you for all your disciples who, with surrendered hearts, deny themselves, take up crosses daily and follow you wherever and whenever and to whomever a witness of grace is needed. Such were those whose patience and love introduced us to you, Lord Jesus, Lover of our souls. Thank you that yours is the unshakable kingdom that has no end and the immeasurable love that will never be exhausted. Amen.

WEEK FOUR

Day 1

I rejoiced with those who said to me, "Let us go to the house of the LORD." (Psalm 122:1)

O God, I thank you today for the covenant relationship and fellowship in Christ we enjoy as the Church; for the faith tradition that has been lived and passed down throughout the ages; for students and Sunday School teachers, pastors and mission workers, schools and seminaries who love and share your Word; for the Holy Spirit working over us and in us and through us for your eternal purposes; for bringing us closer to one another and closer to your divine plan to redeem the world with the gospel of Jesus Christ. Today, I pray that I will be more open, more surrendered, more giving, more available, and more loving to all for whom you gave your only Son. May I weep with those who weep, laugh with those whose joy overflows, and embrace those with troubled souls. And let me not love only those who love me, but also those who are indifferent and may even despise me. I humbly pray in the strong name of Jesus, believing that you are able and willing and ready to do immeasurably more than we can ask or imagine according to the mighty power of the Spirit at work in us. Amen.

DAY 2

Very truly I tell you, whoever believes in me will do the works
I have been doing, and they will do even greater things than
these, because I am going to the Father. (John 14:12)

There is your work, Lord, and there is my work, but it seems that I am consistently anxious that my work is never done while you patiently and deliberately go about your work. Jesus, I want your prayer to become my daily prayer: "My food is to do the will of him who sent me and to finish his work" (John 4:34). That sounds so right and so good. May I seek to do your will, O Lord, with an undivided heart, and in so doing I shall make my work your work and be at peace. May it be so, to the honor and glory of your holy name. Amen.

DAY 3

Now the Lord is Spirit, and where the Spirit of the Lord is, there is
freedom. And we all, who with unveiled faces contemplate the Lord's
glory, are being transformed into his image with ever-increasing glory,
which comes from the Lord, who is the Spirit. (2 Corinthians 3:17–18)

Holy and loving God, I praise you for I am fearfully and wonderfully made. You fashion the unique dreams of my soul. You place within me the delights of my heart. I do not know all that lies deep within my spirit, but you have created me for yourself, and I am never satisfied apart from you. There is more to life than I have known, more to love than I have explored, more faith than I have dared to exercise, and more beauty than I have ever imagined. O Lord, release me from the anxieties that bind my soul. Free me from the fears that enslave me. Save me from the sin that tempts me. Help me to trust what I profess to know and act boldly on what I believe: that you are the God of grace, and therefore, there is always hope; that because of Jesus, I am loved and forgiven, and therefore capable of loving and forgiving; that you know me better than I know myself, and therefore, I can pray freely about anything and everything; that I am a child of God who is uniquely created and gifted for divine reasons, and therefore I will live my life with purpose today. Wherever your Spirit is, there is freedom. O how I pray that my liberated spirit may soar today, easily praising you and joyfully sharing this life in the Spirit with those for whom Jesus gave his life. In his strong and wonderful name I pray. Amen.

DAY 4

And you, my son Solomon, acknowledge the God of your father, and serve him with wholehearted devotion and with a willing mind, for the LORD searches every heart and understands every desire and every thought..... (1 Chronicles 28:9a)

O Lord, you see and know all things. Give me grace today to see you more clearly and know you more dearly, and in knowing you I may know myself even as I am known. Give me today some clear vision of my life as you intend for me to be. Show me my smallness so I may be in awe of your infinite greatness. Show me my fallenness so I understand my need of your righteousness. Show me my lack of love so I can repent and ask for the fullness of your divine love. Show me that I can take refuge in your goodness, as needy as I am, abiding in your forgiving love. Cause my thoughts today to dwell much less on myself and much more on the amazing grace and redeeming love of our Savior, Jesus Christ, in whose name I pray. Amen.

DAY 5

Those who trust in the LORD are like Mount Zion, which cannot be
shaken but endures forever. As the mountains surround Jerusalem, so
the LORD surrounds his people both now and forever. (Psalm 125:1–2)

Thank you, Jesus, for being with us in our saddest moments and
our happiest days. You know our deepest heartaches and share
our greatest joys. You go with us through the valley of the shadows
when fear is so near, and you never leave us when faith is distant
and doubt is so strong. There are moments when your Presence is so
real and our self-interests are so irrelevant. There are days when we
are consumed by uncertainty and other days when we sing songs of
blessed assurance. O Lord, Lover of our souls, teach us to walk in what
we hope rather than what we fear. May your Presence be the delight of
our souls. May heaven be the reality by which we measure all else in
our world. May trust overcome doubt, and may we learn to pray with
greater hope. May we discover our life together in you today is the life
you desire for us to share forever. May we understand the times and
know what to do for the sake of your kingdom and all that you love.
You are the Lord of all, even in the shadows and shadowy days. By
your death we are saved; in your Presence we have hope. Now and
forever. Amen.

DAY 6

Then you will call upon me and come and pray to me, and
I will listen to you. You will seek me and find me when you
seek me with all your heart. (Jeremiah 29:12–13)

Lord Jesus, I want to praise you this morning, but how do I begin?
All kinds of wandering and random thoughts cross my mind as I
try to pray. This is one of those days when it seems that I cannot sort
out what is important, what is necessary, or even what is next. Where
do I begin? Do my prayers affect world peace, national politics, church
conflict? How do I pray for the sick and the suffering, the homeless
and the helpless, the lonely and the lost? Here I am again, wanting
to pray, needing to pray, and ready to pray. So, please teach me how

to pray as you taught your disciples to pray. I must not pray with well-rehearsed phrases, but in the Spirit, where even wandering and random thoughts can lead me into a deeper fellowship with you. Yes, this is where I am, Jesus, so let us begin. Amen.

DAY 7

"Call to me and I will answer you and will tell you great and hidden things that you do not know." (Jeremiah 33:3)

I greet you this morning, my Lord and my God, thankful for restoring my soul and body through the night. I praise you for mercies renewed again today and for your faithfulness even when I am thankless. As I begin this day, I lay all the cares that weigh heavily on my heart before you, trusting in your forgiving love, healing grace, and comforting presence. Make me keenly aware of others, of the sights and sounds of the world around me, and of your Spirit who is here to comfort and counsel. Show me how I can be a servant to those whom you love and who need me today. Give me courage to follow faithfully wherever you lead and strength to do whatever is required. Convince me that I can do more than I could ever ask, think or imagine by the power of your grace at work in me. May your peace rule in my heart, and I will be thankful. May this be one of the most amazing days of my life for your sake and for the sake of all you love I pray, in Jesus' name. Amen.

WEEK FIVE

DAY 1

"This is the day the LORD has made; We will rejoice and be glad in it." (Psalm 118:24 NKJV)

Thank You, O God, for another day filled with possibilities of grace, renewed mercies, and boundless hope. This day also will be filled with your Presence; you are here, and you will be there. Thank you for every gift that will be enjoyed today: the community of faith, the comfort of home, the joy of work, the love of friends, the laughter of children, the wisdom of the aged, the beauty of music, the smiles of strangers, the gift of life. But we also pray for those who are in harm's way, threatened by circumstances beyond their control and helpless to improve their lives. Abide with those who are ill and all whose hearts are broken. Make your Word clear to us that we may know your will and understand your heart and respond with compassion and courage. Fill us with your Spirit so that all to whom Jesus is a stranger will see in our witness the possibilities of grace, renewed mercies, and boundless hope. This we pray for the sake of all you love, in the strong name of Jesus. Amen.

Day 2

In the morning, LORD, you hear my voice; in the morning I lay
my requests before you and wait expectantly. (Psalm 5:3)

In the beauty and stillness of this morning, O God, I feel your Presence. Thank you for being near. Before I begin the day, I ask for a fresh anointing of your Spirit for it will become difficult to feel you near during the ordinariness of this day. There will be much that will trouble my soul, challenge my faith, try my patience, and test my resolve. I will work under stress and possibly be misunderstood and fail in my good intentions. Yet, practicing your Presence, moment by moment, I am confident that your grace is more than sufficient and your peace is deeper than my greatest need. And so, I rise with assurance that all I need to do today will be possible through Christ whose strength is made perfect in my weakness. This I pray in his holy name. Amen.

Day 3

Follow God's example, therefore, as dearly loved children and walk in the way of love, just as Christ loved us and gave himself up for us as a fragrant offering and sacrifice to God. (Ephesians 5:1–2)

This, I believe, Lord Jesus: My life is never without direction or purpose, for you are the Way, and you direct my path. My uncertainty is my own; my way is clear to you, for you are the Truth. In you I live and move and have my being, for you are the Life. Help me to remember that you work through me better when I am still and know that you are God. I can walk patiently, deliberately, steadily on this spiritual journey day after day, for you are the Author and Finisher of my faith. And so, yes! I believe that I can do all things required of me in the strength of your grace at work in my life. May whatever I do today in word or deed, privately or publicly, be miracle-work, eternal-work, satisfying-work, for your sake and for the sake of your kingdom. Amen.

Day 4

Trust in the LORD with all your heart and lean not on your own understanding; in all your ways submit to him, and he will make your paths straight. (Proverbs 3:5–6)

With every passing day, O Lord, I more fully understand that there is a time and a season for every purpose under heaven. There are times to be thankful for the pure joy of being alive and times when I feel so overwhelmed with life that I plead for mercy. There are times when I need to pour out my heart with endless words, and there are times to be still, sit quietly, and wait. There are times when I am so anxious to seize the opportunity that is at hand, and there are times when I am so slow to make even the simplest choice. I admit, Lord, there are times when I cannot unravel the complexity of my experiences. I do not understand the moment and cannot comprehend the purpose of the season. But even then, I can hold to this: You are our Heavenly Father, and like a good father, you are sensitive to our needs, concerned about our predicaments, and ready and willing and able to provide the courage and faith and strength we need to face the challenges of each and every kind of day. So, teach us to live wisely well! For the sake of all who love you and long for your kingdom to come, we pray in Jesus' name. Amen.

DAY 5

A shoot will come up from the stump of Jesse; from his roots a
Branch will bear fruit. The Spirit of the LORD will rest on him—
the Spirit of wisdom and of understanding, the Spirit of counsel
and of might, the Spirit of knowledge and fear of the LORD—
and he will delight in the fear of the LORD. (Isaiah 11:1–3a)

Lord Jesus, you came into our fallen and rebellious world to open our eyes that we may see, to open our hearts that we may believe, and to open our lives that we may experience and express the reality of your kingdom—embracing what is truthful and graceful, forgiving and serving one another, turning the other cheek, and going the second mile. Show us the importance of our witness before those who don't believe, that they and we may be part of your glorious Rule when the lion sleeps peacefully with the lamb and all kingdoms and nations of this world are the kingdom of Christ. This is what we hope and pray in the name of Jesus, whose kingdom will never end and whose love will never be exhausted. Amen.

DAY 6

And without faith it is impossible to please God, because
anyone who comes to him must believe that he exists and that
he rewards those who earnestly seek him. (Hebrews 11:6)

I am discovering, Jesus, that my primary task as your follower is not what I do or say or what I value or even what I believe. At the heart of your invitation to follow you on this journey to spiritual wholeness is to seek you with my whole heart. My passion is not to be satisfied with my faith experience; rather my faith is always the means to experience your satisfaction with my desire to want more of you. I find my greatest joy in knowing you are pleased that I, like

Mary, am seeking the one thing necessary, the good portion that will never be taken away. O Lord, Lover of my soul, help me wholly believe that in my longing to love you I will learn how to best honor you with my heart, mind, soul, and strength, and faithfully love and serve my neighbors across the street and around the world. This is my prayer, to your glory and praise and for the sake of all you love, in your holy name. Amen.

DAY 7

But those who hope in the LORD will renew their strength.
They will soar on wings like eagles; they will run and not
grow weary, they will walk and not faint. (Isaiah 40:31)

Hear my prayer, O Lord, as I quiet my soul before you. In this quietness, I know you are near. I speak, and I know you will listen. I also know that as you speak, I need to listen. And so, I am still, waiting for your peace where anger and hurt are found; for your healing where open wounds of disappointment and pain remain; for communion where I am separated from you and others; for wisdom as I do not understand; for courage to do what I clearly understand. You are good and great. You are patient and kind. You are loving and forgiving. You help me in times of trouble and help me to live with trouble when it cannot be handled. You offer me mercies every morning and sufficient grace for this day and every kind of day. And so, with an undivided heart set on you, I will embrace this day and all that it holds in the peace of Christ and in the power of the Holy Spirit. Amen.

WEEK SIX

DAY 1

Even the sparrow has found a home, and the swallow a nest for
herself, where she may have her young—a place near your altar,
LORD Almighty, my King and my God. Blessed are those who dwell
in your house; they are ever praising you. (Psalm 84:3–4)

O Lord, I owe the gift of this day to you. I offer all my moments
in worship and praise of your holy name. I ask that you fill me
with the Holy Spirit, breathing into my heart your perfect love and
pure desires. Let your truth inform my mind. Let your righteousness
rule over my errant will. Let Christ be formed in me, and let me learn
humility, gentleness, faithfulness, and obedience in doing your will.
Help me to draw upon every opportunity today to grow in grace. Give
me a stout heart to bear my own burdens. Give me a willing heart to
bear the burdens of others. Give me a believing heart to cast all cares
on you. Glory to you, Father, Son, and Holy Spirit. Amen.

DAY 2

Let us not become weary in doing good, for at the proper time
we will reap a harvest if we do not give up. Therefore, as we have
opportunity, let us do good to all people, especially to those
who belong to the family of believers. (Galatians 6:9–10)

M y Lord, is it morning already? How inviting it is to stay in this
warm bed and ignore the responsibilities that are mine and mine
alone; to shrink from the burden of doing what is right and good; to
avoid the risk of being misunderstood or perhaps clearly understood;
to complain about my situation in life; to remind you of those whose
lives are easier than my own; to hoard the gifts you have given me;
to close my eyes and my mind to the suffering, pain, and brokenness
of the world; to let someone else take up the cross and follow you.
But you call me to deny myself, take up my cross, and follow you and
experience this new day that is full of the possibilities of your grace

and renewed mercies. There has never been a day like today, and I would be a fool to miss it. So, I will say, *Good morning, Lord! Great is your faithfulness. This is the day you have made. I will rejoice and be glad in it. And may the words of my mouth and the meditation of my heart throughout this day be pleasing to you, O Lord, my Rock and my Redeemer.* Amen and amen.

DAY 3

Above all else, guard your heart, for everything
you do flows from it. (Proverbs 4:23)

Lord Jesus, save me from the false impression that I can follow the leading of your Spirit, love as you loved, live as you lived, and obey as you were obedient in my own strength. Help me to examine my life honestly in the light of your holy Presence this morning, confessing the immensity of my need and the supremacy of your grace. Then lead me from this place of self-examination and confession to the fire of your sanctifying Spirit to the end that with a holy heart I will follow you closely, love others dearly, live the gospel faithfully, and obediently do whatever honors your holy name. Amen.

DAY 4

Blessed are those who have learned to acclaim you, who walk in
the light of your presence, LORD. They rejoice in your name all day
long; they celebrate your righteousness. (Psalm 89:15–16)

Lord Jesus, you invite us to join you on the narrow path, choosing to live life as servants. You showed us the way of a true servant, one who humbly seeks not to be served but to serve. I confess, Lord, how difficult it is to walk that fine line between obedience and performance, devotion and reputation, faith and presumption. My nature is to wander from the path rather than embrace the wonder of your grace that is greater than any misstep I may take along the way. O Lord, increase my faith, confirm my hope, and fill me with such love that my earthly nature gives way to your nature and I learn to love and serve and walk with you every day. Teach me how to bear the burdens of others that I may share the weight of your heart. Show me how to release everything I am and have and hope to be for the sake of your kingdom. May those who are brokenhearted find in me a patient and caring companion. At the end of the day, may the words of my mouth, the meditations of my heart, the work of my hands, and the journey of my feet be expressions of my love for you and for all whom you love. Amen.

DAY 5

All this is from God, who reconciled us to himself through Christ and gave us the ministry of reconciliation: that God was reconciling the world to himself in Christ, not counting people's sins against them. And he has committed to us the ministry of reconciliation. (2 Corinthians 5:18–19)

Lord Jesus, you commanded us that we should love our enemies. You assumed that we would have enemies because there would be those who oppose what we represent. We desperately need patience with an obnoxious coworker, forgiveness for a domineering boss, long-suffering with a rebellious child, understanding toward a bitter neighbor, forbearance with those with whom we disagree. You call us to be reconcilers, knocking down walls and building bridges between us and others. When others pursue a hostile course toward us, guide us to choose a path that leads to making peace possible rather than concluding that conflict is probable. Help us always to allow for the possibility that there are those we consider enemies who wish peace and security as much as we. May we take the initiative to lay the first planks in bridges of reconciliation. Today, we recommit ourselves to the long view of your kingdom, pursuing peace with all others and embracing holiness without which we will never see you. For your sake and for the sake of all you love we pray. Amen.

Day 6

And he who searches our hearts knows the mind of the
Spirit, because the Spirit intercedes for God's people in
accordance with the will of God. (Romans 8:27)

Show your mercy and kindness today, O Lord, to my loved ones
who stand in need of your help. Where their faith is weak, give
them a word of hope. Where they are lonely, comfort them with your
Presence. Where they are distracted, quiet their hearts, and give them
peace. Where there is need, be gracious and kind and generous with
your provision. Remind them that you came into our space and time
and flesh, experienced our hurt, heartache, and heartbreak; that the
troubles of this world are but a season; that this body of flesh that
sorely wears on us will one day be imperishable. To your care today
and forever, Holy Spirit, I commend my soul and the souls of all whom
I love and who love me. Give us your peace, I pray, in the name of
Jesus, our Savior and the Hope of the world. Amen.

Day 7

May God himself, the God of peace, sanctify you through and
through. May your whole spirit, soul and body be kept blameless
at the coming of our Lord Jesus Christ. The one who calls you
is faithful, and he will do it. (1 Thessalonians 5:23–24)

Holy and loving God, you fashion the dreams of my soul. You place
within me the delights of my heart. I do not understand all that
lies deep within my spirit, but you have created me for yourself, and I
am restless and dissatisfied apart from you. There is more to life than
I have experienced, more to love than I have explored, more faith than
I have dared to exercise, and more beauty than I have ever imagined.
Too much of my life is lived so much smaller than I feel it can be. O
Lord, release me from the anxieties that arrest my spirit. Free me from
the fears that cause me to doubt. Help me to trust what I profess to
know and act boldly on what I believe. Sanctify me wholly. Wherever
your Spirit is, there is freedom, and I pray that my liberated spirit may
soar today, rightly praising you and joyfully sharing this life with all

who love and cherish your holy name, Father, Son. and Holy Spirit. Amen.

WEEK SEVEN

DAY 1

But thanks be to God, who always leads us as captives in
Christ's triumphal procession and uses us to spread the aroma
of the knowledge of him everywhere. (2 Corinthians 2:14)

O Lord, we thank you for the wonder and joy of life. How good and right it is to begin this day praising you and honoring your holy name. Thank you for every opportunity to serve you and all you love. Thank you for faithful servants whose loving kindness yet bold witness has been the means of healing, saving, and sanctifying grace in our lives. Thank you for the knowledge that Jesus is the Savior of the world; that in him we have complete forgiveness of all that is past, assurance of your abiding Presence now, and eternal hope in the future; that the power of the Holy Spirit in us is greater than all that is evil and destructive in this world; that we have the opportunity to make a significant difference today as we give witness to this peace that passes understanding, the peace of Christ the world longs to know. We choose to be thankful, hopeful, joyful, and peaceful because we are confident that you are the Faithful One, and this is your will for the sake of all you love. In Jesus' name. Amen.

DAY 2

But you will receive power when the Holy Spirit comes on you;
and you will be my witnesses in Jerusalem, and in all Judea
and Samaria, and to the ends of the earth. (Acts 1:8)

L et me go into this week, O Lord, as a Spirit-filled witness of your love, renewed by your mercies, strengthened by your grace, and content in your Presence. Let me be more like you not only with my words, but also with my actions and reactions. Let me carefully listen for your voice and obediently follow your footsteps wherever they lead. Let my thoughts be keen and my heart be tender. Let me courageously pursue truth and gladly embrace holiness. Lord Jesus, help me to forsake anything in my life that does not honor you or bless all that you love, for yours is the kingdom that has no end and the love that cannot be exhausted. Amen.

DAY 3

"For my thoughts are not your thoughts, neither are your ways my ways," declares the LORD. "As the heavens are higher than the earth, so are my ways higher than your ways and my thoughts than your thoughts." (Isaiah 55:8–9)

I wonder, O Lord, what amazing things you want me to know about yourself, the deeper beauty and wonders of this world and the glory and majesty of your will? I wonder what I could learn if I began every day seeking your heart and mind, considering the possibilities of your grace, and daring to pray bold prayers? And I wonder how differently I would view the world, treat others, live in the present, and prepare for the future if thinking your thoughts became my primary business? I want to love you, Lord, with an undivided mind as well as an undivided heart. Save me from the satisfaction of my own understanding as well as the distractions that can easily preoccupy my mind. I ask for the mind of Jesus, lest I think too highly of myself, my opinions, my experience, and my conclusions and too little of you and all that you love. Lord, I will dare to be heavenly-minded every day as we continue on the journey together. For the sake of your kingdom, I pray in Jesus' name. Amen.

DAY 4

But seek first his kingdom and his righteousness, and all these things will be given to you as well. (Matthew 6:33)

O God, I ask you to remind me every day that you are closest when I feel that I am farthest from you, and that you are near even when

I feel that I have given you every reason to forsake me. I want to be more assured of your presence and power and become less absorbed with my lack and weakness. Each morning help me as I pray to have a deeper awareness and a fuller appreciation of eternal life. May I look more and more for the reality of your kingdom here and now and worry less about matters over which I have no control. May my desires become more of what you desire—whatever is holy, pure, and good. May my love become more perfect—that I may love what you love and do whatever you would have me to do. May I be more like Jesus, for the sake of your kingdom and all that you love. Amen.

DAY 5

Praise be to the God and Father of our Lord Jesus Christ, the Father of compassion and the God of all comfort, who comforts us in all our troubles, so that we can comfort those in any trouble with the comfort we ourselves receive from God. (2 Corinthians 1:3–4)

You, O Lord, are the God of all comfort and tender mercies. I thank you that you hear me as I pray this morning from the valley of shadows. There is so much I do not understand. Life can be so disappointing, unpredictable, and confusing. Nevertheless, I praise you for being the light that never dims and the warmth that never cools. In you and only you I find refuge when the unexpected disturbs my soul. You are where I find a peace that is deeper than understanding, where my heart is touched again by hope and love. Others come to mind this morning who are not well, grieving in their spirits, devastated by tremendous loss, suffering in their bodies, minds, and souls. Anoint them, and anoint me, Lord Jesus, with your Spirit, that in the chaos and confusion we may see glimpses of your kingdom and promises of new life and better days. In the name of Jesus, the One who makes all things new. Amen.

Day 6

There is one body and one Spirit, just as you were called to one hope
when you were called: one Lord, one faith, one baptism, one God and
Father of all, who is over all and through all and in all. (Ephesians 4:4–6)

In your will, Lord, we have peace. In your love, we are at rest. In your
service, we discover joy. In your presence, we share in the fellowship
of the Holy Spirit: friends with whom we will spend this day; family
who care and pray for us; the broken-hearted and grieving who seek
your face; caregivers who bear the burdens of the needy; pastors and
teachers and mission workers who give witness to you in difficult and
lonely places; seekers who long to belong; newborn babies, aged saints,
and everyone in between who loves your name. Draw near to us this
morning, O Lord, as we draw near to you. Graciously watch over our
souls as we seek to do your will, remain in your love, celebrate your
joy, and care for the souls of others with glad and generous hearts. We
pray, in the strong name of Jesus, that the fellowship of your Spirit
may fill the earth. Let it be, O Lord, let it be. Amen.

Day 7

"For I know the plans I have for you," declares the LORD,
"plans to prosper you and not to harm you, plans to
give you hope and a future." (Jeremiah 29:11)

O God, you rule the worlds from everlasting to everlasting, and
you desire for your peace to rule in our hearts today. Speak to us
when courage fails, when we faint for fear, when our love for others
grows cold, and when neighbors rise up against neighbors. Keep us
grounded in the things that cannot be shaken, abounding in hope and
knowing that no effort we make in serving you is in vain. Restore our
faith in the ultimate triumph of what is right and true and good; renew
the love that never fails; help us to look beyond the things that are seen
and temporal to see the things that are unseen and eternal. This we
choose to believe and hope and pray, in the name of Jesus Christ our
Lord. Amen.

WEEK EIGHT

DAY 1

Shout for joy to the LORD, all the earth. Worship the
LORD with gladness; come before him with joyful songs.
Know that the LORD is God. (Psalm 100:1–3a)

O Lord, our Lord, how majestic is your name in all the earth! You created the light of the first morning and saw that it was good. At the dawn of creation of this new day:

> I praise you for the morning light that beams through my window;
>
> I praise you for your Presence that stirs in my soul;
>
> I praise you for this beautiful world you created for us to enjoy together;
>
> I praise you for the work you have given me to do;
>
> I praise you for all that brings pure delight and unalloyed joy to children;
>
> I praise you for my family and friends;
>
> I praise you for Jesus, Savior of the world, and the Holy Spirit, the Giver of life;
>
> I praise you for your Word that is a lamp unto my feet, a light for my pathway.

And I pray for those to whom the morning light brings little or no joy. Shine your light upon their pathway that they may find hope, peace, and redeeming grace. Let there be nothing within me to darken the brightness of this day. I pray in the name of Jesus, the Light of the World, the Bright, Morning Star. Amen.

DAY 2

Yet you, LORD, are our Father. We are the clay, you are the
potter; we are all the work of your hand. (Isaiah 64:8)

Into your hands, almighty and merciful Lord, I commit the anxieties
that distract my mind, spoil my sleep, and disrupt my relationships.
Into your hands I commit my inappropriate desires for power and to
control and possess. Into your hands I commit the suffering of my
body, my mind, and my spirit that you may bear with me what I cannot
bear alone. Into your hands I commit all that concerns me regarding
my family, that prayer will accomplish what worry cannot. Into your
hands I commit my plans, knowing that you are able to accomplish
far more than I could ever ask or think or imagine. Into your hands
I commit my future, trusting that you will complete all you desire for
me, plans for the good and not for evil. Into your hands I commit the
many endings of my life, that I may release the past, live fully in this
moment, and embrace the future with courage and hope. Into your
hands I commit my life, almighty and merciful Lord—all that I am, all
that I have, and all that is yours. May I live every day in your peace, die
in your grace, and rise into the likeness of Jesus, my Savior, in whose
name I pray. Amen.

DAY 3

Then he said to them all: "Whoever wants to be my disciple must deny
themselves and take up their cross daily and follow me." (Luke 9:23)

Do I dare pray for patience, Jesus? Do I dare submit to your
Lordship, trust your timing, and wait on you? Do I dare speak to
the invisible, listen for the inaudible, believe the incredible, and act
upon the implausible? Do I dare fight the greatest battles on my knees?
Do I dare give in order to receive, stoop down to be lifted up, confess
weakness to become strong? Do I dare praise you when you are silent
and give thanks to you when I have nothing? Do I dare speak your
name when no one cares and no one listens? Daring to deny myself
each day, taking up a cross of responsibility and following your leading

is not natural. I prefer a broader and an easier path, something much less daring. Yet, this is the Great Adventure which you came to reveal, a journey through life that demands and embraces the possibilities of your saving and sanctifying grace. As I dare to follow you today, Jesus, I do not pray for an easy life; I pray to be strong in power and love, faith and obedience, wisdom and compassion. Wherever you lead, my Lord, I dare to go only if you are with me. Let it be so. Amen.

DAY 4

If we confess our sins, he is faithful and just and will forgive our sins and purify us from all unrighteousness. (1 John 1:9)

We confess, O Lord, that we can do better. We can do better than hold grudges and harbor angry thoughts and direct aggressive words against each other. We can do better than thinking so highly of ourselves that we easily think poorly of others. We can do better than filling our minds with negative thoughts and cynical attitudes. We can do better than flippantly using words of faith to express what we believe, then realizing how hollow those words are when we face the shadows and dark storms of life. We can do better than drawing lines and building walls and retreating from each other. Yet we also confess that we will never do better without your redeeming love and the power of your Spirit that delivers us from the tyranny of our self-centeredness. We want to do better, Lord, and so we pray that you will do for us what we could never do on our own. Forgive us of our sins, as we forgive those who have sinned against us. Deliver us from the power of sin, that we may love you and all that you love. Then, we will be amazed at what we become and what we can do because of your grace at work in and through us. Lord Jesus, have mercy on us and hear our prayer. Amen.

DAY 5

Two are better than one, because they have a good return for their labor: If either of them falls down, one can help the other up. But pity anyone who falls and has no one to help them up. (Ecclesiastes 4:9–10)

Thank you, Lord Jesus, for all the faithful servants who have shared a season on our path and whose presence made us more aware of your Presence in every season along the path. To think of them now causes us to praise you. How shallow our lives would have been without their companionship on life's journey. In every conversation, they were a means of grace. Although we grieve that we no longer share this journey with them, needy as we are of the generosity of their grace and wisdom and love, we thank you for the ways these saints made the Way so plain for us. As we continue on our journeys, we ask for the comfort of your abiding Presence and for the conviction of the Holy Spirit that we, too, will be the faithful and obedient and loving companions for others who need us in this season of their lives. In this, we will honor your servants and, we pray, bring glory to your holy name. Amen.

DAY 6

May the God of hope fill you with all joy and peace as you trust in him, so that you may overflow with hope by the power of the Holy Spirit. (Romans 15:13)

Jesus, your name is above every name, the only name by which we are saved. Your love exceeds all that we have ever hoped or believed or expected. We begin this morning, bowing our heads and lifting our hearts before you, confessing our absolute need of your mercy and grace. Apart from you, we realize that our way becomes confused and our instincts are unreliable. Refreshed by your Spirit, confidence is renewed and hope is restored as we intercede for others: the sick and disabled, the poor and discouraged, the least and the lost; leaders who are given the sacred charge to shape our world into a community of peace and justice for all; faith communities around the world who are the distinctive witness of your redeeming love and sanctifying grace.

May the Gospel you preached and taught and lived fill us with hope today and in every kind of day. For the sake of all you love, we pray in your holy name. Amen.

DAY 7

Create in me a pure heart, O God, and renew a steadfast spirit within me. Do not cast me away from your presence or take your Holy Spirit away from me. Restore to me the joy of your salvation and grant me a willing spirit, to sustain me. (Psalm 51:10–12)

Lord Jesus, make me big enough to love my enemies and pray for those who plot against me. I know when I have been hurt; give me grace to endure the pain. I know about doubt when I have felt shaken to the core of my being; wander with me in that darkness and deliver me from the depths of despair. I know when my heart is breaking; do not let such sadness overwhelm me that I forget the rumble of joy at the heart of the universe. I know it seems that I am asking for a lot, Lord, but I also know that you are more willing to give gifts of the Spirit to your children than we are to ask for them. So, I come to you in this moment of prayer, believing that you are more gracious than I can imagine and closer than the air I breathe. This day, make me an instrument of your peace so that where there is hatred, I can love, where there is injury, I can pardon. By your Spirit I pray, and in your name I rise to embrace this day. Amen.

WEEK NINE

DAY 1

Let us hold unswervingly to the hope we profess, for he who promised
is faithful. And let us consider how we may spur one another on
toward love and good deeds, not giving up meeting together, as
some are in the habit of doing, but encouraging one another—and
all the more as you see the Day approaching. (Hebrews 10:23–25)

O Lord, we love because you first loved us. We opened our hearts
to your life-changing grace and our lives to your loving presence
because you made the first move. And now we are learning that
it is in our life together, in the fellowship of all true believers, that
we experience the reality of holy love and express the unalloyed joy
of belonging to you and one another forever. May we embrace this
moment with grateful hearts as we pray for those who do not realize
what they are missing in neglecting this covenant community of faith.
We pray for ourselves and each other as we encourage each other and
continue this journey together, that what we say and how we say it,
what we do and how we do it, what we have and how we share it, who
we are and how we live honor Jesus Christ as Lord, to the glory of the
Father and praise of the Holy Spirit. In our lives, Lord, be glorified
today. Amen.

DAY 2

Therefore, I urge you brothers and sisters, in view of God's mercy,
to offer your bodies as a living sacrifice, holy and pleasing to
God—this is your true and proper worship. (Romans 12:1)

O Lord, you were with us wherever and however we gathered in
your name. We praised you with our voices and shared in the
joy of your Presence among your people. We drew near to you as we
prayed and nearer to each other as we prayed together. We heard your
Word proclaimed and pondered how to respond. We experienced
forgiveness for our waywardness that has diverted us from your

path and confessed our need of your healing spirit that repairs our brokenness, our lack of trust, and our unbelief. And so, I begin this day with renewed hope and confidence and enthusiasm to meet the demands of life, whatever comes my way today. I will bind myself again to you, O Lord, that I may seek justice, love mercy, and walk humbly with you through the ordinariness of this day and every kind of day. For yours is the kingdom and the power and the glory forever and forever. Amen.

DAY 3

Humble yourselves, therefore, under God's mighty hand,
that he may lift you up in due time. (1 Peter 5:6)

In the stillness of this moment, I thank you, O Lord, that you watch over me in my restlessness. You are here when I feel most alone, and you are there when I feel so unworthy. Your peace remains even when I am most anxious, and your love is deeper than my troubled soul. Help me to accept the truth that I am worthy not because I love you, but because you first loved me. Free me of self-doubt and fear and angst. Break the sin that dulls my spirit, and baptize my soul with unalloyed joy. There is so much you want to give and so little I have been willing to accept or even expect. As I pray today, I choose to believe and receive what you have been waiting and wanting to give, the riches of your grace made available to us all through the tender mercies of Jesus, our Savior and Lord. Amen.

DAY 4

See, I am doing a new thing! Now it springs up; do you
not perceive it? I am making a way in the wilderness
and streams in the wasteland. (Isaiah 43:19)

Lord, here I am again, asking for your help. You call me to embrace the fullness of life, but I am afraid to be openhearted, fearful of what others may think of me. You call me to believe, but I am afraid to let go and trust. You call me to love, but I have been hurt, betrayed, and abandoned. Do I dare to be so vulnerable? God of the loving heart, I want to trust you. I want to do what you want me to do. I want to respond to others in love. I want to be more like you. Stand by me when the shadows of doubt surround me. Support me when the road seems long and difficult. Help me to accept your Presence and discern how very near you are every moment of every kind of day. Steady my footsteps and lead me in your way, wherever that leads. Deliver me from the tyranny of trying to please others, that I may find pure joy in simply being close to you. This I pray, Jesus, for your sake and for the sake of your kingdom. Amen.

Day 5

To the Jews who had believed him, Jesus said, "If you hold to my teaching, you are really my disciples. Then you will know the truth, and the truth will set you free." (John 8:31–32)

O God, we wait on you this morning as we realize how weak we are and how much we need you. We are so frail and fickle; we need strength to do what is necessary. We are so foolish and feeble; we need wisdom that we might understand. We are so vain and oblivious; we need unfiltered Truth to humble us. We plead with you for this, O Lord, because only your Life gives life, and your Spirit is able to make us more and better than we are. You invite us to choose your way as our way, living in your Truth, experiencing your Life, confronting the harsh realities of a fallen world, confessing that we need a Savior, and finding grace that is more than sufficient to satisfy our deepest need. We truly need you, O Lord, for you alone speak the words of eternal life. In Jesus' name and for his sake we pray. Amen.

Day 6

You will keep in perfect peace those whose minds are steadfast, because they trust in you. (Isaiah 26:3)

Almighty God, in this quiet hour, I pause and seek the peace of your Presence. All week long I have run here and hurried there, but now in the stillness of my heart and in the clear light of eternity, I am content to leave my life in your hands; the very hairs upon my head are numbered by you. I am content to leave all my loved ones to your care; your love for them is greater than my own. I am content to leave in your hands all the causes of truth and justice in the world; my desire for peace is but a shadow of your divine purpose and love for the world. To you, O God, Father, Son, and Holy Spirit, be all honor and glory and praise forever. Amen.

DAY 7

Very truly I tell you, whoever believes in me will do the works I have been doing, and they will do even greater things than these, because I am going to the Father. And I will do whatever you ask in my name, so that the Father may be glorified in the Son. You may ask me for anything in my name, and I will do it. (John 14:12–14)

O God, in a world that is so complicated and so stressful and so uncertain, help us to unashamedly profess that Jesus Christ is Lord. In a world that is driven by competition and comparison and commercialism, help us believe in the simple things that make life so good and meaningful. In a world that defines its own reality and redefines what is holy and good, help us proclaim the Truth that sets us free. In a world that regressively embraces the worst of human nature as the new normal, stir within us righteous indignation along with our broken hearts. Reorient our lives toward spiritual wholeness and radical obedience. Renew our hearts to care more for things that are eternal than momentary pleasures and short-term solutions. Re-instill in us a sense of personal responsibility for the salvation of our neighbors, the wellbeing of the less fortunate; authentic compassion for victims of injustice; and the just treatment of wrongdoers. Remind us that as your Church we are called not to build walls but to storm the gates of hell. May the Spirit who raised Jesus from the dead make us fully alive and fully engaged in the world as a witness of hope to the discouraged, of love to the lonely, and of courage to the faithless. May we choose to live every day in the fullness and power of the Holy

Spirit because yours is the unshakable kingdom that has no end and the immeasurable love that will never be exhausted. Amen.

WEEK TEN

DAY 1

Submit yourselves, then, to God. Resist the devil, and he will flee from you. Come near to God, and he will come near to you. (James 4:7–8a)

Our Heavenly Father, we come into your Presence because you are love, and there is nothing in all creation that can separate us from such love. We come without fear, because perfect love casts out fear. We come with confidence, because we know that we already are loved. Yes, we come with questions and confusion and emptiness, because when we come into your Presence we find peace. We come because you have called us to come, and we have a longing to praise you. We come in the name of Jesus, the One who has opened our eyes to grace and filled our hearts with your love. Amen.

DAY 2

Every good and perfect gift is from above, coming
down from the Father of the heavenly lights, who does
not change like shifting shadows. (James 1:17)

I praise you, O God, from whom all blessings flow! I praise you with all creatures here below! I praise you with all the heavenly hosts! You have created this day, and it is good because it is filled with your Presence. Yet there are so many today who are not convinced of your goodness and are unaware of the infinite riches of your grace. O Lord, make me aware of those in my sphere of influence whose hearts are breaking, whose bodies are hurting, and whose hope is ebbing. Engrave your Word on my heart, fill me with your Spirit, and use me on this good day as one of your servants through whom your gospel is seen and heard and believed and applied for the sake of all you love.

May your blessings flow as far as the curse is found. This I ask in the strong name of Jesus Christ whose kingdom has no end and whose love cannot be exhausted. Amen.

DAY 3

This is what the LORD says: "Stand at the crossroads and look;
ask for the ancient paths, ask where the good way is, and walk
in it, and you will find rest for your souls." (Jeremiah 6:16a)

You have given us the grand privilege and awesome responsibility, O Lord, to choose. There are many days I prefer to chill, make few decisions, let go, and let the world keep spinning without my help. But you stir my soul and will not allow me to do that. Your design for my life is not to be a spectator, but a participant. I cannot follow you if I am sitting on my hands. I am reminded that I am fearfully and wonderfully made, that my unique thumbprint is to be placed upon this world. I am in the game, and others are depending on me to do my part. You believe in me, you trust me, you have bought my soul, and I am forever in your debt. And so, I choose to stand up and speak rather than sit and complain; I choose to live by faith rather than fear; I choose to let go of the past and be forgiving rather than cling to the hurt and be unforgiven; I choose to pursue holiness and righteousness rather than momentary pleasures at the expense of others. I choose to be part of the solution rather than contributing to the problem. I choose Jesus, and on this Rock I stand. Amen.

DAY 4

Therefore, since we are receiving a kingdom that cannot be shaken,
let us be thankful, and so worship God acceptably with reverence
and awe, for our "God is a consuming fire." (Hebrews 12:28–29)

Holy and loving God, I pray for grace today to trust you more deeply. I pray for faith to believe that you rule the world in truth and righteousness, even when there is so much untruth and unrighteousness in the world. I pray for faith to believe that in seeking first your kingdom and righteousness in all things, you provide for our lesser needs. I pray for faith to not worry about tomorrow, confident that as you have been faithful, you are faithful and always will be faithful. I pray for faith to believe that there is no greater power than Calvary love to melt hard hearts and destroy the power of sin. I pray for faith to see your holy and loving purpose unfolding in the daily stuff of life, especially when life is confusing and chaotic and complicated. I pray for faith to be calm and brave in the face of whatever dangers and trials may meet me in the course of this day. I pray for faith to take the high road rather than stooping to a lower nature that offends you. I pray for faith to believe in the final victory of your Spirit over every enemy of our souls and bodies. And I pray for faith to trust all whom I love and all who love me into your eternal love and care. This I pray, thankful that your kingdom has come and full of hope that it will come in all its fullness. Alleluia and amen.

DAY 5

Since ancient times no one has heard, no ear has
perceived, no eye has seen any God but you, who acts
on behalf of those who wait for him. (Isaiah 64:4)

O Lord God, you are beyond my comprehension and understanding, yet I know you are very near. There is that within me that longs to reach out to you and pray. I want to feel that I am in touch with the Divine, something and Someone beyond myself. I want to lean upon something Eternal, something steadier than my wobbling spirit and erratic will. I need a Strength that is greater than my own, a Power that is greater than any task. I am easily upset by events over which I have no control. I am secretly unsure that I can manage my own life. I often am terribly confused and uncertain in a world that disrupts and disregards peace. I struggle to make sense of chaos, calamity, and catastrophe. O Lord, my Rock and my Redeemer, I ask for serenity—to hang on to hope in spite of my fears. I ask for openness—to respond to your Word and obey the leading of the Holy Spirit in spite of my doubts. And I ask for courage—to hold fast to your eternal Truth in spite of critics, adversaries, and hope-extinguishers. In your Presence I can ask for these things, for you know how badly I need them, and

I know that you are faithful to give good things to those who ask, believing in the name of Jesus. Amen.

DAY 6

"You are worthy, our Lord and God, to receive glory and honor and power, for you created all things, and by your will they were created and have their being." (Revelation 4:11)

O God, your love is forever, and your grace is beyond measure. Praise your holy name! This morning I pray that the reality of your kingdom will come and that your will shall be done in my life as it is in heaven. Move upon my mind and heart in such an indubitable way that I will not mistake your glory as something for which I claim credit. Capture my undivided attention as you captured that of Moses at the burning bush. Inspire my mind to think of things above and beyond this world as Isaiah was inspired in the temple. Free me from the lethargy of ordinariness that staggered the souls of the disciples on the Mount of Transfiguration. Do I dare pray that you become the Supreme Reality without rival in my life? Am I ready for all other so-called realities to be swept aside in the beauty and awe-fullness of your holiness? Help me, Lord, to be done with lesser things, and help me cling to you as if my life depended upon it, for it surely does. May my aim today be first and foremost to hear your voice and obey your will. You alone are God, and I am not. With all the saints and angels I worship you, Father, Son, and Holy Spirit, because yours is the unshakable kingdom that has no end and the immeasurable love that will never be exhausted. Amen.

DAY 7

So Christ himself gave the apostles, the prophets, the evangelists, the pastors and teachers, to equip his people for works of service, so that the body of Christ may be built up until we all reach unity in the faith and in the knowledge of the Son of God and become mature, attaining to the whole measure of the fullness of Christ. (Ephesians 4:11–13)

In every age, O God, you have called faithful women and men to be pastors—shepherds of the sheep—whose ears are attuned to hear a voice most others do not hear; whose words stir emotions and tug the conscience; whose lives are honored yet pitied, considered distinguished yet afflicted; whose humanity is obvious and whose holiness is seldom appreciated; whose hearts are willing to bear the burdens of your heart and be broken with the burdens of those under their care. Thank you for those pastors who have been occasions of the Holy Spirit in our lives. Through their encouragement to trust in your mercy and grace, we know that you are the God of love. Through their faithful preaching of the Word, we have heard the Truth, repented of sin, and believed the gospel, trusting Jesus Christ as our Savior and Friend. Through their example as servants of Christ, we know that following Jesus is a daily experience of divine worship, spiritual growth, and loving service. Through their humility and longsuffering, we have seen the reality of sanctifying grace. And with our prayers, presence, gifts, service, and witness we pledge to be the community of faith and the fellowship of the Holy Spirit that surrounds them in steadfast love. Thank you, Lord, for these your servants. Amen.

WEEK ELEVEN

DAY 1

Therefore, as God's chosen people, holy and dearly loved, clothe yourselves with compassion, kindness, humility, gentleness and patience. Bear with each other and forgive one another if any of you has a grievance against someone. Forgive as the Lord forgave you. And over all these virtues put on love, which binds them all together in perfect unity. (Colossians 3:12–14)

In the quiet of this hour, O Lord, I pray to be at peace. In the beauty of your holiness, I pray to be in awe. In the wonder of your love, I pray to be content. But first, I must pray that my spirit will be refreshed by the Holy Spirit, my thoughts renewed by the mind of Christ, and my soul restored with the joy of your salvation. Grant me a teachable spirit that I may worship you in spirit and truth; that I may learn well the lessons I need; that I may act well with friends and those less friendly; that I may respond generously toward those afflicted by grief or illness or injury; that I may care for the poor, the hungry, and the victims of injustice; that I may share the burden of the weight of your grief for a lost and lonely world that is longing to know your redeeming, holy love. Lord Jesus, I wait on you in prayer and with praise, for yours alone is the kingdom and power forever and ever. Amen.

DAY 2

I am not ashamed of the gospel, because it is the power of God that brings salvation to everyone who believes: first to the Jew, then to the Gentile. (Romans 1:16)

Save me, Jesus, from taking on responsibilities today I was never intended to assume. Save me from wasting time worrying about matters over which I have no control. Save me from the tyranny of the urgent that robs me of the calmness of your abiding Presence and the joy of those with whom I share this life journey. Save me from the slavish fear of the unknown and the dread of what I do understand.

Save me from the paralysis of grief and the bitterness that eats away at my soul. Save me from all sin that dulls my spirit and aborts my ability to love. Save me from the power of sin that perpetuates a sense of frustration and futility. Above all, teach me that your saving grace empowers as well as delivers, inspires as well as forgives, reveals as well as relieves. May the joy of your salvation be my strength, my Lord and my Redeemer. Amen.

DAY 3

He says, "Be still and know that I am God...." (Psalm 46:10)

Quiet me down, Lord. Quiet my restless soul so I can remember how many times you have been there to keep me going when I thought could not make it. Quiet my troubled mind so I can relive those moments when I found hope to be steadfast and strength to keep on keeping on. Quiet my anxious spirit so I can accept my limitations without fear or panic, acknowledging that you are God, and I am not. Quiet my trembling heart so I can rest and be at peace. May I be assured that what I do today matters and what I say makes a difference for your sake and for the sake of those you love. Help me believe that I can do all things through Christ who gives me strength and that you will give me the serenity to accept things I cannot change. Grant me peace, O Lord, and the wisdom to know the difference. Amen.

DAY 4

Sing to the LORD a new song; sing to the LORD, all the earth.
Sing to the LORD, praise his name; proclaim his salvation
day after day. Declare his glory among the nations, his
marvelous deeds among all peoples. (Psalm 96:1–3)

There has been no day, O God, ever before like this day, filled with promises of mercy renewed, grace received, and hope restored. Thoughts that have never been thought may find their expression soon in books, letters, texts, or song. Friends that have never met eventually will form an eternal fellowship of kindred minds and spirit. Prayers that have never been uttered, but once said, will become a means of grace to the hurting, the grieving, the poor, the hopeless, and the lost. And so I pray, do not let me miss the possibilities of grace which this day holds. Rather, help me be alert in all my being to recognize the wonder of it all! Fill my heart with praise to you and my spirit with exuberance as a witness of your Presence to all. I will stand on tiptoes to welcome you into my life, ready to walk with you, my faithful Friend, my Sovereign Lord, my blessed Redeemer. This is the day you have made. I choose to rejoice and be glad in it, as a child of the covenant, created, called out, and commissioned by the One whose name is above every name, Jesus, my Lord. Amen.

DAY 5

Therefore confess your sins to each other and pray for each
other so that you may be healed. The prayer of a righteous
person is powerful and effective. (James 5:16)

Jesus, Friend of sinners, I pray this morning for those whose hearts and lives are overwhelmed with a sense of their own unworthiness; for those who are aware of some great wrong they have done, some secret sin of which they are ashamed; for those who feel guilty for the hurt and pain they have caused others. I pray for those who have become hard and cynical, those whose souls have become so calloused and indifferent that they feel no remorse at all for the dire consequences of their sin. And I pray for those who long ago made promises to you and vows before a faith community to care and love and be faithful as your disciples, but for whom those words now are ignored and meaningless. Jesus, Friend of all who need to be made whole, hear my prayer and have mercy on us. Speak truth to our souls. Convict our hearts and convince our minds that there is no sin so great that your grace is not greater still. May heaven rejoice all day long as wayward children come to their senses and turn their hearts toward home. Let it be so, Jesus, our Savior and Friend. Amen.

DAY 6

There is a time for everything, and a season for every
activity under the heavens. (Ecclesiastes 3:1)

There are times, O Lord, that trouble our souls more than others—
the death of a loved one, a child who is ill, a distressed marriage, a
stressful job, financial needs, social injustice, political chaos, spiritual
dryness, emotional confusion. There are times when our spirits
are glad—the birth of a long-awaited child, the joy of newlyweds,
a promotion at work, an unexpected bonus, a wrong made right,
competent and compassionate leadership, an infilling of the Holy
Spirit, an undivided heart. Thank you for this life, O Lord, in which we
cry and sing, work and rest, grieve and rejoice, hope and pray, question
and trust, share and love together. It is in the difficulty of living, not
in the absence of conflict, that we find your grace, your peace, your
power, your Presence, your joy, your holiness. "For the LORD is good
and his love endures forever; his faithfulness continues through all
generations" (Pslam 100:5)—and that includes this generation on a
day like today and every kind of day. Thus, we continue to pray with
confidence in the name of Jesus, and therefore, we have hope. Amen.

DAY 7

Rejoice in the Lord always. I will say it again: Rejoice! Let your
gentleness be evident to all. The Lord is near. (Philippians 4:4–5)

Because of you, Jesus, I know that God is love. Your Spirit is the
witness that keeps me from despair. I do not need to pray as
though you are far away from me. You are very near. I have known
you in an unexpected moment when I felt a Presence more than my
own. I have believed in a Comforter who gives a peace that passes
my understanding. You are very near. You have come to me in my
discomfort when I have wronged another and betrayed love. You have
come to me in the hope I have held in those times that I somehow
managed to make it through another day. You have come to me in
singing and sighing, praising and praying. You are very near, for you

have breathed the breath of your Spirit into my soul. Therefore, I will praise you for such experiences of joy, peace, love, and hope. And may I be grateful enough and joyful enough to share with others this experience of you, Lord Jesus, the One who always is very near. Amen.

WEEK TWELVE

DAY 1

How lovely is your dwelling place, LORD Almighty! My soul yearns, even faints, for the courts of the LORD; my heart and my flesh cry out for the living God. (Psalm 84:1–2)

Holy and loving God, your presence will be celebrated in worship services across the earth this week by singing and praying, clapping and dancing, proclaiming and communing. Thank you for holy moments that remind us of our mortality and your divinity, our human need and your saving grace, our hope and your peace. We praise you for your loving kindness, your steadfast faithfulness, your enduring mercy, and the joy your presence brings to our souls. We love you, Lord, because you first loved us. As we begin a new week, we pray for the anointing of your Spirit that we may generously express the love we have experienced. Be glorified in us today. In the strong name of Jesus and for the sake of your kingdom we pray. Amen.

DAY 2

Know therefore that the LORD your God is God; he is the faithful God, keeping his covenant of love to a thousand generations of those who love him and keep his commandments. (Deuteronomy 7:9)

Holy and loving God, with our human eyes we cannot gaze upon you in all your glory, but in the glory of all you have done we see who you are. We do not find you in nature, but we see your fingerprints in all you have created. We cannot find you by ourselves, but we can know your mind because you have revealed yourself to us through the

Spirit and your Word. We do not know if we have enough faith to face the challenges of this day, but we have found you to be faithful. We will not complete everything today that we hope or plan, but we can trust your heart even if we do not see your hand. As so, we come to you this morning in the wonderful name of Jesus, our Lord and Savior, who came to us revealing your glory. This much we know, this we believe, and that is enough for today and every kind of day. Amen.

DAY 3

I urge, then, first of all, that petitions, prayers, intercession and thanksgiving be made for all people—for kings and all those in authority, that they may live peaceful and quiet lives in all godliness and holiness. (1 Timothy 2:1–2)

M ost gracious and loving Lord, your generosity exceeds our ability to receive. Your grace is greater than the worst of our sins. Your mercy is beyond our deepest despair. Our lives are blessed every day in ways we do not acknowledge. Thank you that the desire for such love is stamped in every human heart, and any heart can be satisfied with your generous grace and boundless mercy. I pray that you will help me to see in each face the object of your eternal love. I pray that you will help me understand more deeply how you love every person, that you came into our world of space and time to live our life, to be burdened with our pain, to take our sin, to give us eternal hope, and to love us so completely that we might love one another adequately. I pray that you will stamp on my heart your concern for persons across the street and around the world who will not hear this gospel unless we share it. O Lord, as I lift my hands in prayer this morning, I bring to you the people you love, in Jesus' name. Amen.

DAY 4

And I pray that you, being rooted and established in love, may have power, together with all the Lord's holy people, to grasp how wide and long and high and deep is the love of Christ, and to know this love that surpasses all knowledge—that you may be filled to the measure of all the fullness of God. (Ephesians 3:17b–19)

I am tired, Lord. I am tired of the chaos over which I have little or no control. I am tired of trying to understand the current normal while I ponder a new normal. I am tired of being tired. Yet, is this not the moment and place you have wanted and waited for me? You want me to want more than comfort, rest, satisfaction, and happiness. You want me to want you to be at the center of the great longing of my heart, because you are Perfect Love. I am restless and will be weary until I find rest in you, the One who wanted me first and last and forever. That rest is possible when my desire is to love you with all my heart, mind, soul, and strength, not because I am good or capable of such love. No, I can love you only because you first loved us. I am tired of trying to order and make sense of my life. Rather, I choose to be rooted and rest forever in the breadth and length and depth of your love. Thank you, Jesus. Amen.

DAY 5

The greatest among you will be your servant. (Matthew 23:11)

O Lord, how deeply I respect your humble servants for their faithful self-giving; their availability to care for others in need; their desire to be lifelong learners; their honesty to admit their sin; their complete reliance on your grace; their patience to wait on you; and their ability to trust you. Thank you, Lord, for these who do not follow the advice of the hateful or spend time with the hurtful. Rather, they find delight in doing what they understand your will to be. These faithful disciples make me think of you, and I want to be more like you having been around them. Their love of you is revealed in the way they love others. Their humility is obvious in their non-anxious presence and in the pure joy of your Presence. And so, I pray that through all the experiences of this day you will find me also to be faithful, available, teachable, and responsible as a true follower and servant of Jesus, reflecting your Spirit in all I do and say. Should I fail in word or deed, hear my confession and restore the joy of your salvation to my heart. This I pray for the sake of your kingdom and all that you love, in Jesus' name. Amen.

DAY 6

Blessed are those who hunger and thirst for righteousness, for they will be filled. (Matthew 5:6)

Our Heavenly Father, we pray this morning for all who are hungry: those who are needing physical bread and sustenance for themselves and their loved ones because of the dire conditions where they live; those who are hungry for more material possessions, mistakenly thinking that the accumulation of "stuff" brings satisfaction and contentment; those who are hungry for happiness, filling their days with endless activities and pleasures that actually provide only momentary thrills; those who are hungry for life, but only know how to take and not give, receive but not share, expect yet not express thanks; those who are hungry for peace, whose hearts are troubled by anger and hatred, guilt and shame, disappointment and despair; those who are hungry for love, having known neither the amazing grace of God nor the authentic fellowship of the community of faith. We pray that the fullness of Christ, the Bread of Life, will satisfy the deepest longing in every heart with the food that endures to eternal life, for yours is the kingdom and the power and the glory forever. Amen.

DAY 7

Do not be anxious about anything, but in every situation, by prayer and petition, with thanksgiving, present your requests to God. (Philippians 4:6)

I thank you, Jesus, that you watch over me even in my restlessness. When I feel most alone and unworthy, your everlasting arms sustain me. When worries flood my mind, you patiently listen to my troubles.

Help me to feel good about myself, that I am worthy not because I love you but because you first loved me. Heal me of self-doubt, fear, and anxiety. May your Spirit be so strong in me that to spend this moment with you is to feel my soul baptized in love, hope, peace, and joy. There is so much you want to give and so little I have been willing to accept. Do in my heart today, Lord Jesus, what you have been willing and waiting to do, that through me you will do whatever others need of me. Let it be so for your sake and for the sake of all you love. Amen.

WEEK THIRTEEN

DAY 1

For you once were darkness, but now you are light in
the Lord. Live as children of light. (Ephesians 5:8)

Lord Jesus, when there is a cross, we will carry it.
When we are desperate, we will hope.
When our peace is broken, we will persevere.
When we mourn, we will weep together.
When we feel overwhelmed, we will hold on to your promises.
When we lose our way, we will stop and pray.
Whatever we face today, whatever may happen, wherever we go,
we choose to walk with you,
for you are the Way, the Truth, and the Life.
Hallelujah and amen.

—Author unknown—

DAY 2

I desire to do your will, my God; your law is within my heart. (Psalm 40:8)

I find it more comforting than troubling, O Lord, that nothing in my life is beyond your thoughts. With the Psalmist I shout, "How precious to me are your thoughts, God! How vast is the sum of them! Were I to count them, they would outnumber the grains of the sand"

(Psalm 139:17–18a). This I know, and yet you well know that my mind is prone to wander and disregard you. Help me center my thoughts on you and order my activities into an orbit around you, that I may be constantly connected and alive in the Spirit. I begin this day relinquishing control of the universe to you, my Lord and my God. Help me to assume no more responsibility today than I am intended to have, yet may I set my mind to do whatever you require of me with passion and conviction. For the sake of your kingdom and your perfect will, I humbly pray in Jesus' name. Amen.

DAY 3

I have been crucified with Christ and I no longer live, but Christ lives in me. The life I now live in the body, I live by faith in the Son of God, who loved me and gave himself for me. (Galatians 2:20)

Lord Jesus, there are many days when following you on this journey as your disciple is not easy or pleasant. I often find it difficult to know what to say or do. Even when the path is clear and I know what is right, I am tempted to be nice and inoffensive rather than faithful and risk offending someone. I fear that others see too much of me and very little of you because of my reticent witness. I thank you that you fully understand every trial I face and that you are faithful to show me the way through whatever temptation is near. I thank you for the strength and the assurance of your Presence when the way is lonely and I am discouraged because others resist and reject me. I thank you for those who seek me out and forgive me when I do not deserve their compassion. And I thank you for those faithful witnesses who inspire me and others as they continue on this journey regardless of the cost. At the end of the day, may we, your disciples who choose to follow you, be found faithful for the sake of your kingdom and all who follow after us. Amen.

DAY 4

The way of fools seems right to them, but the
wise listen to advice. (Proverbs 12:15)

O Lord, help me to listen well. It is in listening that I hear that still, small voice that speaks to my heart, that whisper of faith that summons me, and the quiet murmur of hope that convinces me that all will be well. Help me to listen and respond well not because I am so wise or so good but because I am loved and wanted and therefore capable of loving and wanting what is wise and good. Help me to listen to others who want to tell me they love me and also to those who are trying to tell me they need my love. Help me to listen to the stranger who could be an angel in disguise and to the friend who may be lonelier and more lost than I realize. Help me to listen more carefully to the angry voices with whom I disagree, as the cry of their hearts may be what I need to hear. And may I be able to sort out whatever I hear, not threatened by the careless tongues of others, yet encouraged by the inspired words of your messengers. I want to become more like you, O Listener of my prayers, so I may hear and understand the prayers of others in the words they speak. In the name of Jesus who forever intercedes for us I pray. Amen.

DAY 5

This is love: not that we loved God, but that he loved us and sent
his Son as an atoning sacrifice for our sins. Dear friends, since God
so loved us, we also ought to love one another. (1 John 4:10–11)

As we were being formed in our mothers' wombs, O Lord, you thought of us. When we struggled as children to understand the world in which we lived, you were there, watching over us. And now, as each of us deals with complications and difficulties as adults, remind us that you are still with us, ready to share our burdens and give us strength to endure the heartaches and heartbreaks of life. How can we not love you and be grateful? How can we fail to love others with the love you have given us? How can we not strive to alleviate the suffering of the poor, pray for the wellbeing of the sick, embrace the lonely with loving arms, encourage the discouraged and hopeless, offer Christ to the spiritually lost and confused, comfort the dying with the blessed assurance of a Savior whose gaze has been upon them forever? O God, help us to rearrange our lives to make more room for you, for true joy, for prayer, for each other, and for all others who touch our lives. As your creation and objects of your love, help us to grow up into your likeness that we may love perfectly as we have been loved. May it be so, Lord Jesus. Amen.

DAY 6

So do not fear, for I am with you; do not be dismayed, for I am your God. I will strengthen you and help you; I will uphold you with my righteous right hand. (Isaiah 41:10)

This we believe, O Lord: You have been our help in ages past, and you are our hope for years to come. Then, why is waiting in this present moment so difficult? What we feel with such anxiety today, you see perfectly through the lens of eternity. What we expect to happen on our terms, according to our plans, and on our timetables must amuse you. How often do we sincerely pray for your kingdom to come and your will to be done only to disregard the fact that your kingdom is coming steadily, assuredly, and your will shall be done ultimately, completely. Not by might nor by power but by your Spirit, it surely will come. Help us to be still and know that you truly are God. Help us to cultivate silence in the midst of the cacophony of our lives, that we may hear your whisper, reminding us that your desire for us to know your will is greater than our desire to know what you will. We acknowledge that it will take a lifetime to grasp this, O God of the ages, but we are thankful that you are willing to patiently wait on us. Because of Jesus. Amen.

DAY 7

Cast all your anxiety on him because he cares for you. (1 Peter 5:7)

Thank you, Lord Jesus, for your patience with me. Thank you for understanding my fears and frustrations, my failures and my faithlessness. Thank you that even when I feel surrounded by absence, your Presence is greater, closer, and available whenever I call on your name. Thank you for the calm assurance that your grace is sufficient for every need, that disappointment has an end, and that there is no experience in our lives beyond your power. Thank you that there is no darkness too deep, no brokenness so painful, and no loss so final that you cannot meet us there and lead us into hope and a future where there are no more tears, no heartaches, and never a heartbreak. Thank you, O Lord, that this day, I can place the full weight of my care into your hands, knowing how deeply and completely you care for all of us as if there was only one of us. I live in the joy of this hope today, praising your holy name for bearing the full weight of my sin and carrying the great burden of my sorrow. I love you, Lord Jesus. Amen.

WEEK FOURTEEN

DAY 1

Again Jesus said, "Peace be with you! As the Father has sent me, I am sending you." And with that he breathed on them and said, "Receive the Holy Spirit." (John 20:21–22)

O Lord, we are aware that our primary task as the Church is to make disciples who will rightly worship you, boldly proclaim the message of your saving grace, faithfully encourage one another, generously care for those in need, and diligently reach out to others who are yet to be disciples. We have this great responsibility to be in the world but not of the world, to live in covenant relationships but never live out our faith in isolation. Help us become the Church you desire, a Spirit-filled fellowship where love abounds and your Word is loved. In times of gladness and sadness, may our hearts be one. In our disagreements and disappointments, may we listen and learn. In confusion and conflict, may we be gracious and truthful. Help us walk the ancient path as your faithful servants who stayed the course, kept the faith, and now have completed their journey. Come, Holy Spirit. Fill the hearts of all your disciples with the unquenchable fire of your love that we, too, may be found faithful for such a time as this. In Jesus' name and for the sake of all you love we pray. Amen.

DAY 2

For God, who said, "Let light shine out of darkness," made his light shine in our hearts to give us the light of the knowledge of God's glory displayed in the face of Christ. (2 Corinthians 4:6)

I begin this week, O Lord, by praising your glorious name. You are glorious because you care about the small things as much as the great things: children with minor hurts and adults with major disappointments; families who are close and single adults with no family or friends nearby; the joyful newlyweds and the lonely widower in a rest home; the soft glow of a lamp by which I read your Word and the brilliance of the sun by which once again morning has broken. Your glory is present with us in places and moments we often do not look for you: in difficult conversations, in periods of unanswered prayer, in the midst of pain, in the agony of heartache and heartbreak, in the anxiety of political turmoil, and in the fear of the unknown. The praise of your glorious name is on my lips today, O Lord, overflowing from my heart in every place, that what has been stunted or broken in my life may begin to heal and become whole again. Holy is your name, Father, Son, and Holy Spirit, for yours is the kingdom and the power and the glory forever. Amen and amen.

Day 3

Blessed are the pure in heart, for they will see God. (Matthew 5:8)

My mind is stayed on you, Lord Jesus. You are my Helper in weakness, my Savior from sin, my Redeemer from indifference, my Healer from resentment. May I never be satisfied comparing myself to others, thinking more highly of myself that I ought to think. Rather, I pray to be a single-minded servant with an undivided heart, a Spirit-filled and Spirit-led disciple on the journey to spiritual wholeness, a child of God who is growing into your likeness and sanctified by your holy love. I pray in your name, believing that you are able to do immeasurably more than all I could ever ask or imagine. Amen.

Day 4

Let the peace of Christ rule in your hearts, since as members of one body you were called to peace. And be thankful. (Colossians 3:15)

Today, Lord, I pray for peace. Deep peace. Real peace. Not as the world gives, but the peace that only you can give. I pray that I will know this day that at the heart of all my cares, concerns, conflict, and confusion, there is that deeper calm that comes from the assurance of your abiding Presence. When I leave this place of prayer in a few moments, I pray that I will go with the confidence that nothing can happen that will interrupt that peace. Out of that peace may I have conviction to do what is right and just, compassion to care for the poor in body and spirit, and the courage to be a peacemaker and peace giver wherever I am needed. For your sake and for the sake of all you love, I pray in the name of Jesus, the Prince of Peace. Amen.

DAY 5

Since, then, you have been raised with Christ, set your hearts on things above, where Christ is, seated at the right hand of God. Set your minds on things above, not on earthly things. (Colossians 3:1–2)

Lord, I greet you with praise and a thankful heart. I want to live today as a witness of a life well-lived in Christ. Forbid that my thoughts should become preoccupied with anything that displeases you. Forbid that I should be content with only the things that satisfy my wants and my needs. Forbid that I should love anyone less than I have been loved by you. Rather, may it be evident in my words, thoughts, and actions that my heart is set on things that are eternally significant. May I grow more confident of this gift of eternal life that is my life because of you. And may I recognize opportunities each and every day to gladly share with others this hope that lies in my heart. This I pray for the sake of your kingdom and for the sake of all you love, in Jesus' name. Amen.

DAY 6

Seek the LORD while he may be found; call on him when he is near. Let the wicked forsake their ways and the unrighteous their ways and the unrighteous their thoughts. Let them turn to the LORD, and he will have mercy on them, and to our God, for he will freely pardon. (Isaiah 55:6–7)

O God, your love is from everlasting to everlasting. Your truth endures forever. Your way is filled with peace, and your mercies never end. Your glory fills the heavens, and your majesty rules the earth. Yet, this is a broken world. Our greed has overtaken common sense and the common good. Our reluctance to share has caused the poor to become poorer. Our politics have led us into incivility, bitterness, and division. Even our faith is branded not by love, mercy, and forgiveness but pride, prejudice, and anger. Lord, have mercy on us. We regret our hard hearts and repent of our rebellious spirits. We want to walk together with you on paths of righteousness along still waters, so near that your Spirit may restore our wayward souls. Only then will our homes be havens of peace and our communities centers of hope. Only then will unbelievers be willing to listen to what we sing and speak. O Lord, heal our brokenness, fill us with your Spirit, and restore our joy for the sake of all you love across the street and around the world. In Jesus' name. Amen.

DAY 7

Yet a time is coming and has now come when the true worshipers will worship the Father in the Spirit and in truth, for they are the kind of worshipers the Father seeks. God is Spirit, and his worshipers must worship in the Spirit and in truth. (John 4:23–24)

Holy and loving God, I thank you for sanctuary, holy moments in holy places, that set us apart from our past with all its sin and shame; from a noisy world that is often hard and confusing and indifferent; from the wearisomeness of fear and worry, busyness, and work. I especially thank you for the sanctuary where I gather with family and friends and the faith community, where we pilgrims rest along the journey, our souls are refreshed, sin is confessed, burdens are shared, and hope is renewed. I praise you for the many places you provide sanctuary across this globe, holy ground where your Word is preached, sacraments are received, and the faithful are lost in wonder, love, and praise. We desperately need sanctuary, O Lord, where we can step aside and worship you in the beauty of holiness. And so, we continue to pray daily for your kingdom to come and your will to be done on earth as it is in heaven to the end that we no longer will need sanctuary, for your dwelling place will be with us. In the name of Jesus, the One who came into our space and time that we may enjoy your Presence forever. Amen.

WEEK FIFTEEN

DAY 1

Let the morning bring me word of your unfailing love,
for I have put my trust in you. Show me the way I should
go, for to you I entrust my life. (Psalm 143:8)

Almighty God, holy is your name. You have set your glory above the heavens. You are above all things, created all things, and sustain all things. You command the morning and cause the dawn to know its place. How majestic is your name in all the earth! And yet, you are involved in every moment and every matter that concerns every one of us. You are not unaware, unfeeling, or unmoved. You are here in our world of space and time, and we praise you for that. The reality of Jesus' life, suffering, death, and resurrection assures us that we not only can know you but also that you know us and that you desire for us to be immersed in your mercy, grace, and redeeming love. Even more amazing is that you choose to impart the presence and the power of the Holy Spirit to us, working in us and through us your divine will. And so, we do not simply pray for miracles. We make ourselves available to be miracles of your mercy, grace, and redeeming love in a world so desperately in need of your presence and power. As you command today, O Lord, I thank you for every person who makes your love and presence real and for every person who generously shares the riches of your grace with others. May your holy name be lifted up and honored through my life today for your sake and for the sake of all you love. In Jesus' name. Amen.

DAY 2

They will enter Zion with singing; everlasting joy will crown
their heads. Gladness and joy will overtake them, and
sorrow and sighing will flee away. (Isaiah 35:10)

Flood my heart today, Lord, with the unalloyed joy of your Presence. Inspire my thoughts. magnify my imagination, and frame my decisions. Occupy the center of my will. Help me be still in the silence and thoughtful with every word I speak. As I rush about and when I relax, when I am with others and when I am alone, in the freshness of the morning and in the weariness of the afternoon, may your peace rule in my heart. In moments I am able to pause and pray today, rekindle the joy of your salvation and remind me of your Power in my life that is greater than any task at hand. May all that I do be an offering to you and a witness to others of your truth, justice, and grace. This I pray in the strong name of Jesus. Amen.

Day 3

Forgetting what is behind and straining toward what is ahead,
I press on toward the goal to win the prize for which God has
called me heavenward in Christ Jesus. (Philippians 3:13b–14)

Lord Jesus, I pray that your thoughts would flood my mind, soften my heart, and fill me with your peace. Cast out any seeds of bitterness, resentment, or anger that have taken root and cause me to be resistant to love, compassion, patience, and understanding. I confess that there is much about present circumstances that confuse me, and I grieve for what once was but is no more. Every day I am confronted with arguments and pretensions that are designed to cause doubt, fear, and uncertainty. Yet, your promise remains that no eye has seen, nor has any ear heard, nor has any heart begun to imagine the things you have in mind for those who love you. O Lord, help me set my mind on things above and beyond the shadows of this life, that I might capture every thought and make it obedient to you. As your mind fills my thoughts, I will gladly embrace the reality of hope, the contentment of peace, and the healing power of your love. This I pray for your sake and for the sake of all you love, in your holy name. Amen.

DAY 4

Great are the works of the LORD; they are pondered by all
who delight in them. Glorious and majestic are his deeds,
and his righteousness endures forever. (Psalm 111:2–3)

O Lord, my God, this I believe, and therefore, I have hope: Morning
by morning, you renew your mercies. Great is your faithfulness.
How good and gracious you are. Every day is a new creation, a gift
to embrace, share, and celebrate. If I miss anything today, it will be
because of my own blindness or calloused heart. Forgive me for too
many days of doubting your goodness, nullifying your grace, and
abandoning faith. Rekindle the sparks of hope from the ashes of my
disappointments. Fan the flame of your Presence, and create the
warmth of your Spirit in me. Remind me of important things I have
forgotten, wonderful things that surround me, and eternal things that
reveal an amazing future that is your promise and my dream. This is
the day that you have made, Lord, and I choose to rejoice and be glad
in it. This I believe, and therefore, I have hope. In Jesus' name. Amen.

DAY 5

Therefore, if you have any encouragement from being united
with Christ, if any comfort from his love, if any common sharing
in the Spirit, if any tenderness and compassion, then make
my joy complete by being like-minded, having the same love,
being one in spirit and of one mind. (Philippians 2:1–2)

O merciful and loving God, I thank you today for all the merciful
and loving people through whom you made yourself known: for
parents who first became the gospel I understood through their words
and songs and hugs; for friends who accepted me as I am and did not
feel the need to change me into what I am not; for teachers who saw in
me potential and challenged me to attempt to reach it; for pastors who
welcomed me into the fellowship of faith when my faith was so weak
and uncertain; for my wife who has cared for me more than I have
cared for myself; for my children and grandchildren who will never
cease to love me, even when I am no longer with them. And I also pray

for all who are not so merciful or loving, asking your mercy on them, for they know not what they do. May the Spirit of Truth convict us all of our need and the redeeming love of Jesus convince us of the better way, so we will not only believe the gospel but also will become the gospel for the sake of all you love. I pray in the strong name of Jesus, our Savior and Lord. Amen.

DAY 6

Be completely humble and gentle; be patient, bearing with one another in love. Make every effort to keep the unity of the Spirit through the bond of peace. (Ephesians 4:2–3)

O Lord, let me never lose hope for the best in others nor a passion to seek to understand those who are not understood. Let me never lose the willingness to examine my own heart and test the spirits that I may walk along the path of righteousness and in the fellowship of your Spirit. Let me always have an ability to weep with those who weep, rejoice with those who rejoice, and bless all others, even those who reject me. Renew my faith in the ultimate triumph of your goodness, love, peace, and justice. Let me see life as it is, not relieved of its pain and suffering, betrayal, and loss. Rather, give me courage to pray, work faithfully, and wait patiently for the reality of your kingdom amid the worst that we experience, because you are faithful and good, and your mercies endure forever. This I pray in the strong name of Jesus for the sake of all you love. Amen.

DAY 7

To the weak I became weak, to win the weak. I have become all things to all people so that by all possible means I might save some. I do all this for the sake of the gospel, that I may share in its blessings. (1 Corinthians 9:22–23)

L ord Jesus, make me an instrument of your peace today. For those who are weak, help me to be their strength. For those who are discouraged, help me to offer hope. For those who are hurting, help me to stop and listen. For those who are lost, help me to introduce them to you, the Good Shepherd. For those who are empty, help me to be overflowing with love. For those who have made a mess of their lives, help me to be patient. For those who have nothing, help me to be extravagantly generous. For those who have no peace, help me to be a non-anxious witness of your Presence. For your sake and for all you love, I pray. Amen.

WEEK SIXTEEN

DAY 1

Like cold water to a weary soul is good news
from a distant land. (Proverbs 25:25)

How blessed, O Lord, are the feet of those who publish the Good News! Today we bless those messengers who have been to the Cross and are willing to cross seas and cultures to speak your words and bring hope to those who otherwise might not hear the gospel of Jesus. We pray for their needs as they often endure hardships in difficult places, far from the comforts of family and friends. Help us to do what we can to provide whatever is necessary for their witness. We pray that you would protect them from harm to their bodies and souls. Help them not to despair of the work when they see little fruit of their labors. Comfort them with the assurance that nothing they do in your name is done in vain, that in due season the harvest will come. May we be inspired, challenged, and engaged by their witness, sharing their burden for the least, the last, the loneliest, and the lost. It is in your strong name, Lord Jesus, that we pray for all who serve you today, across the streets and around the world, for the sake of your kingdom. Amen.

DAY 2

For in Scripture it says, "See, I lay a stone in Zion, a chosen
and precious cornerstone, and the one who trusts in
him will never be put to shame." (1 Peter 2:6)

This we believe, Lord Jesus: You willingly came into our world of space and time, taking on our flesh and blood to live our life, suffer our pain, share our sorrows, bear our sins, and die our death. In your passion, you opened the way to forgiveness. By the Spirit, you opened the way to Paradise. Help us today to experience and express your transforming resurrection power—to silence the evil word, to forbid the evil deed, to break the evil habit, and to banish the evil thought. Flood our souls with perfect love, and make our lives shine as a light in the darkness. We pray in your holy name for the sake of your kingdom and all that you love. Amen.

DAY 3

If you remain in me and my words remain in you, ask whatever you
wish, and it will be done for you. This is to my Father's glory, that you
bear much fruit, showing yourselves to be my disciples. (John 15:7–8)

This I believe: Before I embrace each day, O God, I must pause and let you first embrace me. Too often I ignore this divine moment and let the tyranny of the urgent crowd out the friendship you desire and I need. But here, in the quiet, my heart is moved. I am at peace, and I find hope, purpose, fellowship, and love. Here you remind me that you are God, and I am not. Because of Jesus, my life is changed, now and forever. You remind me that I can pause and draw near throughout this day so I may be prepared, ready to engage the world in the power of the Holy Spirit. As I reflect on your Word, I am inspired to pray more deeply, obey more readily, and serve more thoughtfully. Here and now, I offer you my worship, pausing in your amazing Presence, embraced by eternal love, content and confident, for yours is the kingdom and the power and the glory forever and ever. Amen.

Day 4

Whether you turn to the right or to the left, your ears will hear a
voice behind you, saying, "This is the way; walk in it." (Isaiah 30:21)

This I believe: I will not be called upon this day, O Lord, to face
any task or challenge or issue alone. In every moment I will be
accompanied by your Presence and empowered your grace. Through
the eyes of faith, I will see Jesus walking the path before me, carrying
my burdens, and marking the way for me to follow. I will think of
faithful witnesses who have inspired and encouraged me, those saints
who once walked this path with you and who now rest from their
labors. I will remember how they welcomed me, prayed for me, and
loved me into your kingdom. I will be reminded throughout the day
that I am on this journey with other pilgrims, brothers and sisters in
Christ with whom I share this fellowship in the Spirit. I will thank you
for all who cheer me on when I am lonely, pray for peace when I am
anxious, guard me when I am tempted, and counsel me when the way
is unclear. Established by your Word and surrounded by steadfast love,
I begin another day as a follower who seeks to be worthy of your holy
name, caring for the poor, praying for the broken-hearted, defending
the helpless, welcoming the stranger, and sharing the story of Jesus
and his love. In my life, Lord, be glorified today. Amen.

Day 5

For this is what the Sovereign LORD says: I myself will search for my
sheep and look after them. As a shepherd looks after his scattered flock
when he is with them, so will I look after my sheep. (Ezekiel 34:11–12a)

This I believe: You are the Good Shepherd who walks with me beside
still waters and into green pastures. You supply my needs, restore
my soul, and lead me in the way of everlasting Life. I am grateful for
the gifts of grace throughout the years—salvation and strength, health
and happiness, wisdom and joy. Your love surpasses my imagination,
and your faithfulness amazes me every day. Help me to recall your
goodness in the moments of disappointment, believing that even

misfortune can be an occasion for me to grow deeper in knowledge and grace. Give me faith that I may learn to walk with you through the shadows and not be afraid of evil. Let your mercy and goodness fill my cup to overflowing, enabling me to bless others this day and in every kind of day. Lead me step-by-step on the journey home, O Lord, for yours is the unshakable kingdom that has no end and the immeasurable love that will never be exhausted. Amen.

DAY 6

Though you have not seen him, you love him; and even though you do not see him now, you believe in him and are filled with an inexpressible and glorious joy, for you are receiving the end result of your faith, the salvation of your souls. (1 Peter 1:8–9)

This I believe: The joy of the Lord is my strength, and therefore, today I will choose to take joy with me wherever I go. To whom much is given, much is required, and I should not—I cannot—be ungrateful by keeping joy to myself. I can be joyful because others have shared their joy with me. Others need the joy I can and should share with them in word and deed. Lest I get lost in the dull, disappointing, discouraging, and disheartening occasions of the day, I will choose to celebrate the unalloyed joy in the laughter of children, the pure sweetness in the smile of the aged, the unbridled courage of youth, and the holy whispers of saints in prayer. Yes, my Lord, this is a day that you have made. With all who love you and all whom you love, I will rejoice and be glad in it! In Jesus' name. Amen.

DAY 7

We demolish arguments and every pretension that sets itself up against the knowledge of God, and we take captive every thought to make it obedient to Christ. (2 Corinthians 10:5)

This I believe: It is your desire to give me your mind that I might have your perspective and gain your understanding. Too quickly I come to conclusions that often lead to disappointments and discouragement simply because of my nearsighted spirituality. It is as if I am trying to see through dark glass or merely observing a dim reflection in a mirror. My thoughts are not your thoughts, and so my ways cannot be your ways. Yet, your Spirit can open my heart to the depth of your love, my mind to the breadth of your compassion, and my life to the possibilities of your grace. May I not think too highly of myself but think rightly toward all others. May I be slow to speak but quick to obey. May I make decisions today in the light of eternity and be comforted every moment of every day with the assurance that I and all that I love are forever in your thoughts. For your sake and for all you love, I ask these things in your holy name. Amen.

WEEK SEVENTEEN

DAY 1

But God demonstrates his own love for us in this: While we were still sinners, Christ died for us. (Romans 5:8)

We begin this new day and week praising and thanking you, O God, for the depth and breadth of your love. In his living and giving and dying, Jesus proved how desperately and completely you love us. In the power of his resurrection, we understand eternal life as eternal love. In the fellowship of the Spirit, we share our hopes, fears, joys, and sorrows with brothers and sisters who experience and express your love every day. In the creation of every new day, your love and mercy allow us to begin again. And so, we ask for your help to be loving to the unlovely, to care for the lonely, to forgive those who have hurt our loved ones and us. We also ask that you forgive us for not trusting you and allowing love to guide our thoughts, words, and deeds. Today, we choose love, because holy love has chosen us. For your sake, and for the sake of this world you love, we pray. Amen.

Day 2

His divine power has granted to us all things that pertain to
life and godliness, through the knowledge of him who called
us to his own glory and excellence. (2 Peter 1:3 ESV)

We live in a world that responds to power, O God: the power of money, the power of status, the power of influence, the power of weapons, the power of politics. Yet, your power, which this world fails to understand, is the greater power, the true power that changes hearts, heals wounds, mends broken relationships, and gathers us into an eternal community. Forgive us, O Lord, that we have not learned this, have ignored or rejected this, or we have been seduced to hope in that which is ultimately impotent. In the quiet of this moment, as we welcome a day full of possibilities of grace and new beginnings, help us to embrace your promise to live in the power of the Holy Spirit. Whatever our dreams have been, give us better ones. Whatever our path has been, show us a more excellent way. We pray the prayer of St. Francis, "O divine Master, grant that I may not so much seek to be consoled as to console, to be understood as to understand, to be loved as to love; for it is in giving that we receive; it is in pardoning that we are pardoned; it is in dying to self that we are born to eternal life." Through Christ our Lord we pray. Amen.

Day 3

If you then, though you are evil, know how to give good gifts
to your children, how much more will your Father in heaven
give the Holy Spirit to those who ask him! (Luke 11:13)

I know the promise, Jesus: "Ask and it will be given to you. Seek and you will find. Knock and the door will be opened to you." But more than once I have asked, and it was not given to me. I have sought sincerely and come away disappointed. I am not sure I really want to know what is on the other side of that door after all. Surely there is more to this promise, these amazing words that suggest your willingness, readiness, and ability to respond to my prayers. Ah, but as I look deeper, I see there is something more here. "Keep asking," you actually said, "and it will be given to you. Keep seeking, and you will find. Keep knocking, and the door will be opened." So, prayer is work, an ongoing conversation that is more about you and me than those things, more about trust than answers, more about obedience than obtaining. O Lord, help me to practice the promise rather than simply to claim it. Surprise me with your response rather than merely satisfying my wants and desires. May I experience the overflowing joy of the Holy Spirit and the deep assurance of your pleasure as I pray. So here I am, Lord, asking, seeking, knocking, waiting, trusting, and loving this moment with you. This is time well spent. Thank you. Amen.

DAY 4

For you created my inmost being; you knit me together in my mother's womb. I praise you because I am fearfully and wonderfully made;
your works are wonderful, I know that full well. (Psalm 139:13–14)

I thank you, O Lord, for this life I enjoy even when I do not understand it. Whatever you do is marvelous, and how well I know it. I am created in your image, and I am discovering on this journey what all that means. I want. I wonder. I reach. I pray. I imagine. I hope. I dream. I love. I am mortal, but I have a longing for heaven. I am not always brave, but I sometimes show courage. I am not always honest, but I desire the truth. I am not always loving, but that is my heart's desire. O Lord, deliver me from discouragement when things do not go my way and when I do not go your way. Keep me from losing faith when I am confused and I do not understand. May I act boldly on what I do understand. When it seems that I cannot hold on to you, help me to let go and let you do the holding, because you are able to accomplish infinitely more than we would ever dare to ask or hope. This I believe, my Lord and my God, for yours is the unshakable kingdom that has no end and the immeasurable love that will never be exhausted. Amen.

Day 5

Praise be to the God and Father of our Lord Jesus Christ! In his
great mercy he has given us a new birth into a living hope through
the resurrection of Jesus Christ from the dead, and into an
inheritance that can never perish, spoil or fade. (1 Peter 1:3–4a)

Help us, Lord Jesus, when we live on the wrong side of Easter. We worry about things that are so unnecessary in light of your Resurrection. We forfeit the benefits of life in the Spirit you have made possible to all who believe. Our timidity restrains us from living more daringly, more expectantly, and more joyfully. Out of fear of challenges and disappointments, we miss holy moments and divine appointments through which we can discover the adequacy of your provision, power, and peace. Help us, O Lord, to give up small ambitions that are self-serving and self-oriented for pure hearts that are committed to love you and love others as you have loved us. May we be your answers to the prayers of many as we feed the hungry, clothe the poor, care for the sick, welcome the outcast, teach the illiterate, and share the story of Jesus and his love across the street and around the world. May your Resurrection Power be contagious among us because we simply cannot keep silent or still! We are not among those who have no hope. We are Easter people, loving graciously, living expectantly, serving joyfully on the other side of Calvary and an empty tomb. Let it be, Lord Jesus, let it be, for yours is the unshakable kingdom that has no end and the immeasurable love that will never be exhausted. Amen.

DAY 6

The LORD bless you and keep you; the LORD make his face to
shine upon you and be gracious unto you; the LORD turn his
face toward you and give you peace. (Numbers 6:24–26)

Lord, in your mercy, hear our prayer this morning as we intercede
for these you love:

- Friends who are in great pain and facing serious health issues.
- Loved ones who are not coping well with circumstances
  beyond their control.
- Relatives whose hearts are far from you and have no sense of
  redeeming grace.
- Spouses who have lost their life companions and best friends.
- Colleagues who are filled with fear, anger, depression, and
  disbelief.
- Young adults who are consumed by a sense of unworthiness.
- Children who have been abused, misused, abandoned, and
  feel they are to blame.
- Prodigals who think they are unloved, unwanted,
  unforgiveable, and unacceptable.
- Addicts who are enslaved by their weaknesses and guilt,
  longing to be free.
- Young professionals who are overwhelmed by the pursuit of
  wealth and social status.
- Widows and widowers who sit alone, longing for someone to
  simply sit with them.
- Pastors who wonder how they can provide for their
  family's needs.
- This younger generation to be filled with delightful hope,
  unalloyed joy, unlimited faith, and perfect love—that such
  children will be your witnesses of the way to heaven.

Have mercy on us, O Lord, and hear our prayers, in Jesus'
name. Amen.

DAY 7

There remains, then, a Sabbath-rest for the people of God;
for anyone who enters God's rest also rests from their
works, just as God did from his. (Hebrews 4:9–10)

I need a quiet place today, Lord, holy ground beside still waters where you can restore my soul. I need to find that thin space between my life and the eternal where I can let go, relax, rest, and wait on you. After a hectic week of fighting without and fear within, others losing their calm and making unreasonable claims, news that suggests that life is out of control, I need to be still. I need to be truthful. I need strength to begin again. I need to remember your gift of Sabbath-rest. "Draw near to God, and he will draw near to you" (James 4:8 ESV). Time apart with you becomes a divine moment. When you are near, ordinary places become sacred space and all that is unhealthy and unhelpful and unholy has no space. I praise and thank you, Father, Son, and Holy Spirit, for the divine appointment and the holy ground of Sabbath-rest. Amen.

WEEK EIGHTEEN

DAY 1

When I consider your heavens, the work of your fingers, the moon and
the stars, which you have set in place, what is mankind that you are
mindful of them, human beings that you care for them? (Psalm 8:3–4)

O Lord, our Lord, how majestic is your name in all the earth! We praise you for your greatness, which embraces our smallness. We praise you for your majesty, which was once clothed in our humanity. We praise you for your sovereignty, which embraces our frailty. We praise you for your holiness, which overwhelms our sinfulness. We praise you for your glory, which heals our brokenness. We praise you for your love, which gives us life, abundant and eternal. We praise you for Jesus, who came into our world of space and time to claim us for his own. We praise you for the Spirit, who gives us power to honor you and bless others. We praise you that your mercies are renewed every morning, your grace is more than sufficient, and nothing in all creation is able to separate us from your love. O Lord, our Lord, may your name be praised in all the earth! Amen.

DAY 2

From the rising of the sun to the place where it sets, the name of the LORD is to be praised. (Psalm 113:3)

On this day, O Lord, may my first thought be of you, my first word be your name, and my first action be praise. "Morning has broken, like the first morning," we sing. This is just another morning, yet it is a new morning, the first of its kind, like the first morning. There has never been a day like this one. I have never lived a day like this one. So, let me anticipate new beginnings, seek out new relationships, welcome new adventures, embrace new opportunities, and discover new possibilities of your grace. Set me free from the regret of past failures, the despair of disappointment, and the fear of an unknown future. "Behold, I make all things new" (Revelation 21:5 NKJV). This I believe. Therefore, make me keenly aware of the ordinary gifts of this day and the extraordinary evidence of your grace. Stir in me a new eagerness for life, a new openness to love, and a new passion to serve. This I pray, for thine is the kingdom and the power and the glory on this morning and forever. Amen and amen.

DAY 3

May the words of my mouth and this meditation of my heart be pleasing in your sight, LORD, my Rock and my Redeemer. (Psalm 19:14)

Words often come easily to me, Jesus. I sing along with familiar songs and hymns. I join the creeds and the model prayer you taught your disciples to pray. I remember phrases of poems, lines from movies, and popular clichés. I enjoy conversations with loved ones and engaging in small talk with strangers. It is more difficult, however, to find words when I need to confess my sin, offer an apology to someone I have hurt, or speak the truth in love to another. I stammer and stutter or remain strangely quiet when I could say a good word for you. O Word of God, save me from uttering careless words that hurt, and fill my mouth with words that heal. May all my conversations today be seasoned with grace, to the honor and glory of the One who has the words of eternal life. Amen.

DAY 4

Whoever does not take up their cross and follow me is not
worthy of me. Whoever finds their life will lose it, and whoever
loses their life for my sake will find it. (Matthew 10:38–39)

I dare to pray a rather dangerous prayer today, Heavenly Father. I ask to have the mind of Christ. I want to be aware of you in every moment as Jesus set his mind to do your will. I want to know your heart of love, the power of your righteousness, and the contentment of your Presence. I want to see the world as Jesus sees it, people who need healing and hope, peace and justice, saving and sanctifying grace. I also want to see his vision of the kingdom as it is intended and will be one day, how it reorders our lives and reorganizes my priorities, how you are ready to redeem what is lost and what seems hopeless. I know this is a dangerous prayer, because it opens me up to specific responsibilities, radical obedience, and inevitable inconveniences. No doubt it will cause me to be thought of as many others have thought of Jesus—annoying, unpredictable, foolish, offensive. I ask for courage to live out this prayer today, not counting the cost but satisfied that being of one mind with Jesus is to be an answer to the prayers of others. May it be so in my life, in his name and for the sake of all you love. Amen.

DAY 5

Little children, you are from God and have overcome them, for the one who is in you is greater than the one who is in the world. (1 John 4:4)

Lord Jesus, you have walked where we are walking. You have stood where we are standing. You have faced what we are facing. You have been tempted as we are being tempted. Thank you for your obedience, faithfulness, and strength over all that seeks to kill, steal, and destroy. I praise you that by grace and in the power of the Holy Spirit you have given us the ability to stand firm. We are not victims but more than conquerors. We are not strangers but friends. Even in the darkest moments of our lives, you are there with us. You have given us not a spirit of fear but of power, love, and self-control. Thank you for this reality of new life, renewed hope, and a certain future. Throughout this day and every day help us to be channels of faith, hope, and love for all who are tempted by fear, uncertainty, and evil. This we pray for the sake of your kingdom and all for whom you laid down your life. Amen.

DAY 6

Now may the God of peace, who through the blood of the eternal covenant brought back from the dead our Lord Jesus, that great Shepherd of the sheep, equip you with everything good for doing his will, and may he work in us what is pleasing to him, through Jesus Christ, to whom be glory forever and ever. Amen. (Hebrews 13:20–21)

O God, your Presence is our peace. Your Love is our hope. Your Truth is our salvation. We wait on you this morning in quietness and humility. May your Spirit fall upon us as the morning mist covers the earth. Lift the burdens of troubled souls. Still the hearts of the fearful. Encourage the desperate with hope. Gird up the weak with confidence. Give vision to those whose lives are dull and joy to those who are mired in sadness. May the sick receive healing grace and the curious, godly wisdom. Give us the power to live today in the world without loving it more than we love you and to live in you so we may love all that you love in the world. May we be your servant people, caring for the poor and the rich, the young and the old, the saints and the sinners, walking among them as Jesus walked, making plain the gospel in word and deed. Help us to see the abundance of what you have given us and the little we need for daily living, and may the surplus be yours for the blessing of the world. This we pray in the name of Jesus, who loved us and gave himself for us, the Lamb of God who takes away the sin of the world. Amen.

DAY 7

I love those who love me, and those who seek me find me. (Proverbs 8:17)

O Lord, my God, we come to this hour purely by your grace. Thank you for speaking through life and light, in thoughts and memories, in stillness and revelation, in love and joy, and even in sorrow. You have sustained us throughout every day and every kind of day, and we are grateful. We ask for your forgiveness for spiritually unhealthy attitudes and unholy actions. We pray for your healing touch, making our hearts pure and our bodies strong. We pray for friends and family whose lives have been touch by death, illness, or misfortune. Help them to trust in your abiding Presence and the comfort of the Holy Spirit. Help us want to hear and understand your Word so that our hearts will burn within us, and we can give witness to the joy for which Jesus died and is now ours through his living Presence. This we pray in his strong name. Amen.

WEEK NINETEEN

DAY 1

Remember this: Whoever sows sparingly will also reap sparingly, and whoever sows generously will also reap generously. Each of you should give what you have decided in your heart to give, not reluctantly or under compulsion, for God loves a cheerful giver. (2 Corinthians 9:6–7)

O God, our Creator and Redeemer, we praise you for your goodness and mercy. Great is your faithfulness! We ask for your blessing not out of a false sense of our own worthiness or entitlement, but that we will be blessed to be a blessing to all whom you love. All good gifts come from you. They are yours to give, and they are yours to withhold. They are not ours to keep. We hold them in trust. May we learn to be content with what we have, remembering that we do not need most of what we want and that true joy is found in simplicity and generosity. Only as we continue to depend on you for all things and be thankful for everything can we truly and rightly enjoy anything. And may we always keep in mind the words of your faithful servant, Jim Eliot, that "he is no fool who gives what he cannot keep to gain what he cannot lose." Let it be so, O Lord, in all our living and giving. Amen.

DAY 2

Show me your ways, LORD, teach me your paths. Guide me in your truth and teach me, for you are God my Savior, and my hope is in you all day long. (Psalm 25:4–5)

Good morning, Lord! I awake to this new day with all its possibilities, its uncertainties, its many faces, and its underlying mystery. Such is every day, but this is today, another gift of life to share with others. Every day is a new creation of yours, and I am amazed and thankful. May I be able—in your strength—to move through this day free of anger or bitterness so that when I meet my neighbor or encounter a stranger, I may recognize your face. Confirm the truth by which I rightly live; confront me with the truth from which I wrongly turn. I do not ask for what I want but for what you know I need, as I offer this day and myself back to you, Blessed Redeemer and Creator. Be glorified in my life today. Amen.

DAY 3

But the fruit of the Spirit is love, joy, peace, forbearance, kindness, goodness, faithfulness, gentleness and self-control. Against such things there is no law. (Galatians 5:22–23)

Be with me today, Holy Spirit, wherever I go and particularly be with me here at home. Be with all whom I love and help me to show those nearest to me the care and concern I show to others for whom I am responsible beyond my home. Help me to show politeness to my own household, the courtesy which I understand is proper and right to show to strangers. Lord, each day may I learn better how not to presume upon the kindness of those whom I love and who love me. Let perfect love begin at home today—no, let it begin with my heart. I humbly ask this through Jesus Christ, our Lord and Lover of our souls. Amen.

DAY 4

All this I have spoken while still with you. But the Advocate, the Holy Spirit, whom the Father will send in my name, will teach you all things and will remind you of everything I have said to you. (John 14:25–26)

Lord, have mercy on me. Too easily I become overly committed, and too often your peace does not rule in my heart. And so, as I begin this day I pray that you would come with heavenly calm into the clutter of my everyday world. Come with your strength into my weakness. Come with your holiness into my self-centeredness. Come into every corner of my heart and make your home in me. Let your abiding Presence that stilled the hearts of saints calm my soul. Let the courage that inspired them inspire me. Let the imagination that possessed them to pray past the ordinary into the unusual possess my mind so that I may transcend what I think I know of myself and my circumstances and devote myself truly and completely to the glory of your name. May others see your life through me, steadying those who have slipped along their journey, encouraging those who have forgotten their way, comforting those who grieve, and opening all hearts to love, hope, and eternal joy. I pray believing that yours, O Lord, is the unshakable kingdom that has no end and the immeasurable love that will never be exhausted. Amen.

Day 5

Truly my soul finds rest in God; my salvation comes
from him. Truly he is my rock and my salvation; he is my
fortress, I will never be shaken. (Psalm 62:1–2)

O Lord, we wake up every morning to a world that is changing. Every day is fraught with uncertainty. We encounter twists and turns of life we do not see coming. We often feel out of control over matters that affect our lives and the lives of our loved ones. We wonder as our thoughts wander over the unknown. This is our world as we know it and our life as we were born into it. It is what it is, but we also know this is not all there is. You have set eternity in our hearts, and we always are longing for that "something more." We praise your holy name that we also can know that the One who made our hearts, with all its hopes and dreams, also is able to satisfy its deepest longings. Therefore, our Lord and our Savior, we can begin this day, the first day of the rest of our lives, with the confidence you will never leave us or forsake us. We will kneel before we stand, bow before we rise, let go so we can be held, and pray before we enter into a day unlike any other. Today, we will fear no evil, change, or uncertainty, for you are with us. Alleluia! Alleluia! We go forth, in your name in quietness and confidence, to serve you with glad and grateful hearts. Amen.

DAY 6

Be kind and compassionate to one another, forgiving each
other, just as in Christ God forgave you. Follow God's example,
therefore, as dearly loved children. (Ephesians 4:32–5:1)

Our Heavenly Father, you never intended us to journey through life alone. Created in your image, you stamped on our hearts a restlessness that will not be satisfied if we are apart from you and choose to distance ourselves from one another. Through the eternal covenant by the blood of Jesus we draw near and are reconciled to you. Through his life, death, and resurrection we can draw near to one another, remove barriers and tear down walls that divide us. Freely we have received, freely we can give. Fully we have been forgiven, fully we can forgive. Perfectly we are loved, perfectly we can love. May we who claim your name love and live among all others in such a way that in observing us, they see the resemblance, are drawn to you, and give you praise. For the sake of all you love, we pray in Jesus' name. Amen.

DAY 7

The Word became flesh and made his dwelling among us. We
have seen his glory, the glory of the one and only Son, who
came from the Father, full of grace and truth. (John 1:14)

Lord Jesus, how marvelous it is to know that you came so near to us in the flesh that we heard the eternal Word through your voice and gazed into the eyes that have watched us forever. We marvel at the thought that you began the liberation of sinners from the burden of guilt, welcomed all those on the lonely edges of life, and proved the rule of your eternal kingdom as bodies were healed, evil was broken forever, and a new community formed to continue your mission to every tongue, race, nation, and tribe. Until that great day when the arrival of your kingdom interrupts all our work and we are ushered into the fullness of all that you have made possible as the faithful Promise and true Revelation of God, we offer ourselves in praise, honor, and thanksgiving, for you alone are worthy. Amen. (Adapted from Phil Thraikill)

WEEK TWENTY

DAY 1

For those who are led by the Spirit of God are children of God. The Spirit you received does not make you slaves, so that you live in fear again; rather, the Spirit you received brought about your adoption to sonship. And by him we cry, *"Abba*, Father." The Spirit himself testifies with our spirit that we are God's children. (Romans 8:14–16)

I begin this day, O Lord, meditating on the eternal plan that invites me to know you in such a personal way that I can call you Father. You desire that all may enjoy such a relationship with you forever. May I do nothing today to disrupt the deep peace and abiding joy of your Presence. With the whole of creation that groans to be set free from its limitations, pains, and struggles, I, too, groan to be free, healed, and at rest. I welcome every influence of the Holy Spirit upon my spirit today to that end. When you knock on the door of my heart, may I not keep you waiting without but welcome you readily within. Do not let me harbor anything in my heart that offends you or brings shame to your holy name. May no corner of my heart be closed to your Presence. Change me as you will, make of me what you can, and use me as you wish, that as your beloved child and devoted servant, I honor you and bless others. This is my hope and my prayer throughout this and every day, in Jesus' name. Amen.

DAY 2

He says, "Be still, and know that I am God...." (Psalm 46:10)

I really want to be able to do that, Lord, to be still for a few moments, but stillness is so difficult for me. My world is filled with clanging and clattering, noises and voices, interruptions and disruptions. Even in church I prefer sound. I am not comfortable being still. But, you do not simply invite me to be still; you command it! Be quiet! Be still! Help me, O Lord, to embrace the stillness that I may grow steadier and surer. It is in this quietness that I become more aware of your endless activity, more confident that you move faster than I, and that you hear my prayers above all the clatter in my life. You never sleep nor slumber. You are always present, forever accomplishing what you desire. You remain with me. You heed my unspoken prayers and anxious hopes. I rest in you in the stillness of this moment. Thank you, Jesus. Amen.

DAY 3

You do not delight in sacrifice, or I would bring it; you do not take pleasure in burnt offerings. My sacrifice, O God, is a broken spirit; a broken and contrite heart you, God, will not despise. (Psalm 51:16–17)

Forgive us, Lord, when we harden our hearts lest we become vulnerable and enter the pain of those who suffer. Forgive us when we close our minds lest we be confronted with truth that demands repentance. Forgive us for our selective hearing lest we are moved by the cries of our neighbors who do not look like us. Forgive us for quick tempers and angry words that build walls of distrust and barriers of resentment. Forgive our unkind thoughts and our lack of generosity toward the less fortunate that we too quickly judge and too often blame. Forgive our indifference to the grief, pain, and sorrow of the poor in spirit. Forgive us for our lack of courage and compassion to be friends of sinners. Forgive us, O God. Have mercy on us, Jesus. Fill us, Holy Spirit, lest we grieve you and wander away from your Presence. Let our hearts break for what breaks yours. For such a time as this, O Lord, we offer ourselves in spirit, mind, and body as your witnesses of hope and instruments of healing. We pray in the name of Jesus for the sake of our nation, our world, and all that you love. Amen.

Day 4

Therefore, since we are surrounded by such a great cloud of witnesses, let us throw off everything that hinders and the sin that so easily entangles. And let us run with perseverance the race marked out for us, fixing our eyes on Jesus, the pioneer and perfecter of faith. For the joy set before him he endured the cross, scorning its shame, and sat down at the right hand of the throne of God. (Hebrews 12:1–2)

Thank you, Jesus, for sharing your story with us. Thank you for teaching us of your kingdom of love and truth. Thank you for living your life so clearly before us. Thank you for your compassion, healing, forgiveness, and love. Thank you for stories of a lost coin, a lost sheep, and a lost son that end with great rejoicing when they were found. Thank you for coming to us even before we knew we were lost. Thank you that through your suffering, death, and resurrection you opened the door for us to share in your kingdom forever. Thank you for those who told us your story, those whose lives and example have inspired us to want to know more about you. Thank you that it is not just a story we hear and enjoy; you are the Story, the Eternal Word, the Author and Finisher of our faith. Jesus, continue to write your story on my heart and help me so to live and speak that others will come to know and love your story, too. In your name, and for the sake of all who have yet to hear your story I pray. Amen.

Day 5

I love the LORD, for he heard my voice; he heard my cry for mercy. Because he turned his ear to me, I will call on him as long as I live. (Psalm 116:1–2)

How should I pray today, Lord? Should I wait until all is calm and right and pleasant in my soul? Should I choose my words carefully and thoughtfully express my concerns so as not to offend you and others? Should I sit straight or fall on my knees or even lay prostrate on the floor? How should I pray about matters for which I have no words? For such things I have questions rather than petitions, more doubt than confidence that there are answers. How should I pray? I am not really sure, but this I can do. I can come just as I am and offer whatever I can, in whatever words I can muster, with whatever amount of faith I have. I can pray as Jesus taught, asking for daily bread, forgiveness, and deliverance. I can pray with grace because no posture or petition earns your attention. And I can pray as best I can, knowing that whatever I have left unsaid that should have been said, O Lord of my heart, you already have heard. This is my prayer, with praise to your holy name. Amen.

DAY 6

But we have this treasure in jars of clay to show that this all-surpassing power is from God and not from us. We are hard pressed on every side, but not crushed; perplexed, but not in despair; persecuted, but not abandoned; struck down, but not destroyed. We always carry around in our body the death of Jesus, so that the life of Jesus may also be revealed in our body. (2 Corinthians 4:7–10)

Life is hard, Lord. We struggle in a world that is filled with deceit and betrayal, envy and sloth, hardship and violence. Yet it is the world you have made, the world you love, the world we all share, and the world you are still creating with renewed mercies every morning and gifts of grace throughout the day. We long for that day when all the kingdoms of this world will have become the kingdom of Christ and all our struggles in human relationships will give way before your eternal love. Help us to live today in this hope, that because of Jesus we can be forgiven of all the ways we have offended you and that we can be free to forgive all who have offended us. Remind us of the long line of faithful servants who embraced the Cross and triumphed over adversity to glorify your name. Teach us how to be the Church, the Body of Christ, a living presence in the midst of a fallen world, fully devoted to you and all you love. May we be constantly amazed at what you can do through us by the grace of our Lord Jesus at work within us. It is to him we give all honor, glory, blessing, and praise as we pray in his name. Amen.

DAY 7

Paraphrase of Habakkuk 3:17–19

Though my finances are inadequate, and my health fails and the forces of evil flourish; though my teams always lose and my preferred candidates are never elected to office; though I am unappreciated, ignored, and even the target of malicious slander; though all the world seems to be falling apart, I will not resent you, Lord. I will not let go of you. In fact, I will find my joy in you, the God who saves. You are my strength, and I am confident that you will take me to heights I never imagined were possible. Amen. (Unknown)

WEEK TWENTY–ONE

DAY 1

These are they who have come out of the great tribulation; they have washed their robes and made them white in the blood of the Lamb.... Never again will they hunger; never again will they thirst. The sun will not beat down on them, nor any scorching heat. For the Lamb at the center of the throne will be their shepherd; he will lead them to springs of living water. And God will wipe away every tear from their eyes. (Revelation 7:14, 16–17)

On this day I come to you, Jesus, absolutely desperate and yet full of hope. I share the burden of suffering for members of my family, friends in my church, neighbors in our community, the least, last, lost, and lonely across the world. My heart is weighed down with such grief, hurt and pain, illness, loneliness, and spiritual darkness. But I also pray with unalloyed joy and unbridled hope, praising and thanking you for all that you are, all you have done, and all you promise to those who love you. Even as I try to pray with a troubled heart, I love and trust you. My weakness is your moment to give me your strength so that your peace and wholeness rule over my heart. And so, today I pray, *Come with power, Lord Jesus, bind our wounds and heal our brokenness. Come with peace and banish all envy, fear, and selfish ambition. Come with a vision of your unshakable kingdom that has no end, and we will live and share forever in the immeasurable love that will never be exhausted. Come, Lord Jesus.* Amen.

DAY 2

Praise the LORD, my soul; all my inmost being, praise his holy name. Praise the LORD, my soul, and forget not all his benefits—who forgives your sins and heals your diseases, who redeems your life from the pit and crowns you with compassion, who satisfies your desires with good things so that your youth is renewed like the eagle's. (Psalm 103:1–5)

O God, I begin this day remembering. I remember shining moments of happiness and shattering moments of grief. I remember times when faith was easy and times when doubt was so strong. I remember hours when I was thrilled with life, and I remember days that were filled with disappointment. I remember the ebb and flow of ordinary days, the tug and pull of life that define our days. And I remember how often in the midst of the ordinariness of those days I felt the presence of the Holy Spirit, assuring me, comforting me, reminding me that you are there. And so, I go into this day remembering your grace that strives with us, your strength that sustains us, and the eternal promise that you will be with us always, everywhere. I remember. And I marvel. And I am grateful. Because of Jesus. Amen.

DAY 3

Now to him who is able to do immeasurably more than all we ask or imagine, according to his power that is at work within us, to him be glory in the church and in Christ Jesus throughout all generations, for ever and ever! Amen. (Ephesians 3:20–21)

M ost merciful Lord, you know what I desire before I ask. You give much more than I need before I even think of it. You are great and you are good, and I am thankful. I do not have the vocabulary today to express how worthy you are of all praise and honor, nor, regrettably, do I have the ability to explain convincingly the beauty of holy love. Ah, but you invite me simply to bow in your Presence, releasing all that I am and ever hope to be, knowing that you are able to save me to the uttermost. Abiding in your Presence right now, help me to unclench my hands, relax my tense muscles, and recondition my thinking about myself and the world around me. Shape me by your truth and grace that I may love others with Christ-like love. Give me glimpses of your kingdom that cast out selfish vision and slavish fear. Make me more willing to follow Jesus even when bearing my cross seems to be an impossible task. I do not want to simply talk the talk but walk the way when I pray, *Here I am, Lord; mold me and make me after your will.* Then I truly will bless your name and sing your praises with my whole heart. I pray this in the name of Jesus, for yours is the unshakable kingdom that has no end and the immeasurable love that will never be exhausted. Amen.

Day 4

Brothers and sisters, I do not consider myself yet to have taken hold of it. But one thing I do: Forgetting what is behind and straining toward what is ahead, I press on toward the goal to win the prize for which God has called me heavenward in Christ Jesus. (Philippians 3:13–14)

Lord, I am thankful for the assurance that I am never, ever alone on this journey. You are always near. You know the beat of my heart, the pulse of my spirit, the words spoken, and the words unspoken. Hear me, as I pray into this day, seeking first and foremost to live into your holiness, throwing off anything that hinders our relationship and desiring everything that I may experience and express the maximum measure of your grace available. As I rise in the morning, I will be done with the past, facing a new day with roads to walk, hills to climb, songs to be sung, people to be loved, tears to be shed, pain to be endured, and, above all, the assurance of your Presence every step of the way. Thank you, Jesus. Amen.

Day 5

We who are strong ought to bear with the failings of the weak
and not to please ourselves. Each of us should please our
neighbors for their good, to build them up. (Romans 15:1–2)

Today, holy and merciful Lord, we pray for the poor in spirit who search for a life worth living but do not know where to look; for the suffering in mind and spirit who long for rest and release from pain; for the sick whose bodies cry out for relief and recovery; for the grieving who need to know you have not failed them or their loved ones; for the poor and hungry who need compassion and a fair chance; for the persecuted who are perishing without justice; for the anxious who worry without ceasing and without faith; for the addicted who struggle in bondage to forces they cannot control; for the fearful who do not have the courage to rejoice in the blessings of the moment; for the lonely who slip away for the lack of friendship; and for the refugee who has nowhere to lay his head. For these people we know and for those whose needs are known only to you, Lord Jesus, we ask for your saving and amazing grace. Amen.

Day 6

I will not leave you as orphans; I will come to you. Before
long, the world will not see me anymore, but you will see
me. Because I live, you also will live. (John 14:18–19)

Come, Lord Jesus, come. Come and hush our distracting thoughts. Come and speak into the din of our chaos and confusion. Come and whisper words of hope and strength. Come in compassion and assure us that justice will roll down like the waters. Come and be merciful to us. Come and occupy our souls and give us peace. Come and open our hearts to the unalloyed joy of your Presence. Come and open our eyes to behold your incomparable beauty. Come and stir the dying embers of our spirits that we may be fully alive in your Spirit. Come, Lord Jesus, come. Come and redeem this world you died to save. We wait for you. Amen.

DAY 7

Let us then with confidence draw near to the throne of grace, that we may receive mercy and find grace to help in time of need. (Hebrews 4:16 ESV)

Teach us to pray bold prayers, O Lord. As we come before you in quietness and humility, help us to shut out of our minds all that disturbs our souls so that we may become so filled with your Spirit that you are the supreme Reality who fills every fiber of our being. Help us to take hold of the Power that moves mountains and casts them into the sea. Better yet, let that Power take hold of us so we become expressions of grace and answers to prayer. And then, as we pray, filled with your Spirit and motivated with holy hearts, we understand and speak the language of your kingdom. O Lord, teach us to pray bold prayers for the sake of all you love. Amen.

WEEK TWENTY–TWO

DAY 1

But if we walk in the light, as he is in the light, we have fellowship with one another, and the blood of Jesus, his Son, purifies us from all sin. (1 John 1:7)

Our Heavenly Father, through the blood of Jesus you have redeemed us from the sin that drives us apart and have reconciled us with the love by which all things are held together. Thank you for making us partners with you in this eternal covenant. Thank you for the vision of your kingdom that blesses and inspires us. Thank you for a vision of divine love for all that does not diminish your love for each. Thank you for the vision of us as sheep that even when we wander away, the Good Shepherd goes looking for us. Thank you for the vision of the community of believers, the Church, whose history of division and dissension does not alter your desire for the salvation of the world. Thank you for the vision of the world whose greed and lust for power does not silence your demand for peace and holiness. Help us to so live in your vision before others that they, too, will believe and receive

the gospel, worship and adore you, love and obey your Word, and represent Jesus to the least, the last, the loneliest, and the lost across the
street and around the world. Amen.

DAY 2

When the Lord saw her, his heart went out to her
and he said, "Don't cry." (Luke 7:13)

Do I dare ask you, Lord Jesus, to break my heart with the things
that break your heart? I think of the depth of your compassion
in these stories of human suffering, and I know I could not handle
that. On one hand, I truly want to be more like you, fully human and
able and willing to suffer with those who suffer. On the other hand,
every day we are confronted with the pain of the human condition.
We eventually feel helpless and too easily learn not to listen much less
respond and get involved. Forgive us, Lord, for feeling less of what
breaks your heart and losing our capacity to love as you love. Help us
deny ourselves, take up our crosses daily, and embrace suffering as
obedient disciples who walk with you, Lamb of God, on the journey.
Wherever and to whomever you lead us today, may our hearts overflow
with compassion as we are your hands and feet and voice. For the sake
of your kingdom and all that you love, we pray in your holy name.
Amen.

DAY 3

So then, just as you have received Christ Jesus our Lord, continue to live
your lives in him, rooted and built up in him, strengthened in the faith as
you were taught, and overflowing with thankfulness. (Colossians 2:6–7)

O Lord, I thank you for the love that opens every morning, for
the quietness that begins each day, and for the enthusiasm that
comes to my heart in these quiet times together. I thank you for the
things I see with my eyes and the things I see only with my mind.
Help me to love your loved ones in this world in the noblest way, that
I will be a witness of your saving, sanctifying, and serving grace. Help

me to love your Spirit so that I am renewed every day with the things that you love. Teach me to love your will, that I may honor your name and bless others in the power of your Spirit. And may the joy of your Presence break upon me time after time today, Lord Jesus, my Friend and my Redeemer. Amen.

DAY 4

May our Lord Jesus Christ himself and God our Father, who
loved us and by his grace gave us eternal encouragement
and good hope, encourage your hearts and strengthen you in
every good deed and word. (2 Thessalonians 2:16–17)

No eye has seen nor any ear heard nor has entered into the heart of any person what you, O Lord, have prepared for all who love you. We see glimpses of holy love in the best of human relationships, in the beauty of family, and in the community of faithful believers. For the sake of this world, we who claim your name pray that we will see your way more clearly, love one another more dearly, and follow you more nearly. May the expression of resurrection hope that lies in us be gracious, redemptive, and winsome in all the words we speak and the service we offer others today and every day. Through Christ, the Light of the World, we pray. Amen.

DAY 5

Then Job replied to the LORD: "I know that you can do all things,
no purpose of yours can be thwarted. You asked, 'Who is this that
obscures my plans without knowledge?' Surely I spoke of things I did
not understand, things too wonderful for me to know." (Job 42:1–3)

Lord, after we so diligently make our plans, do you really laugh? After all, in your eternal design, knowing the end and the beginning, our plans surely appear childish and myopic. Ah, but you delight in us when we ask for wisdom. You are ready to show us that in yielding to your way, we grow beyond where we are now and discover a Power that transcends earthly barriers and limitations. Our problems become opportunities for discovering your Presence and your way through them. Your grace gives strength to those who are troubled, tired, and weak; those who are no longer able to cope with unrewarding jobs, dysfunctional relationships, and unending loneliness; those whose lives have spun out of control; those who no longer know where to turn or to whom. Good Shepherd, hold them, comfort them, inspire them, and let their lives be different because your touch has given them hope and a future. Help us to step out of our preconceived notions so we, too, may experience your glory, which transcends our fondest dreams and imaginations. For you alone are God, and you only are our guarantee of eternal joy. In Jesus' name we hope and pray. Amen.

DAY 6

Just as a body, though one, has many parts, but all its many parts form one body, so it is with Christ.... Now you are the body of Christ, and each one of you is a part of it. (1 Corinthians 12:12, 27)

We praise you, O Lord, for the body of Christ that has been a means of your grace all along our spiritual journeys. We remember the strong arms of the saints who prayed beyond the ordinary, carrying the weight of our troubled souls to you day and night as we were seeking, knocking, and asking for you to do for us what we could not do for ourselves. We have felt the welcoming arms of brothers and sisters who ushered us into the fellowship, nurtured us in the faith, corrected us in our immaturity, and prepared us to make the next generation of disciples. And we have run into the open arms of the faithful who patiently and prayerfully waited on us when we wandered away from the fellowship into the far countries and then embraced us when we became homesick for the family of God. It is in the body of Christ that we hear the call to begin our journey to spiritual wholeness, we belong eternally to the family of God in a covenant relationship, and we become the hands and feet and voices of Jesus for a world that is longing to be loved and welcomed home. All praise and glory be to you, O Lord, that you do immeasurably more than we ask or imagine, according to your power that is at work within us. Alleluia and amen!

DAY 7

But when the kindness and love of God our Savior appeared, he saved us, not because of righteous things we have done, but because of his mercy. He saved us through the washing of rebirth and renewal by the Holy Spirit, whom he poured out on us generously through Jesus Christ our Savior. (Titus 3:4–6)

In your marvelous wisdom and according to your amazing grace, O Lord, we are uniquely created in your image, capable of receiving and giving love. In the deepest experiences of the heart, we can know that we are accepted, loved, desired, and forgiven. This is love, that you love us not because we are lovable; we are lovable because you choose to love us. We may think we are unlovely, but we are never unloved. We may fear that we are resisted, rejected, or removed from your grace, but you are perfect in love, and perfect love casts out all fear. This is love, not that we rightly love you or consistently love one another as you commanded, but that you first loved us, even in our unloveliness and our unlovingness. And so we pray, Holy and Loving God, that you would save us from the heartaches and heartbreaks of pursuing love as something to be earned, acquired, held, guarded, or deserved. Through your Spirit, free our spirits to believe, receive, and give love as a pure gift, perfectly revealed in Jesus who gave his life so that we might enjoy an intimate relationship with you forever. This is love. This is my need. This is my prayer. Amen.

WEEK TWENTY–THREE

DAY 1

But from everlasting to everlasting the LORD's love is with those who fear him, and his righteousness with their children's children—with those who keep his covenant and remember to obey his precepts. (Psalm 103:17–18)

Alleluia! Today, O Lord, my Lord, I choose praise rather than blame, joy rather than sadness, confidence rather than fear. I praise you for life, love, and laughter. I praise you for the beauty of the earth and the serenity of the heavens. I praise you for the best of human relationships and the redemption of broken hearts. I praise you for the hymns of the saints and the songs of children. I praise you for the history of service and sacrifice of those who loved you more than life itself. I praise you for the dreams of early Christians that are being fulfilled across the world. I praise you for your Holy Presence as I pray, reminding me that eternal life is intermingled with the life I now live in this jar of clay. Alleluia! I choose to surrender all my cares and anxieties to you today and be gathered up in hope and in the power of the Holy Spirit. I choose to walk humbly with you, loving mercy and doing justice with others. For when all is said and done, yours is the kingdom and the power and the glory forever. Alleluia and amen.

DAY 2

He remembers his covenant forever, the promise he made,
for a thousand generations, the covenant he made with
Abraham, the oath he swore to Isaac. (Psalm 105:8–9)

O God, you have been a Friend to all the faithful throughout the generations, and today, in every circumstance and time of need, you will be my Friend. I am at peace, knowing that you are near. You watched over me through the night; let me not go through any part of this day without knowing your presence. I commend to you my body and soul as a means of your grace. To your love and care, I commend my family, friends, church family, fellow workers, neighbors, and those who are strangers—friends yet to be—but loved by you. I commend to you the community of faith, that the reality of the eternal covenant, sealed by the blood of Jesus, will equip and inspire us to do what pleases you and honors those you love throughout this day and every day. This I pray in the name and to the glory of our Savior, Jesus Christ, whose kingdom never ends and whose love will never be exhausted. Amen.

DAY 3

Is anyone among you in trouble? Let them pray. Is anyone happy?
Let them sing songs of praise. Is anyone among you sick? Let them
call for the elders of the church to pray over them and anoint
them with oil in the name of the Lord. And the prayer offered in
faith will make the sick person well; the Lord will raise them up.
If they have sinned, they will be forgiven. (James 5:13–15)

I pray, O Lord, that you will prepare my heart and mind for all this day holds. Help me to see your fingerprints in the beauty of the day. Help me listen carefully and hear you speaking in the cries for help that may not be spoken. Give me a deeper appreciation for the people with whom I share this day. You will touch me through human hands. May I also offer your touch to those who suffer but do not know how to ask for help: lonely people who bear their pain alone, anxious people who fear they can't make it, spiritually lost people who long for a Savior. Help me to look, listen, reach out, embrace, and pray with others who long for the healing grace and redeeming love of Jesus. For your sake and for the sake of all you love, I pray in your holy name. Amen.

DAY 4

And forgive us our debts, as we also have forgiven our debtors.
And lead us not into temptation, but deliver us from the evil one.
For if you forgive other people when they sin against you, your
heavenly Father will also forgive you. (Matthew 6:12–14)

Holy God, how good it is that your mercies are renewed every morning because every day I need strength and courage to do what is pleasing in your sight. I need grace to forgive those who have wronged me and to care for those who are distant from me. I need faith as I pray for the sick and attempt to bind up the brokenhearted among my friends. I need new power to proclaim the gospel and speak truth to the world. Help all of us today who claim your name to be more Christ-like in thought, word, and deed. May we be channels of your grace and mercies to all whose lives intersect with ours today. May your peace prevail over the hurry and worry that will tempt us to ignore you. O Lord, fill me with the Holy Spirit that love may break out of my life, giving witness of renewed mercies and amazing grace offered to all. In Jesus' holy name I pray. Amen.

DAY 5

As obedient children, do not conform to the evil desires you had when you lived in ignorance. But just as he who called you is holy, so be holy in all you do; for it is written: "Be holy, because I am holy." (1 Peter 1:14–16)

Heavenly Father, in the ups and days of each day, the good times and the bad, the sunshine and the clouds, the moments of inspiration and the agony of despair, you are always the same—with love and forgiveness, with healing and help, with promise and hope. Thank you for your activity in the world, for the creation of every day, the reconciliation of relationships, and the healing of bodies. Thank you for striving with us in our reluctant sanctification as your Church. My prayer today is for marriages where there is brokenness and disagreement, for parents whose hearts are wounded by their children, and for children who are apart from their parents. Help us, Lord, not to fear rejection or disillusionment when we pray. You made us and know us better than we know ourselves, so help us as we pray the prayer of Jesus—"Not what I will, but what you will." In full surrender of our hearts and faith believing in your saving and sanctifying grace, O God, fill us with the Holy Spirit. Make us pure in heart, strong in faith, powerful in love, generous in spirit, and grant us your peace. For the sake of your kingdom and all you love, we pray in Jesus' name. Amen.

DAY 6

But when you pray, go into your room, close the door and pray to your Father, who is unseen. Then your Father, who sees what is done in secret, will reward you. (Matthew 6:6)

Lord, there are many times I am not sure how to pray. Honestly, I am not very good at being still and listening. There is so much chatter and competing voices that shout out the quiet. Even when

I pray, I do not always pray with a trusting, believing heart. Afraid of not being heard and then being disappointed, I pray with a timid heart. And then as I pray, do I really want to be changed into what I do not know or control? Am I prepared for the answers to my prayers? I am very good at making excuses but less skilled in prayer. So, Lord Jesus, teach me to pray not pious-sounding phrases but in the Spirit and truth as you taught your disciples to pray this prayer:

> Our Father in heaven, hallowed be your name. Your kingdom come, your will be done, on earth as it is in heaven. Give us today our daily bread, and forgive us our debts as we forgive our debtors. And lead us not into temptation, but deliver us from evil. For the kingdom, the power and the glory are yours, now and forever. Amen.

DAY 7

We all, like sheep, have gone astray, each of us has turned to our own way; and the LORD has laid on him the iniquity of us all. (Isaiah 53:6)

Our Heavenly Father, you love us even when we are at our worst: when we have broken the rules of life, when we have injured our health, when we have mistreated our families and betrayed our friends, and when we have hated ourselves and complained about you. But you loved us all so much that you would not leave us at our worst. You see us for who we are meant to be not what we have become. You sent Jesus to redeem us, to deliver us from the deadly consequences of our own making. Amazing Love! How can it be that you would suffer our sin, brokenness, and rebellion, unworthy as we are? Oh, how I need to allow such love to flood my soul, that out of the overflow of being loved I may be capable of loving others even when they are at their worst. I choose the way of the Cross—the forgiveness of sins and the freedom from sin—as a follower of Jesus. O God, help me to leave behind all regrets, that in the embrace of holy love, I may embrace that which you love without reserve. This I pray because Jesus loves me, and this I know. Amen.

WEEK TWENTY–FOUR

DAY 1

Better is one day in your courts than a thousand elsewhere; I
would rather be a doorkeeper in the house of my God than dwell
in the tents of the wicked. For the LORD God is a sun and shield; the
LORD bestows favor and honor; no good thing does he withhold
from those whose walk is blameless. (Psalm 84:10–11)

I praise you, O Lord, for the community of faith with whom I share
this daily journey of life. I praise you for those who have cared for
me in my need, given comfort in my grief, forgiven my actions and
attitudes, and lifted me to your throne of grace in prayer. I praise you
for those whose lifestyles have made your love real and inspirational,
a beacon of hope in a dark, troubled world. I praise you for those who
have borne witness to the One who lived, laid down his life, and was
raised to make us whole, all who told the stories of Jesus that we might
love him, too, and trust him as Savior. I praise you for the fellowship
of the warm heart, those lives who reveal the power of the Holy Spirit,
demonstrating the fruit and gifts of the Spirit's Presence. I praise you
for those faithful servants whose courageous obedience and humble
service in years gone by made it possible for me to worship, pray,
serve, and share life in the community of faith today. O Lord, grant
us wisdom, grant us courage for the facing of this hour and for the
living of these days, lest we miss thy kingdom's goal. Forbid that we
fail to honor these whom you love or rightly serve you whom we adore.
Amen.

DAY 2

How priceless is your unfailing love, O God! People take refuge in
the shadow of your wings. They feast on the abundance of your
house; you give them drink from your river of delights. For with you
is the fountain of life; in your light we see light. (Psalm 36:7–9)

Lord Jesus, I thank you for mercy that opens every morning, for
quietness that welcomes each day, and for the enthusiasm that
comes to my heart in your Presence. I thank you for the wonders I see
with my eyes and the possibilities I see in my mind. I am a captive of
your unfailing love. Help me to love all others in the noblest way, that
my obedience to truth and full surrender to grace will be a witness to
this and future generations. Help me to love your Spirit so that I am
renewed every day with the things that you love. Teach me to love your
will, that I may serve you and others in the power of your Spirit. May
Resurrection joy break upon me and overflow to others throughout
this day, O Lord, my Friend and Redeemer. Amen.

DAY 3

A new command I give you: Love one another. As I have loved
you, so you must love one another. By this everyone will know
you are my disciples, if you love one another. (John 13:34–35)

Jesus, we have heard in your words and we have seen in your life
and death the witness of divine love. "Amazing love! How can it
be, that Thou, my God, shouldst die for me?" Nothing in all creation
can separate us from the reality of perfect love. But it is not enough to
know or talk or sing about your amazing love. You command that all
who are born of your Spirit and are partakers of your divine nature
must speak and live and express such love to others. Our love for you
means we deliberately identify ourselves with your interest in others—
all others. And that is not an option, is it? You bring across our paths
the kind of people who remind us of who we have been to you so that
we can learn to love them as we understand you have loved us. "As I
have loved you" so now we must love others—all others—and therein
we reveal whose disciples we are. O Lord, help me to love completely

all who need to hear and see the breadth and length and height and depth of your love. This I pray for the sake of your kingdom and for all that you love. Amen.

Day 4

Blessed is the one whose transgressions are forgiven, whose sins are covered. Blessed is the one whose sin the LORD does not count against them and in whose spirit is no deceit. (Psalm 32:1–2)

O Lord, as I pray today, I dare not ignore thoughts of hurts received and hurts given. I cannot come into your Holy Presence without confessing the deep sorrow I feel for the latter. Forgive me for the wounds I have inflicted and the grief I have given people whom I've loved. In the power of your Spirit help me learn to touch others with gentler hands and kinder words. Keep me from being so insensitive as to inflict pain with careless and thoughtless comments. Forgive me for being the problem rather than part of the solution. Let me be a witness to the truth that to whom much is given, much is required. And may the words of my mouth and the meditations of my heart be acceptable unto you and a means of grace to all others today and always. For your sake and all that you love. Amen.

Day 5

Make every effort to live in peace with everyone and to be holy; without holiness no one will see the Lord. (Hebrews 12:14)

O God, so much of our life is rather common and ordinary. We live by routine and habit most days, and we are comfortable with that. But in our complacency, we too easily allow mediocrity to become our new normal. We desperately long for Something More, but we have not because we ask not. Good and gracious Lord, we need interruptions of grace that remind us of the Divine Normal. We need to be aware— even anticipate—glory moments that come to us in the ordinary stuff of life: the unalloyed joy in the eyes of a child, the relentless hope in the witness of a wise teacher, the self-giving love in the touch of a caregiver, the stubborn faith in the prayer of an elderly saint. Help us to embrace what is true, honorable, just, pure, lovely, and gracious—things worthy of praise and evidence of the Holy Spirit at work among us. O God, give us holy hearts that we may experience and express the possibilities of your grace in every moment of every day for your sake and for the sake of all you love. In Jesus' name. Amen.

DAY 6

The Spirit of the Sovereign LORD is on me, because the LORD has anointed me to proclaim good news to the poor. He has sent me to bind up the brokenhearted, to proclaim freedom for the captives and release from darkness for the prisoners, to proclaim the year of the LORD's favor.... (Isaiah 61:1–2a)

Gracious Lord, we pray this morning for all who sincerely want to take steps of faith but whose minds are filled with doubt and despair. With hopes crushed by life circumstances and joy damaged by the actions of others, we pray especially for family members and friends who are finding it hard to believe and begin again. Their heartaches and heartbreaks are a stumbling block to deeper commitment. They are offended by the certainties that others seem to have in the face of their own insecurities and doubts. Their fear will not allow them to ask questions, lest they be seen as weak, inadequate, and thus, unworthy. But you, O Lord, are rich in mercy and lavish with your grace. Come and heal these broken spirits. Encourage and strengthen these weary souls. Confirm hope and restore joy in these troubled hearts. Transform these loved ones to become witnesses of Calvary Love and Pentecostal Power to this weary, doubting, damaged, heartbroken world. This we humbly ask in your name, Lord Jesus, for their sake and for the sake of all you love. Amen.

DAY 7

You make known to me the path of life; you will fill me with joy in your presence, with eternal pleasures at your right hand. (Psalm 16:11)

O Lord, in the stillness of this moment, hear the confident prayers of children who are so close to your kingdom and the worried voices of adults who fear they are not. Comfort those whose hearts are heavy with grief today, that they may live and pray again with hope. Bind up the hurts of the wounded, the lonely and the disappointed, that they may discover healing, love, and joy. Give us your peace, that we may be at peace with ourselves and become peacemakers with all others. Forgive us where our shortsightedness has blinded us to the least, the last, the lonely, and the lost in our midst. Create in us clean hearts, O God, and renew a right spirit within us, that we as a loving community of faith may demonstrate how the kingdoms of this world become the kingdom of Christ. We pray in the name of Jesus Christ our Lord, the Alpha and Omega, the beginning and the end, who was and is and is to come. Amen.

WEEK TWENTY–FIVE

DAY 1

Satisfy us in the morning with your unfailing love, that we may sing for joy and be glad all our days. (Psalm 90:14)

J esus, thank you for pauses in our lives when we gather, reconnect, reminisce, and are reminded how brief this life is. Over these years that seem like hours we have learned how to live with joy and sorrow, delight and disappointment, blessing and brokenness. We confess that at times we have been unwise, have lost our perspective, and have wandered away from you and each other. We want to come back and walk with you, our Eternal Companion, the One who knows the way home. Jesus, we pray that you would refresh our spirits as we awake every morning with renewed mercies for a new day and the assurance of your unfailing love for every kind of day. May our children and our children's children see who you are in the beauty of holiness and what you do best in the lives of all who have an intense desire to experience and express the fullness of your redeeming and sanctifying grace. Give us hearts of wisdom so that the rest of our days may be the best of our days. For the sake of your kingdom and all that you love, we humbly pray in your holy name. Amen.

DAY 2

My Father's house has many rooms; if that were not so, would
I have told you that I am going there to prepare a place for
you? And if I go and prepare a place for you, I will come back
and take you to be with me that you also may be where I am.
You know the way to the place I am going. (John 14:2–4)

I thank you, Heavenly Father, that you have set eternity in my heart so that nothing of this world will ever satisfy me wholly. I thank you that every good gift I enjoy is but a foretaste of a greater, more gratifying joy yet to come. Above all, I thank you for the sure hope of an abundant and endless life because of Jesus, the Lamb of God and Lord of Life. As I journey through this day with all that it holds, help me to rest well tonight, knowing that I am but a stranger and pilgrim here on earth, preparing for the purer joys of heaven. I have this peace, hope, joy, and love, now and forever, because of Jesus, and I am grateful. Amen.

DAY 3

All the believers were together and had everything in common. They
sold property and possessions to give to anyone who had need. Every
day they continued to meet together in the temple courts. They broke
bread in their homes and ate together with glad and sincere hearts,
praising God and enjoying favor of all the people. And the Lord added
to their number daily those who were being saved. (Acts 2:44–47)

I love the thought, O God, that you came into our world of space and time, walking in the cool of the day, seeking out fellowship with the first couple. That you prefer us as companions is such a wonder-filled thought, I too often do not even allow my mind to think it. Most of my days are rather lonely, some intentionally designed and others not expected or planned that way at all. Surely, I need times of solitude and privacy, but if I were not able to hear voices other than my own and see faces and bump up against other people, I would wander and wonder in a world of my own creation. I thank you for the face-to-face life of the Christian community, companions on the journey, who are physical reminders of your gracious Presence. I must embrace this divine reality so I can fully experience your saving and sanctifying grace. O Lord, it has always been your desire to share this life experience with us, and so I pray that in the fellowship of the community of faith we all will find our way forward together in the light of your love and the joy of your companionship. In Jesus' name. Amen.

DAY 4

I will give you a new heart and put a new spirit in you; I will remove from you your heart of stone and give you a heart of flesh. And I will put my Spirit in you and move you to follow my decrees and be careful to keep my laws. (Ezekiel 36:26–27)

Lord, today I wait upon you, knowing that without the fullness of your Spirit dwelling in me, I am vulnerable to the consequences of sin. I become anxious and self-centered. My needs and desires become excessive. I become less caring, less civil, and less concerned with others, especially those who do not serve my needs or agree with my opinions. I do what I do not want to do, and I cannot do consistently what I want to do. But in your love you never let go of me! Your Spirit pursues me in my need, ready, willing, and able to break the hardness of sin in my life. And so, with the Psalmist I pray, "Search me, God, and know my heart; test me and know my anxious thoughts. See if there is any offensive way in me, and lead me in the way everlasting" (Psalm 139:23–24). This is life in the Spirit, and this is where I want to live throughout this day and every day. Thank you for this reality, all because of Jesus, in whose name I pray. Amen.

DAY 5

This is the confidence we have in approaching God: that
if we ask anything according to his will, he hears us. And
if we know that he hears us—whatever we ask—we know
that we have what we asked of him. (1 John 5:14–15)

In the name of Jesus and in need of your great mercy, O God, we open our hearts to you again this morning. We praise you for all that you are and all that you have done. We thank you that you meet us right where we are and not where we think we should be. We pray today especially with the brokenhearted and troubled in spirit. Comfort those who grieve and give courage where there is fear. Replace the desperation in their hearts with hope and the sickness in their bodies with health. Let your light shine into the darkness of their minds, revealing a way forward beyond the immediate horizon. Make us all aware of the sacred trust we have been given in the love, care, and support of our families and friends, children and parents, neighbors and brothers and sisters in Christ. As we pray for these and others who come to mind, we come boldly to the throne of grace, seeking boundless mercy and asking for redeeming grace in this time of their need. As children of the covenant, created, called out, and commissioned by the name that is above every name, we offer this prayer. Amen.

DAY 6

As Jesus went on from there, he saw a man named Matthew
sitting at the tax collector's booth. "Follow me," he told him,
and Matthew got up and followed him. (Matthew 9:9)

Lord, you call us as your disciples to deny ourselves, take up our crosses daily, and follow you. You call us to openness of heart, but we fear that someone will take advantage of us if we become that vulnerable. You call us to faith, but we are afraid to trust what we cannot control. You call us to love, but we have been betrayed, hurt, and abandoned before, and we really do not want to go through that pain again. Jesus, we want to trust you. We want to follow you. We want to be your disciples, learning and willing to do what you want us to do. We want to respond to others in love. We want to be more like you. We need to know that we are not alone when the shadows of doubt surround us. We need to feel your strength when the road seems long and difficult. We need your peace to steady our footsteps and faith to continue on your way, wherever that leads. Deliver us from the tyranny of pleasing others so that we may find the pure joy of being your faithful servants every day. For your sake, Lord Jesus, and for the sake of all you love, we pray in your holy name. Amen.

DAY 7

Wait for the LORD; be strong and take heart
and wait for the LORD. (Psalm 27:14)

I admit that I am not very good at waiting, Lord. I prefer fast service, quick results, and rapid answers. I get impatient when I am put on hold or get caught at a stoplight or sit longer than planned in a doctor's office. Yet, it is in such moments that I need to be still and wait on you. While I have time on my hands, you have the whole world in yours. When I am impatient, you are in no hurry. As I anxiously ponder the unknown, you are under no constraint. There will be interruptions in my plans today that can become sanctifying opportunities to practice your Presence. Help me to learn that some good things are worth waiting for and that waiting on you always brings good things. With a grateful heart, Lord Jesus, I pray in your name. Amen.

WEEK TWENTY-SIX

Day 1

A strong wind was blowing, and the waters grew rough. When they
had rowed about three or four miles, they saw Jesus approaching
their boat, walking on the water; and they were frightened. But
he said to them, "It is I; don't be afraid." (John 6:18–20)

There are those ordinary moments, Jesus, when we simply enjoy
your Presence, much like those days the disciples experienced
with you along the roads of Galilee and Judea. And there are those
extraordinary moments when we, like the disciples, are troubled,
anxious, and then amazed as you show up unexpectedly in your power
and glory. Nothing in our lives compares to those divine moments
when you make yourself known to us. We are never the same when in
your holiness you come into our world of space and time. Forgive us,
Lord, for other times we have acknowledged your Presence, presuming
you are near, but have failed to honor, respect, and expect you in all
your glory. Today, we ask that you show up and amaze us with the
unalloyed joy of your Presence. Thank you for the promise that you
always will be with us, and we love you for the promise that you are
able to do far more abundantly than all we can ask or think, according
to the power of the Holy Spirit at work within us. And so, we humbly
and simply pray, *Come, Lord Jesus.* Amen.

Day 2

The LORD is righteous in all his ways and faithful in all he
does. The LORD is near to all who call on him, to all who call
on him in truth. He fulfills the desires of those who fear him;
he hears their cry and saves them. (Psalm 145:17–19)

O Lord, our God, we come today to wait before you. We come with
different hopes and fears, different needs and questions, different
dreams and concerns, different hurts and experiences, different
expectations and disappointments. We come to wait for the assurance

PRAYERS FOR THE JOURNEY

of your amazing Grace, the promise of your heavenly Peace, the power of your abiding Presence, and the outpouring of your boundless Mercy. We give you thanks and praise, honor and glory, love and devotion. We wait before you now knowing that one day all our waiting will end, we will see your face, and the deepest longings of our hearts will be satisfied forever. Until that day, we come as we are to wait for the infilling of your life-giving, life-changing, life-renewing Spirit. Come to us, O Lord, in all your fullness, as we wait before you. Amen.

DAY 3

My prayer is not for them alone. I pray also for those who will believe in me through their message, that all of them may be one, Father, just as you are in me and I am in you. May they also be in us so that the world may believe that you have sent me. (John 17:20–21)

I want to thank you today, Lord Jesus, for all who have prayed for me over the years. Many of these I remember from childhood: parents and family, teachers and preachers, friends, and then others I have never known yet for some reason I was on their prayer list. Thank you for these praying saints who took me into their hearts before they shared my name with you. I am praying this prayer because you heard and answered those prayers, and I am so thankful. Now, I ask that you place names on my heart, family and friends and others who need me to bring them to you. Let me share their burdens, celebrate their joy, and intercede for their welfare. In full surrender of everything before your throne of grace, help me to ask anything boldly. I, too, want to be a praying saint who believes that no eye has seen, nor has any ear heard, nor has any heart begun to imagine the things you are preparing for those who love you. Come, Holy Spirit, and help me to pray for all you love, according to your will. In Jesus' name. Amen.

DAY 4

I will instruct you and teach you in the way you should go; I
will counsel you with my loving eye on you. (Psalm 32:8)

O God, there are so many things on my mind today, so many
thoughts that are flooding this hour. Much of what is demanding
my attention is in reaction to what I have read or heard as others
have thought out loud. There also are those murmurings of my heart
that have gone unexpressed, troubling things I have pondered and
wondered about for too long. Before I spend another day—or even
an hour—trying to process all these heart matters competing for my
attention, I need spiritual discernment. I need the mind of Christ.
I need your Spirit to teach me and take me to a deeper place than
my own understanding, my personal preferences, and my myopic
worldview. Thank you that the Advocate has come to be with us and
to teach us all we need to know of your best for our good. Capture my
thoughts, direct my attention, and flood my mind with all that you
have been waiting and wanting and willing to reveal to me. May it be
my absolute delight to know and do your will. In the name of Jesus
and for the sake of all you love I pray. Amen.

DAY 5

Though the LORD is exalted, he looks kindly on the lowly; though
lofty, he sees them from afar. Though I walk in the midst of trouble,
you preserve my life. You stretch out your hand against the anger
of my foes; with your right hand you save me. (Psalm 138:6–7)

My heart is heavy today, O Lord, as I think about so many who
are under the radar and go unnoticed in this crisis moment:
the lonely who do not dare to ask for help; single persons who have
no one with whom they can share their fears and struggles; the quiet
sufferer who has been hurt, disappointed, and marginalized by life
experiences; the elderly whose loved ones and friends have gone
on before; the long-sufferer who has been forgotten over time; the
addicted who are bound by forces beyond their control; grief-stricken
parents, children, and spouses whose fears have become reality. Lord,

I realize that many of these forgotten souls are not far away; they are in my neighborhood, in my family, in my church, on my Twitter feed, and are friends on Facebook. How often do I look at faces without seeing the pain? Or listen to words without hearing the fear? Or read their postings but am clueless to their confusion? Or have I simply paid no attention whatsoever? Forgive me, Jesus, and help me, Friend of all, to open my eyes to see the unnoticed, hear the silent cry of the forgotten, embrace those who have stopped trusting, and befriend the lonely. This I pray for your kingdom's sake and for the sake of all you love. Amen.

DAY 6

Remember the former things, those of long ago; I am God, and there is no other; I am God, and there is none like me. I make known the end from the beginning, from ancient times, what is still to come. I say, "My purpose will stand, and I will do all that I please." (Isaiah 46:9–10)

God of all beginnings and endings, we come to you as the One who renews mercies and restores our souls every day. We offer love to you because you first loved us. We praise you for life in all its abundance, for this world that is so rich and beautiful, and for the human family that is so diverse and amazing. We bless you for Jesus who came into our world of space and time, taking on our flesh and blood, living our life, dying our death, who was raised in power over all that we dread and fear. We ask that you forgive us for meandering through too many days distracted and disappointed, bored and unbelieving. We pray that you would help us to trust you so deeply that nothing can deflect us from enjoying your Presence in the ordinariness of the day. We want to delight in doing your will, serving others, and praising your holy name. This is our hope, and this we pray in the name of Jesus Christ, the Alpha and Omega, the beginning and the end of all that matters. Amen.

DAY 7

But the fruit of the Spirit is love, joy, peace, forbearance,
kindness, goodness, faithfulness, gentleness and self-control.
Against such things there is no law. (Galatians 5:22–23)

I believe your Word, O God, that to everything there is a season and a time to every purpose under the heavens. I understand that I am a participant, not a mere observer or commentator or critic of life. I am expected to be a contributor, not a consumer; a servant, not a master; a doer, not a hearer; a fruit-bearer, not a fruit-inspector. As I grow deeper in grace, I must become more generous in the Spirit. I must be willing to allow the Spirit to invade, occupy, and transform my ordinariness into your extraordinary purposes. I know that you are the Lord of Love, the Giver of all that is good, the One who saves and sets us free to experience the possibilities of grace. I offer my life to you this morning with a willingness to engage in whatever operations of the Holy Spirit you desire for me and your purposes in this season of my life. Because of Jesus, I believe you are able to do this and so much more than I can ever ask or dare to think. Let it be so. Amen.

WEEK TWENTY–SEVEN

DAY 1

And we know that in all things God works for the good of those who love
him, who have been called according to his purpose. (Romans 8:28)

L ord Jesus, I believe that you desire for all things to work together for the good of all, but there are times when it is very difficult to see a divine plan at work beyond the chaos and confusion and mysteries of the day. Today, I ask for grace to trust you; for faith to believe that you rule the world and the Church in truth and righteousness; for faith to believe that if we seek first your kingdom and your righteousness, you will provide for all lesser needs; for faith to not be anxious about tomorrow but believe that your mercies are renewed every day; for faith to believe that there is nothing greater than the power of your love, even the forgiveness and freedom from all sin and shame; for faith to believe in the final victory of the Holy Spirit over every enemy of our souls and bodies; for faith to be assured that in the struggles, doubts, and pain you are very near; for faith to trust that the welfare of all our loved ones is in your hands. I have heard the testimonies of others that you answer these and many other prayers. And so, I ask you to help me endure uncertain days as these faithful servants trusted and refused to allow confusion and anxiety to rule their days. Believing your will for us is holy happiness, I humbly offer this prayer in your name and for the sake of all you love. Amen.

DAY 2

I will praise the LORD who counsels me; even at night my heart
instructs me. I keep my eyes always on the LORD. With him
at my right hand, I will not be shaken. (Psalm 16:7–8)

Dear God, I hear your call to follow, and I am all in, but I need your help. Be Lord of my life. Control all my thoughts and feelings. Direct all my energies. Instruct my mind. Strengthen my will. Take my hands and make them skillful to serve you. Take my feet and make them swift to go where you direct me. Take my eyes and keep them fixed on your holiness. Take my mouth and make my words eloquent in sharing your love. May this day be a day of radical obedience, a day of spiritual joy and peace. Make all the work I accomplish today be an eternal investment in the kingdom of our Lord Jesus Christ, in whose name and for whose sake I pray. Amen.

DAY 3

So from now on we regard no one from a worldly point of view.
Though we once regarded Christ in this way, we do so no longer.
Therefore, if anyone is in Christ, the new creation has come:
The old is gone, the new is here! (2 Corinthians 5:16–17)

I confess, O Lord, that not only have I prayed too little but I have prayed too small. Rather than asking you to pick up mountains and cast them into the sea, I have complained. Rather than believing that you are able to do above and beyond all I could ever think or imagine, I have not bothered to ask you to do more than I expect. Instead of exploring the possibilities of grace, I have resigned myself to mediocrity. I need you to teach me *how* to pray as well as to help me to know *what* to pray. Convict me of my small faith that has become shaped by doubt rather than hope, disappointment rather than promise, self rather than Spirit. Convince me that I have not because I have not asked. And above all, help me embrace the saving and sanctifying grace of Jesus, which not only atones for my sin and shame but also restores "the years the locusts have eaten" (Joel 2:25). You marvelously make my past as if it had never been. This is the miracle I need. This is my prayer, indeed. Amen.

DAY 4

So he said to me, "This is the word of the LORD to
Zerubbabel: 'Not by might nor by power, but by my
Spirit,' says the LORD Almighty." (Zechariah 4:6)

Holy God, your will is right and good and true, sustaining the world by your mercies. You inspire our hope for a new world beyond this one that will make all these struggles worthwhile. We praise you for Jesus who died to make that new world a reality and rose from the dead to usher us into that new world. We pray that in the power of the Holy Spirit you will help us live and give and serve in this old world, that your kingdom may come on earth as it is in heaven. In our life together, help us to sing your praises and humble ourselves as we pray, listen to, and obey your Word. As we embrace one another as brothers and sisters in authentic Christ-centered, Spirit-filled community, may we celebrate a foretaste of the new world that is to come. Come, Lord Jesus, come. Your will be done in us and through us as it is in heaven. Amen.

Day 5

"Everyone who calls on the name of the Lord will be saved." How, then, can they call on the one they have not believed in? And how can they believe in the one of whom they have not heard? And how can they hear without someone preaching to them? And how can anyone preach unless they are sent? As it is written, "How beautiful are the feet of those who bring good news!" (Romans 10:13–15)

Lord Jesus, today I pray for all who have never prayed or been invited to call on your name. I pray for those who acknowledge your existence but deny your power. I pray for those who see evil in the world and conclude that you do not exist. I pray for those who know only anger and judgment. I pray for those who have been wounded by apathy, prejudice, and injustice within your church. I pray for those who have never heard the gospel and for those who labor every day to share your story in word and deed. I pray for my neighbors who search for meaning and purpose every day and then lay their heads on pillows at night with no answers and no peace. Holy and loving Savior, from you every family on earth takes its name, even if they have never heard your name. Send witnesses of your mercy and grace to all people across this planet that they may hear, believe, repent, humbly receive, and then generously share the love and forgiveness that you made possible. Use the conversations and the conduct of my life as a reflection of your holy and loving character. This I pray in your name, the only name under heaven given to us by which we must be saved. Amen.

Day 6

As you come to him, the living Stone—rejected by humans but chosen by God and precious to him—you also, like living stones, are being built into a spiritual house to be a holy priesthood, offering spiritual sacrifices acceptable to God through Jesus Christ. (1 Peter 2:4–5)

Lord Jesus, because we have come to know you as our Savior, we are forever in your debt. Because we have chosen to follow you as Lord, we choose to let that decision shape every other decision we make today. Because we have enjoyed your Presence and experienced your Power, we embrace every day with unwavering hope. Because we have been forgiven and set free from the power of sin, we can pray for those who despise us and forgive those who sin against us. Because you hear us as we pray, we can ask anything of you, anytime, anywhere. Because we are joined here and now to the fellowship of all true believers, we belong to the forever family of God. Because you love us with Perfect Love, we have no fear as we rise and begin each day as your ambassadors to a world desperately in need of your love. In your blessed and holy name we pray. Amen.

DAY 7

God is our refuge and strength, an ever-present help in trouble. Therefore, we will not fear, though the earth give way and the mountains fall into the heart of the sea, though its waters roar and foam and the mountains quake with their surging. (Psalm 46:1–3)

Eternal God, you have been the hope and joy of all generations. To all ages, you have given the power to seek you and do your will. At no time have you been without a witness. Today, we especially need to know you are near to us. We pray that you will give us a clearer vision of your truth, that we may cope well with reality; a greater faith in your power, that we may have courage to do what is right; and more confidence and assurance in your love, that we will be assured we are not alone. When the way gets dark, give us grace to continue the journey. When we are confused, let us be faithful and true in what we understand. When the future is cloudy, we ask only that you shine light on our next step. When we do not understand the full picture, let us hold fast to what you command, confident that you work all things together for the good for those who love you. When we lack faith, let us draw close to one another and go forward in love. We choose to trust you and lean not on our own understanding, for we know your heart, and you will never leave us nor forsake us. We pray in honor, glory, and praise of your holy name, Father, Son, and Holy Spirit. Amen.

WEEK TWENTY–EIGHT

DAY 1

If you love me, keep my commands. And I will ask the Father,
and he will give you another advocate to help you and be with
you forever—the Spirit of truth. The world cannot accept him,
because it neither sees him nor knows him. But you know him,
for he lives with you and will be in you. (John 14:15–17)

Lord Jesus, you did not promise that life would be easy and trouble-free. In fact, you specifically told your followers that in this world there would be trials and tribulations, heartache and heartbreak, grief and groanings that cannot be expressed. Following you includes a cross, a burden that we choose to assume for others as well as ourselves. Today, we recommit ourselves to love you, to trust you, and to walk with you, because you promised to be with us through it all and beyond. In this quiet moment, I have experienced your love; help me to graciously love all others today. I have trusted you here, praising your holy name; help me to respond to every challenge courageously in faith. I have opened my life to your Spirit; help me to go forth in peace and spiritual power that is greater than any task or trial or tribulation. This I pray, Jesus, in your name and for the sake of all you love. Amen.

DAY 2

For this is what the high and exalted One says—he who lives forever,
whose name is holy: "I live in a high and holy place, but also with
the one who is contrite and lowly in spirit, to revive the spirit of
the lowly and to revive the spirit of the contrite. (Isaiah 57:15)

Our Heavenly Father, I bow as I come before your throne of grace today, offering more of my life to you. I bow not because I am worthy to be in your Presence but because you are worthy of all our thanks and praise. I bow not for my own benefit, expecting to receive a blessing, but to give you honor and glory. I bow before you not because I must but because I long to enjoy your Presence. I bow knowing that you will ask nothing of me that I cannot face, nothing I cannot do, nothing I cannot give, as long as I rely on the abiding presence and saving grace of our Lord Jesus. O God, I ask that by the power of the Holy Spirit you will help me rise from this place to worship, love, and serve you in a manner that truly honors you and gives witness of the reality of your kingdom to a watching world. For your sake and for the sake of all you love, I pray in the name of Jesus. Amen.

DAY 3

"Bless the LORD, O my soul, and all that is within me,
bless his holy name!" (Psalm 103:1 ESV)

I praise you, O God, for all that you have made, every mountain and hill, every field and valley, every tree and plant, every creature small and large, every color and shape and design. I praise you for every person I meet, every conversation we have, every laugh and smile, every tear that is wiped away, and every hurt that is shared. I praise you for every experience of genuine friendship and every expression of divine love. I praise you for Jesus, the Lamb of God who takes away the sin of the world. I praise you for the outpouring and infilling of the Holy Spirit. I praise you for the fellowship of the Church and for the communion of the saints. I praise you for the assurance that the love, joy, worship, and fellowship we share here and now are only a suggestion of all that you have in store for us there and then. And I offer this prayer and praise in the wonderful name of Jesus, the Resurrection and the Life. Amen.

DAY 4

And will not God bring about justice for his chosen ones, who cry
out to him day and night? Will he keep putting them off? I tell you,
he will see that they get justice, and quickly. However, when the
Son of Man comes, will he find faith on the earth? (Luke 18:7–8)

There are many days, O God, that I wish life was much simpler: do this, not that; this is right, that is wrong; go this way, avoid that way. However, so much of this journey is not quite clear. I am not always certain what you would have me do. I hold to your promise that everyone who asks receives and, in the meantime, I attend to the nearest responsibility, waiting and watching. I am tempted to take matters into my own hands, according to my own understanding when Heaven is silent. I soon come to my senses and remember that you have much more at stake in your grand plan of redeeming the world than what I perceive from where I sit. I do not know much at all as to what you are doing, but this I know: You are doing the heavy lifting and if in my small, flawed manner, I know how to give good gifts to my children, how much more are you, Heavenly Father, willing to give the Holy Spirit to all who ask? The gift of yourself is the only justification I need that you are good and your timing is perfect. I believe; help my unbelief. In Jesus' name. Amen.

DAY 5

Search me, O God, and know my heart! Try me, and know
my thoughts! See if there is any grievous way in me, and lead
me in the way everlasting." (Psalm 139:23–24 ESV)

We draw near, O Lord, with contrite hearts. Forgive us for those things we have said and done and thought that have grieved you and hurt others. We ask that you forgive us for those things we have failed to say, neglected to do, and should have pondered but did not. Forgive our silence to resist oppressors and our lack of courage to embrace victims of hate and racism. Forgive us for walking by on the other side, choosing not to get involved in someone else's pain, closing our eyes to their despair, and not hearing their cries for help. Forgive us for not believing in the power of the gospel and living out the reality of your kingdom with one another on earth as it is lived out in heaven. Forgive us when we have grieved the Holy Spirit. O Lord, we are desperate, but we are not hopeless. Help us today as we speak, serve, and reason together for your sake and for the sake of all you love. Amen.

DAY 6

Have I not commanded you? Be strong and courageous.
Do not be afraid; do not be discouraged, for the LORD your
God will be with you wherever you go. (Joshua 1:9)

In the midst of this rapidly changing world, O God, you are always there, steadfast and immutable, like an eternal Rock upon which we can anchor our souls. Life happens, the world turns, history marches on, and we come to crossroads where we must decide what is the good way wherein we must walk to experience and express the fullness of life in your Spirit. Forgive us when we have hardened our hearts and strayed from your path, deceiving ourselves that we knew a better way or retreating out of fear for the cost of the journey. We often have stopped trying because the way seemed too difficult. In those moments of truth, O Lord, we pray to be found faithful that we may bring hope to the discouraged. We pray to be prophetic witnesses of your truth and grace. We pray that our passion for all people to know the saving grace of Jesus will inspire us to be more courageous, compassionate, and creative in offering the love of Christ across our streets and around the world. Assure us of your abiding and guiding Presence as we seek to walk with you every day. When we lose our way, let us not be ashamed to ask for help, and when we seek help, may we find in each other faithful and gracious friends. For the sake of your kingdom and all that you love we pray in the glorious name of Jesus. Amen.

DAY 7

Come to me, all you who are weary and burdened,
and I will give you rest." (Matthew 11:28)

We thank you, Lord Jesus, that you understand us just as we are. We come to you when our souls are empty, our hearts are fearful, our minds are troubled, and our bodies suffer pain. We come to you with our questions, even when we are not sure we want to know the answers. We come when we are bewildered by current reality and when we are dreaming of better days to come. We come with sadness and with our "what-might-have-beens." We come with anger and disappointment. We come confused and confessing. We come with wandering thoughts and wondering minds. Yet, right now, in this sanctified moment, we come to worship you and to praise your holy name. We come to honor you as our Savior and to acknowledge you as our Lord. We come to renew our decision to be your disciples, to love one another as you have loved us, and to reach out to our neighbors across the street and around the world in prayer, in presence, in giving, and in serving. We can come to you today because you first came to us, and now there is nothing in all creation that is able to separate us from your love. Thank you, Jesus. Amen.

WEEK TWENTY-NINE

DAY 1

They devoted themselves to the apostles' teaching and to the fellowship, to the breaking of bread and to prayer. Everyone was filled with awe at the many wonders and signs performed by the apostles. (Acts 2:42–43)

Holy Spirit, you are ready and willing to come into every heart that is humble enough to welcome you. Be present and help us as we pray. For all the gracious opportunities and privileges of worship this day, we thank you. For the invitation to live this day in the joy of your Presence, we thank you. For the fellowship and companionship of our church family, we thank you. For the renewal of our souls at the Table, remembering our Lord's death and experiencing his living Presence, we thank you. For all the preaching of the Word and the music that has lifted our souls, we thank you. For the Sabbath rest that restores our souls, we thank you. As we lie down to sleep tonight, we will thank you for this good day and commit ourselves and our loved ones to your unsleeping care. In Jesus' name. Amen.

DAY 2

This day is holy to our Lord. Do not grieve, for the joy
of the LORD is your strength. (Nehemiah 8:10b)

Thank you, O Lord, for the gift of this day with all things bright and beautiful. Drive away the shadows of discouragement and loneliness that linger near. Lift me up from all weariness and dread. Fill me with joy and an excitement for all the possibilities this day holds. Help me trust you with all my heart as I acknowledge you in all my ways. Prepare me for the unexpected, that my words and actions will be seasoned with grace. Above all, let me sense how very close you are and the assurance that you always will be. And now I rise and go forth, a child of God, secure in the grace of Jesus, filled with the Holy Spirit, and sent to make a difference in the world. Amen.

DAY 3

Rejoice always, pray continually, give thanks in all circumstances; for
this is God's will for you in Christ Jesus. (1 Thessalonians 5:16–18)

You are God of the ordinary and extraordinary. Thank you for the miraculous and the routine of this day. Thank you for unalloyed joy and the pleasure of daily work. Thank you for serendipitous moments and the calmness of tedium. Thank you for surprising gifts of love and the faithfulness of old relationships. Thank you for healing of mind and body that I cannot explain and the stamina to keep on keeping on. Thank you for the keen awareness of your Presence and this quiet moment undergirded by faith. Thank you for the atoning work of Calvary Love and the fresh anointing of Pentecostal Power. As I rise to encounter whatever this day may bring, Father, Son, and Holy Spirit, may I bring honor and glory to your holy name. Amen.

DAY 4

Answer me when I call to you, my righteous God. Give me relief from
my distress; have mercy on me and hear my prayer. (Psalm 4:1)

Holy and loving God, I am thinking today of friends who are full of doubt and despair, those who have been deceived into thinking there is no truth beyond what they can see, hear, touch, or prove, those who cannot comprehend the divine gift of love, acceptance, and forgiveness. I am thinking of other friends who have been broken and damaged by the spiteful words and deeds of others so often that they fear trusting anyone again, choosing now to shut themselves off from all others. And I am thinking of families and individuals that have suffered great loss, whose world has crumbled, whose hopes have been dashed, whose hearts are breaking still, not knowing how to begin putting all the pieces of their lives back together again. Holy and loving God, hear their prayers, and hear this prayer for them. Forgive their sin. Heal their brokenness. Comfort them with your Presence. Bless them with gifts of mercy and kindness. Help us, the Body of Christ, to help them in their hour of need. Restore their joy and give them an abiding hope that together we will enjoy forever the sanctifying consolations of the Holy Spirit. This I ask in Jesus' name. Amen.

DAY 5

Therefore, there is now no condemnation for those who are in Christ
Jesus, because through Christ Jesus the law of the Spirit who gives
life has set you free from the law of sin and death. (Romans 8:1–2)

I confess, O Lord, that though I long to be a faithful and loving disciple, I often resist your power to transform my life to be more like Jesus. I make vows to you and promises to others, but I do not always follow through on what I pledge. I want to trust you, to read your Word, and to take time to pray, but it is much easier to fill up my time being expedient. I feel the need to be your servant, to love my neighbor as you have loved me, but seldom is it convenient to go out of my way to reach out to others. Oh, I have great intentions, Lord, to be thankful, to praise you, to make worship of your Holy name the priority of my life, but I become preoccupied with other things. Where do I begin? I admit my double-mindedness. I repent of my good intentions and confess that I have failed to rightly honor your glory. Forgive me for insulting you with my excuses and yielding to my weaknesses rather than seeking your grace. My heart is deceitful, O Lord; you and you only can cure it. Come, Holy Spirit. Create in me a clean heart, singularly devoted to you. Restore the joy of your saving, sanctifying grace. Only then will my life be a lesson to others of redeeming love and spiritual power. In the strong name of Jesus I hope and pray. Amen.

DAY 6

Blessed are the peacemakers, for they will be
called children of God. (Matthew 5:9)

O Lord, you have been with us through all the moments of our lives. When we quiet our hearts apart from the din of this world and the mysteries of life, we sense how near you are, and we are at peace. And now, may your peace rule our hearts as we resume our life together, aware of the differences that divide and polarize us. May we recognize that those with whom we agree eighty percent of the time are still our friends, not our twenty-percent enemies. Certainly, we will have conflicts and struggles, differences and dissension, but may prevenient grace, through the power of the Holy Spirit, lead us to a deeper conviction to become our best selves. And Lord, may that renewal and reconciliation begin in the hearts and communities of your children who profess your name and are led by your Spirit. May it be so, Lord Jesus, and let it begin in me. Amen.

DAY 7

Dear children, let us not love with words or speech
but with actions and in truth. (1 John 3:18)

We praise you, good and gracious Lord, for the many wonderful gifts we enjoy: adequate food, comfortable homes, caring loved ones, meaningful work, joyful recreation, civil liberties, and communities of faith. As we reflect on these and many other good gifts around us, we offer you our praise and love with grateful hearts. We realize that we are blessed to be blessings, stewards of your goodness, witnesses of your grace. We have this moment to share what you have put in our hands and in our hearts with the poor, broken, abused, and neglected. We want to be more than generous in all our giving so others in all their receiving will offer praise to you as they hear the gospel and see love in action. For such a time as this, we will be the hands and feet and voice of Jesus. This we pray for his sake and for the sake of all for whom he laid down his life. Amen.

WEEK THIRTY

DAY 1

Ascribe to the LORD, you heavenly beings, ascribe to the LORD
glory and strength. Ascribe to the LORD the glory due his name;
worship the LORD in the splendor of his holiness. (Psalm 29:1–2)

I pray for your presence, Lord Jesus, to fill the hearts of all who share this prayer. I pray that your glory will be felt wherever people gather in your name. I pray that your Spirit will be the delight of all who seek your face and offer you praise and worship. I pray that wherever your Word is heard, truth will lead to obedience, and obedience will bring healing and hope. I pray that the spiritually lost, the emotionally detached, and the socially outcast will find friends who are generous stewards of your redeeming grace. I pray that wherever your servants are sent across streets and around the world, they will find open hearts and open doors to boldly share your gospel. And I pray that we will live every day with the assurance that your grace is greater than our sin, your peace is deeper than our deepest pain, your strength is stronger than any task required of us, and your will for our lives is better than anything we can ask or think. We pray this, Jesus, believing that yours is the unshakable kingdom that has no end and the immeasurable love that will never be exhausted. Amen.

DAY 2

Surely he took up our pain and bore our suffering, yet we considered him punished by God, stricken by him, and afflicted. But he was pierced for our transgressions, he was crushed by our iniquities; the punishment that brought us peace was on him, and by his wounds we are healed. (Isaiah 53:4–5)

I am thankful this morning, Lord Jesus, that you bore all our grief and carried all our sorrow. I am thankful that you are the Lamb of God who takes away the sin of the world. I am thankful to know that you wept when your heart was broken and that you are near to every broken heart. I am thankful that you share the pain of those whose lives have been damaged by the words and deeds of others. I am thankful that you understand those who are filled with resentment because of what they have suffered. I am thankful that you feel the rejection of those who are hated and bullied by others and made to feel as if their lives do not matter. I am thankful that you know the fears of little ones, the innocents, who suffer from the consequences of evildoers. I am thankful that you will persevere with those who feel unworthy, unloved, and unvalued because of a past that continues to haunt them. I am thankful that you lovingly watch over those whose suffering is unknown and whose tears are unseen. I am thankful, Jesus, that you are Savior of the world. Praise your holy name. Amen.

Day 3

As Jesus and his disciples were on their way, he came to a village where a woman named Martha opened her home to him. She had a sister called Mary, who sat at the Lord's feet listening to what he said. (Luke 10:38–39)

The temptation is very real, O Lord, to assume more responsibility than you intend for me to have. Too easily, distracting diversions are added to daily duties, and before I realize it, I have wandered off the path where goodness and mercy follow me. I have become like Martha, so occupied with many good things that I have forgotten that one thing is needful. In such moments, you call me to come apart and rest awhile, regroup, refocus, and be renewed at your feet. It is there I relearn the one commandment that shapes my efforts to keep all other responsibilities: to love you with all my heart, mind, and strength. As Mary poured perfume upon your head as an expression of pure devotion, I will begin this day with my love and praise to you, and then pour out my devotion in worshipful work and loving service to those whom you love. In your name, to your glory, and for the sake of your kingdom I pray. Amen.

Day 4

In the same way, the Spirit helps us in our weakness. We do not know what we ought to pray for, but the Spirit himself intercedes for us through wordless groans. (Romans 8:26)

Hear us, O Lord, as we pray today. Hear the beat of our hearts, the pulse of our spirits, the words we speak, and the words unspoken. Hear us and help us order our lives, being thankful for the good and despising the evil. Hear us and help us sort out our priorities, holding fast to that which honors you and blesses others and letting go of that which lures us away from loving you and caring for others. Hear us and help us acknowledge our sin, confessing that we are powerless to absolve our sins but ready to embrace freedom from the power of all sin. Hear us and help us rise above the aberrant pride that causes us to regard ourselves as remarkable and unusual. Keep us from dwelling on our weaknesses, as if such a claim is an adequate excuse. Hear our prayer as we come to you just as we are, wanting and needing to know more of all that you are. Holy and loving God, let us rise up today and be done with the past. Help us as we move out from under the clouds of self-pity and self-blame into the brilliance of your glory and the amazing possibilities of your grace. O Lord, hear us as we pray in the name of Jesus. Amen.

DAY 5

On Behalf of Persecuted Christians

Eternal God, in every age you have raised up men and women who have lived and died in faith, responding to your call, believing the gospel, and trusting in your eternal love. You call your followers to proclaim your name unashamedly, to do what is just unapologetically, to live in community lovingly, and to walk with you humbly. Today, as we honor those faithful witnesses who have gone before us, we also pray for our brothers and sisters in the Body of Christ who are under persecution. Forgive us for not interceding for them as they need us to pray. We ask for your strength for those who are weary and suffering because they name you as Lord. We ask for courage for all who stand in danger across this world at this hour due to their faith. And we pray for comfort, Holy Spirit, for those who grieve the loss of loved ones whose unwavering faith caused their deaths. O Lord, as we pray on their behalf, we pray with heavy and broken hearts. May your faithful servants across this planet know that they are not forgotten. And Lord, give us courage to follow you so that, joined with those from ages past and those who serve you with full devotion today, we may inherit the kingdom you promised, through Jesus Christ our Savior and Lord. Amen.

Day 6

In my vision at night I looked, and there before me was one like a son of man, coming with the clouds of heaven. He approached the Ancient of Days and was led into his presence. He was given authority, glory and sovereign power; all nations and peoples of every language worshiped him. His dominion is an everlasting dominion that will not pass away, and his kingdom is one that will never be destroyed. (Daniel 7:13–14)

Eternal God, you have made yourself known throughout all generations by cherished traditions and faithful witnesses. You are still at work in the world today, still ready to befriend all who are willing to do your will. You are the God of tomorrow who holds the destiny of all nations in your hands. You are shaping the future for the sake of your kingdom that will surely come. For this reason, O Lord, I bow before you in the name of Jesus who willingly laid down his life for us all that we, through the blood of the eternal covenant, might have peace with you and be reconciled to one another. We pray for the Church, the Body of Christ, which keeps alive the ministry of the Word for the salvation of all people and the redemption of the poor and needy. Through your Spirit you call us to this mission that is greater than ourselves, promising us the Power to live out that commitment, that even in all our shortcomings, we can love those whom you love and forgive those whom you have forgiven. And so, today, we will do our best to walk responsibly, faithfully, and prayerfully, believing that this is one day closer to the consummation of your divine will throughout the earth. This we pray, in the strong name of Jesus Christ, our Lord and Savior. Amen.

Day 7

Who shall separate us from the love of Christ? Shall trouble or hardship or persecution or famine or nakedness or danger or sword?... No, in all these things we are more than conquerors through him who loved us. (Romans 8:35, 37)

I am thankful, Lord Jesus, that life with you is not immunity from trouble but peace in the midst of difficulties. Your guidance is not always through sunny days and open doors but sometimes through the clouds of unknowing and closed doors. I am learning that joy is the result of faithfully trusting you and accepting your will even when it seems not to be so joyous. I believe the promise in your Word that these light afflictions which seem so final actually are working an exceedingly better and eternal purpose for my wellbeing. So, help me, O Lord, to keep walking through the shadows and banging on closed doors so that I may learn the better way, actually the only way that keeps me close to you, the One whose power and love even the doors of hell could not withstand. I love you, Jesus. Praise your holy name! Amen.

WEEK THIRTY–ONE

DAY 1

Let the message of Christ dwell among you richly as you teach and admonish one another with all wisdom through psalms, hymns, and songs from the Spirit, singing to God with gratitude in your hearts. And whatever you do, whether in word or deed, do it all in the name of the Lord Jesus, giving thanks to God the Father through him. (Colossians 3:16–17)

O Lord, my God, I thank you this morning for everything in creation that speaks of your grace, power, truth, and glory. I am thankful for every person whose life, words, and deeds bring you glory and whose witness leads others to the knowledge of your holy name. I thank you especially for those who preach the good news of Jesus, teach the eternal Truth of your Word, and witness to your redeeming love through compassionate and sacrificial service. I thank you for every person whose life is a means of grace and whose words breathe forgiveness and peace. And I thank you for those faithful servants who first introduced me to Christ and whose worship and service made being a Christian an exciting adventure I would not dare miss. Through your love and by the inspiration of the Holy Spirit I pray that my life, too, will be a song of praise and a prayer of thanksgiving to your honor and glory, today and every day. In the precious name of Jesus I pray. Amen.

DAY 2

Praise the LORD. Praise God in his sanctuary; praise him in his mighty heavens. Praise him for his acts of power; praise him for his surpassing greatness.... Let everything that has breath praise the LORD. (Psalm 150:1–2, 6)

I praise you this morning, O Lord, that you created a world that reflects your love and truth and the beauty of your holiness. I praise you that all of creation is completely reliant upon you for its life, and that even when we turned away from you in our self-centeredness and self-sufficiency, you did not forsake us. I praise you that your love for your creation has no limits, that in Jesus you distinctly demonstrated your mercy to seek and to save a lost world and broken lives. I praise you for the Good News of his life, his words, his death, and his resurrection, this message that you called us to receive and believe, share and make known across every street and around the world. O Lord, I cannot worship you too often nor trust you too much for all you have done for us in the atoning death of Jesus and through the resurrection power of the Holy Spirit. I live today not with fear or frustration, despair or desolation, anger or anxiety, but with heartfelt praise, boundless love, and unalloyed joy. O God, as it was in the beginning, may it now and ever be, world without end. Amen.

DAY 3

But he said to me, "My grace is sufficient for you, for my power is made perfect in weakness." Therefore, I will boast all the more gladly about my weaknesses, so that Christ's power may rest on me. That is why, for Christ's sake, I delight in weaknesses, in insults, in hardships, in persecutions, in difficulties. For when I am weak, then I am strong. (2 Corinthians 12:9–10)

As I pray today, O Lord, I bring you my fears, that you may give me faith. I bring you my self-reliance, that I may let go and learn to trust you. I give you my self-satisfaction, that I might be humbled and changed by grace. I bring you my weakness, that I can be made strong in the Spirit. I give you my heartaches and heartbreaks, that I can know your peace. I offer my emptiness, that you might fill me with joy overflowing. I give you my complete trust, that my soul may be at rest. I offer you my love, that I may never be satisfied with anything else. I give you this moment—it is all I have to give—that I may enjoy every moment with you this day and forever. All that I am and ever hope to be, I offer you, O Lord, my Strength and my Redeemer. Amen.

DAY 4

And I pray in the Spirit on all occasions with all kinds of
prayers and requests. With this in mind, be alert and always
keep praying for all the Lord's people. (Ephesians 6:18)

I love you, Lord, for hearing our prayers when we stammer with the words, get distracted with wandering thoughts, and even when we can only muster up a few familiar phrases. Sometimes the best we can do is offer the words of others as we struggle to express our true feelings. But you, O Lord, are as attentive in those silent places of our hearts where there are no words as you are in the great assemblies when we pray together the time-honored prayers of the Church. There are special divine moments and sacred spaces where we love to pray, yet you invite us to a holy conversation with you on any occasion, in any place, about any matter that matters to us. The more we pray, the better we learn how to pray: expressing praise and worship, lifting personal experiences and concerns, embracing the feelings of others, responding to life events, supporting workers in the harvest, interceding for the salvation of the world. What a privilege it is to carry everything to you, O Lord, in prayer. May we have confidence that every prayer we pray, however and whenever and for whomever, has eternal significance for the sake of your kingdom and all that you love. Amen.

DAY 5

But now, this is what the LORD says—he who created you, Jacob,
he who formed you, Israel: "Do not fear, for I have redeemed you;
I have summoned you by name; you are mine." (Isaiah 43:1)

O Lord, our Creator and Redeemer, help us as we pray today. You alone know us as we truly are. You know the hurt and anger we carry with us, the concerns that fill our minds, and the worries that consume our thoughts. You know the things we have said, done, and thought that grieved you and offended others. You know the emptiness we feel, the anguish that haunts us, and the fear that paralyzes us. You know the sorrow that breaks our hearts and the doubt that troubles our souls. You know the longing for our lives to change, the cry of our hearts to be healed of painful memories, and our unspoken confession of sin. You also know that we are here in your Presence, trusting in your faithfulness, believing that your mercies are fresh and your grace is more than adequate for all we need this day. Come, Holy Spirit, fill the hearts of your faithful, kindle in us the fire of your love, and we shall be re-created to your glory and for the sake of all you love, in Jesus' name. Amen.

DAY 6

Why, my soul, are you downcast? Why so disturbed within me? Put your
hope in God, for I will yet praise him, my Savior and my God. (Psalm 42:11)

H oly and loving God, you are forever drawing near to us, seeking us out, calling to us, beckoning us to trust you and follow you into a deeper, fuller life. We prefer easier paths and responsibilities that are less demanding. We avoid the road less traveled, lest we be excluded from the acceptance and approval of others. We recognize our limitations but do not sense how much we need your blessing. We wallow in guilt rather choosing to believe, confess, and receive the Good News of your forgiving love. Have mercy on us, Lord, have mercy on us. Speak into our souls. Slow us down so we can hear your voice and be convinced that you alone have the words of life, abundant and eternal. O Lord, with the full surrender of our hearts and minds and bodies, show us your way. In Jesus' name. Amen.

DAY 7

My heart, O God, is steadfast, my heart is steadfast; I
will sing and make music. Awake, my soul! Awake, harp
and lyre! I will awaken the dawn. (Psalm 57:7–8)

Thank you, Jesus, for this day of awakening and renewal—for the ways you have awakened my mind to your Presence and goodness and my soul to the renewing of the Holy Spirit in love and power. My prayer again today is for you to work in my life so you can do through me what you have been waiting and wanting to do. By your grace, keep me sensitive to your voice of guidance, assurance, comfort, and hope. Help me absolutely to trust you and radically obey you. My heart is steadfast, my Lord and my Savior. My heart is steadfast. I offer this prayer with hope, believing and receiving, for your sake and for the sake of all you love. Amen.

WEEK THIRTY–TWO

DAY 1

The seventh angel sounded the trumpet, and there were
loud voices in heaven, which said, "The kingdom of the world
has become the kingdom of our Lord and of his Messiah,
and he will reign forever and ever." (Revelation 11:15)

We honor and bless you today, Jesus, for you alone are King of kings and Lord of lords. In you, we have seen the unlikely become reality. We have witnessed you in the unexpected. We believe in the Truth you have lived and spoken. We dare to hope that your kingdom has come among us and continues to come day after day among the poor and the lonely, the sick and the weary, the angry and the abused, the haters and the peace seekers. And we live every day in the power of your resurrection, anticipating that one day all the kingdoms of the world will be your kingdom alone. Lord Jesus, if we catch only a glimpse of your mercy among the hardness of life, if we can sense your presence only for a fleeting moment in the busyness of life, if we can witness that wholeness happens in the midst of the brokenness of life, then we will know surely that your kingdom is coming and your will is being done. This we pray in your name for your sake and for the sake of all you love. Amen.

DAY 2

Remain in me, as I also remain in you. No branch can bear fruit by itself; it must remain in the vine. Neither can you bear fruit unless you remain in me. I am the vine; you are the branches. If you remain in me and I in you, you will bear much fruit; apart from me you can do nothing. (John 15:4–5)

Here I am, Lord Jesus, waiting on you today. Not that you are ever late for this divine appointment—waiting is what I must do. Help me to linger in this place, this moment. There will be time later for the roles and responsibilities required of me—places to go, people to see, things to do—so, I will stay here now and pray and wait. Waiting on you is not doing nothing. This is where I come to understand how to abide in you and experience the wonder of wonders—that you desire to abide in me. This is what is required if I truly want my life to bear fruit: to do that which is eternally significant, for apart from you I can do nothing. This is how I learn to pray, asking anything in your name, assured that you are listening, and then listening as you are speaking. This is when I learn to be still and know more fully that you are God, and I am not. And so, I wait in this divine moment which will order all the other moments of this day as in every kind of day. For your sake and for the sake of all you love, I pray in your holy name. Amen.

DAY 3

And when Jesus heard it, he said to them, "Those who are well
have no need of a physician, but those who are sick. I came
not to call the righteous, but sinners." (Mark 2:17 ESV)

Thank you, Jesus, Friend of sinners. You showed us the full measure
of your love by laying down your life for us. You saw our need,
not our worthiness. You sought our devotion, not our compliance. You
were our Friend even before we knew we needed a friend. Help us to
make such love known to others who need such a Friend. May others
see the reality of your friendship through our forgiveness, faithfulness,
and first love. May our desire to be friends of sinners become the
ordinary, everyday message of our lives. And may the joy of your
companionship, our Savior and Friend, be our strength today and in
every kind of day, for yours is the unshakable kingdom that has no end
and the immeasurable love that will never be exhausted. Amen.

DAY 4

Now listen, you who say, "Today or tomorrow we will go to this or that
city, spend a year there, carry on business and make money." Why, you do
not even know what will happen tomorrow. What is your life? You are a
mist that appears for a little while and then vanishes. Instead, you ought to
say, "If it is the Lord's will, we will live and do this or that." (James 4:13–15)

O Lord my God, I bow before you in the changing of the seasons on
earth and in the unpredictable times of life. I try to appear that I
am in control of the circumstances that surround me, but you know the
vacillations of my heart. I have faith that a new day will dawn, yet how
quickly I doubt your goodness during the day. I depend on sunshine
and rain, but how easily do I complain when I prefer one over the
other! But you, O God, are always the same in all of my yesterdays, this
day, and every tomorrow. I must learn to wait on you in the meantime.
I want to trust you with my whole heart in the dark as well as the
light, in the storms as well as the sunshine. Help me, in the changing
of seasons of life, to feel your strength, to know your peace, and to be

found faithful today and in every kind of day. This I ask in the strong name of Jesus for your sake and for the sake of all you love. Amen.

DAY 5

The secret things belong to the LORD our God, but the things revealed belong to us and to our children forever, that we may follow all the words of this law. (Deuteronomy 29:29)

O God of our fathers and mothers, you were their help in ages past, you are our present help in this time of need, and you are forever the hope of all children yet to be born. There is no other to whom we can turn. We seek your face, O Lord. Forgive our sin and heal our land. Give us peace for today. Give us hope for the future. There is no shadow of turning with you. Over all the changes of our lives you remained unchanged. There is no darkness so dense that hides your everlasting presence from us. Teach us to live wisely. Teach us to live humbly. Teach us how to live well with each other. And teach us to live in the quiet confidence that you are God and only your kingdom is forever. Praise your holy name. Amen.

DAY 6

In my distress I called to the LORD; I cried to my God for help. From his temple he heard my voice; my cry came before him, into his ears. (Psalm 18:6)

Thank you, O God, for hearing the cries of our hearts. No sound escapes you. No tear falls unnoticed. From every corner of this world prayer is poured out, and there is nothing about us that does not concern you. Your thoughts toward us are beyond our imagination, outnumbering the grains of sand! Therefore, we are confident today that you are listening even before we are ready to pray. And we pray that we are ready and willing to listen as you are ready and willing to speak. Thank you for being our Friend with whom we can share the joys and sorrows, celebrations and challenges, blessings and burdens of this day. We offer ourselves as we pray in the strong name of Jesus and in the power of the Holy Spirit who intercedes for us when we all we can do is cry. Amen.

DAY 7

But thanks be to God, who always leads us as captives in Christ's triumphal procession and uses us to spread the aroma of the knowledge of him everywhere. (2 Corinthians 2:14)

I praise you, O God, for your name is above every name, the only name by which we are saved. I praise you for your love that goes beyond all that I have ever hoped or believed or expected. I bow my head and lift my heart before you, confessing I desperately need you. Apart from you, my way becomes confused and my instincts are unreliable. Restore my soul and fill me with your Spirit that I may rise in newness of heart and mind, passion and purpose. Today, with the abilities of my mind, body, and soul, and with the gifts you have entrusted to me, may I honor you and bless others in your name. Use my words, shape my thoughts, and guide my hands to be a winsome witness to the gospel, the saving and sanctifying grace of Jesus Christ. I pray this for the sake of your kingdom and for the sake of all you love, in his name. Amen.

WEEK THIRTY–THREE

DAY 1

Finally, brothers and sisters, whatever is true, whatever is noble, whatever is right, whatever is pure, whatever is lovely, whatever I admirable—if anything is excellent or praiseworthy—think about such things. (Philippians 4:8)

I praise you, O God, Father, Son, and Holy Spirit; I bless your holy name.

I praise you for the twin-beating of my heart that
enables me to experience and express life, to receive
and give, to pray and praise, to be loved and to love.

I praise you for worship that carries us beyond ourselves; for
the preaching of the Word that reveals our need and your
provision; for compassionate service and sacrificial giving.

I praise you for the unalloyed joy of children, the creative
passion of the young, the enduring energy of grown-
ups, and the non-anxious wisdom of the aged.

I praise you for babies crying in church, lessening
the possibility of snoring adults.

I praise you that the worst of human nature is only for
a moment; your deeper work of grace is forever.

I praise you that in giving what we cannot
keep, we gain what we cannot lose.

I praise you for those who admit their needs, confess their sins,
and ask for prayer, thus giving witness to the Church at its best.

I praise you for creation, for Calvary, and for community.

I praise you that your steadfast love endures forever; your
mercies never end; they are renewed every morning.

Great is your faithfulness, O Lord. I bless your holy name. Amen.

DAY 2

Lord, you have been our dwelling place throughout all generations.
Before the mountains were born or you brought forth the whole
world, from everlasting to everlasting you are God. (Psalm 90:1–2)

I lift my heart to you, O God, after hours of rest and renewal. I praise
you that you neither slumber nor sleep, that you keep watch over my
soul through the night. I thank you for the beauty of the morning and
for the opportunities before me during the day. I am burdened with
the special needs of my family and friends. May they experience your

comforting grace, be assured of your abiding presence, and feel their burdens lightened. Our hope is in you and you alone. Renew our sense of expectation today that you will intervene in our lives, calming our fears, showing us your will, and giving us strength to do more than we ever imagined. Through your Son, Jesus Christ, with the Holy Spirit in your holy Church, all honor and glory is yours, Almighty Father. Amen.

DAY 3

His master replied, "Well done, good and faithful servant! You have been faithful with a few things; I will put you in charge of many things. Come and share your master's happiness!" (Matthew 25:23)

Holy God, you are always creating, always working, always making new things. I pray today for wisdom and courage as I seek to be a faithful worker in the harvest, living out my faith in the everyday stuff of life. Help me to sanctify the ordinary, embracing the routine as divine moments and the commonplace as holy ground when I can be a witness for Christ in words and deeds. May I live a life of integrity in the performance of my responsibilities, being sensitive to my coworkers and conscious of anything about our workplace or work that may be demeaning to others and offensive to you. And help me to employ my gifts beyond what is required of my work responsibilities as a good servant who rightly honors the Master. I pray this in the name of the One who is at work even now, interceding for us at the right hand of the Father. Amen.

DAY 4

Teach me to do your will, for you are my God; may your good Spirit lead me on level ground. (Psalm 143:10)

Lord, I have discovered that it is not the position of my body but the devotion of my heart that pleases you when I pray. I have great passion for what I think is right, true, and good, and you have boundless compassion for repentant sinners who have not done what is right, true, and good. I have learned that it is not the measure of my faith but trusting in your faithfulness that gives me confidence. I am finding that there is no heartache or heartbreak that is so deep that your peace is not deeper still. I am discovering every day the depth, breadth, length, and height of redeeming love. And I am realizing that hope is not wishful thinking but a deep longing in our hearts to experience what no eye has seen, no ear has heard, no mind has conceived. Help me to trust you with all my heart and not depend on my own understanding. In all my ways may I acknowledge you, assured that you will guide my steps. May it be so. In Jesus' name. Amen.

Day 5

See what great love the Father has lavished on us, that we should be called children of God! And that is what we are! (1 John 3:1a)

Our hearts grieve, O God, that so many of your children feel unloved, unlovely, and unlovable. So many of us live far below the privileges and pure joy of being loved, accepted, and forgiven. Rather than being renewed by your mercies, we dwell on our failures and focus on our flaws. We feel so unworthy and undeserving of unconditional love. But your grace is deeper than our need, your mercy is broader than our sin, and your faithfulness is greater than our faithlessness. Help us abandon ourselves solely to the economy of your provision in Jesus, whose holy love satisfies the deepest longing of our hearts. Not by our worthiness but according to your boundless mercy and by the renewal of the Holy Spirit we find our rest in you. For your sake and for the sake of all of your children whom you love across the street and around the world, we pray in Jesus' name. Amen.

DAY 6

Teach me your way, LORD, that I may rely on your faithfulness; give me an undivided heart, that I may fear your name. I will praise you, Lord my God, with all my heart; I will glorify your name forever. (Psalm 86:11–12)

How we thank you, O Lord, for this amazing privilege of coming into our holy presence as we pray. What an honor it is to freely express the matters of our hearts to you: our needs and concerns, our sorrows and joy, our pain and praise, our fears and trust. In this sacred moment, you remind us that we must open our hands as we open our hearts, surrendering everything into your hand, not depending on our understanding or expecting answers, but trusting you as the Lord Almighty who was and is and is to come. Our hope is not in our hope but in your promises. Our faith is not in our faith but in your faithfulness. Our love is not in our loving but in being loved. We have not seen, we have not heard, nor could we ever imagine the things you have prepared for all who love you, yet by your Spirit you are ready and willing and able to reveal your heart to us. For this we pray with open hands and open hearts, in the name of Jesus. Amen.

DAY 7

And the peace of God, which transcends all understanding, will guard your hearts and your minds in Christ Jesus. (Philippians 4:7)

You, O Lord, are the calm when gale winds sweep over my soul. You are the rest for my frazzled spirit when my heart grows weary. You are the patience when my anxiety makes demands that I cannot meet. When I feel overwhelmed, remind me that you are my Rock and my Redeemer. When I begin to bend under the strain of life's burdens, give me strength to carry my cross another day. O Master of my life, help me to place my complete trust in you, confident that you are completely trustworthy. Help me to release all my cares to you, contented that I am always on your mind. And help me to follow you, knowing that you will never lead me where your grace cannot keep me. In your holy name, Lord Jesus, I pray. Amen.

WEEK THIRTY–FOUR

DAY 1

For as high as the heavens are above the earth, so great is his love for those who fear him; as far as the east is from the west, so far has he removed our transgressions from us. (Psalm 103:11–12)

> Forgive them all, O Lord: our sins of omission and our sins of commission; the sins of our youth and the sins of our riper years; the sins of our souls and the sins of our bodies; our secret and our more open sins; our sins of ignorance and surprise, and our more deliberate and presumptuous sin; the sins we have done to please ourselves and the sins we have done to please others; the sins we know and remember, and the sins we have forgotten; the sins we have striven to hide from others and the sins by which we have made others offend; forgive them, O Lord, forgive them all for his sake, who died for our sins and rose for our justification, and now stands at thy right hand to make intercession for us, Jesus Christ our Lord. Amen.
>
> John Wesley, Manuscript Prayer Manual,
> c. 1730–34 (Spinckes, "Devotions")

DAY 2

Surely the arm of the LORD is not too short to save,
nor his ear too dull to hear. (Isaiah 59:1)

How grateful we are, Heavenly Father, to come before you at the beginning of this day with so many needs and expectations. We come asking to know the peace of your abiding Presence before we pray, as we pray, and after we pray. We come asking that hurting souls will be healed, heavy burdens will be shared, troubled minds will find comfort, hard hearts will be transformed, and hope will be restored. Come, Lord Jesus, and lift our eyes to see the vision of the world you see, the world you laid down your life to save. Come, Holy Spirit, and renew your church across the world so we will love what you love and love to do what you would have us do. For the sake of your kingdom now and forever, we pray in your holy name. Amen.

Day 3

The Spirit searches all things, even the deep things of God. For who knows a person's thoughts except their own spirit within them? In the same way no one knows the thoughts of God except the Spirit of God. What we have received is not the spirit of the world, but the Spirit who is from God, so that we may understand what God has freely given us. (1 Corinthians 2:10b–12)

Lord, teach me to pray beyond the ordinary and into the extraordinary. Through the Spirit, show me your mind that I may know your thoughts, the deep things of God. Help me as I dare to pray for you to break my heart with the things that break your heart, that I may be more passionately concerned for your kingdom to come on earth as it is in heaven. Then show me how to put my arms around the poor in body and spirit, provide as I can, and unrelentingly plead their case before you and others until they are satisfied. Help me to know how to pray for our leaders and all who make decisions for the common good, that their convictions will be shaped by the values of your kingdom rather than personal interests. By your Spirit, may I pray with the mind of Christ beyond the commonplace and into the eternal. For your sake, O God, and for the sake of all you love, teach me to pray in the language of your kingdom. Amen.

Day 4

He has shown you, O mortal, what is good. And what does the LORD require of you? To act justly and to love mercy and to walk humbly with your God. (Micah 6:8)

Holy and loving God, my prayer this morning is that I live this day in the refuge of your will and the freedom of your grace. Teach me humility that I will not act in my own conceit or self-interest. Give me a greater love for all you love so that I may give witness to the world of the more excellent way. Instill in me a sense of wonder so that I may feel your presence and recognize your fingerprints all around this world. Impart to me deeper trust so that I may embrace the unknown without fear. May I be a healer to the broken, a comfort to the mournful, and a friend to the lonely. Quicken my sensibilities, deepen my compassion, and stir my passion so that I may live as a child of God—created, called out, and commissioned by the One whose name is above every name, Jesus, our Lord. Amen.

DAY 5

I am the good shepherd; I know my sheep and my sheep know me—just as the Father knows me and I know the Father— and I lay down my life for the sheep. (John 10:14–15)

O Lord, our Good Shepherd, we need to know this morning that you are near. From the chaos of this moment, may we find rest beside still waters. As uncertainty clamors all around, restore our souls, and assure us that you are leading us in the way of everlasting life. When disappointment grieves our spirits, help us believe that even adversity can be an occasion of a deeper experience of grace. Give us faith that we may learn to walk with you through the shadows and not be afraid. Let your mercy and goodness nudge us all along our journey home with the promise that there will be better days than our worst days and happier days than our saddest days. Lead us, Good Shepherd, for yours is the kingdom and the power and the glory forever and ever. Amen.

DAY 6

But you are a chosen people, a royal priesthood, a holy nation, God's special possession, that you may declare the praises of him who called you into his wonderful light. Once you were not a people, but now you are the people of God; once you had not received mercy, but now you have received mercy. (1 Peter 2:9–10)

We praise you, O Lord, for the life we have together as the people of God and the joy we share in knowing you as our Savior and

Lord. Faithful servants hoped in you, believed your promise, and prepared the way for the coming of Christ. Devoted disciples walked with Jesus, fell away, and then in the power of the Holy Spirit turned the world upside down. Throughout the years many have stood firm, declaring the name that is above all names in the face of opposition, oppression, and rejection. Through a long line of faith your servants were led into our lives to tell your Story, declare your praises, and invite us to repent, believe, and embrace the name of Jesus. We pray today for all people across this planet who are called by your name. Despite our weaknesses and failures, controversies and contentiousness, by your grace and mercy we are called to be your witnesses and proclaim your kingdom. As we thank you for the fellowship, joy, and hope we share in Christ, we also pray for a renewal of the Holy Spirit in us that through us we may worthily speak your name. This we pray for the sake of your kingdom and all that you love. Amen.

DAY 7

As the Father has loved me, so have I loved you. Now remain in my love. If you keep my commands, you will remain in my love, just as I have kept my Father's commands and remain in his love. I have told you this so that my joy may be in you and that your joy may be complete. (John 15:9–11)

I thank you, O God, for the love that embraces me every day and on every kind of day; for the quiet times I spend alone and the enthusiasm of time well spent with friends and family; for the things I see that inspire my imagination; for the seasons of life, each with its challenges and rewards; for the witness of saints who are praying for me, seeing not only the world as it is but the witness of the Spirit who is among us, above us, and around us, preparing us for heaven. May the joy of your Presence accompany me throughout this day and then break upon my soul as I rise in the morning, enthralled again by this gift of life, abundant and eternal, all because of Jesus, our Savior and Lord. Amen.

WEEK THIRTY–FIVE

DAY 1

Enter his gates with thanksgiving and his courts with praise;
give thanks to him and praise his name. (Psalm 100:4)

O Lord, may my first thoughts each day be about you, my first action be a prayer to you, and my first words be words of praise and thanksgiving for all that you are. I praise you for your goodness and wisdom. I thank you for your love and forgiveness. I praise you for the opportunities before me this day. I thank you for the presence of the Holy Spirit all through the day. I praise you for the gifts of the Spirit that give me the confidence to serve others. I thank you for this quiet moment when joy may be restored and a right spirit may be renewed in me. May I spend this day truthful in all I say, faithful in all I do, generous in my dealings with others, obedient to your Word, and mindful of my eternal destiny as your child. I praise and thank you, Father, Son, and Holy Spirit. Amen.

DAY 2

As the rain and the snow come down from heaven, and do not return to
it without watering the earth and making it bud and flourish, so that it
yields seed for the sower and bread for the eater, so is my word that goes
out from my mouth: It will not return to me empty, but will accomplish
what I desire and achieve the purpose for which I sent it. (Isaiah 55:10–11)

O Lord our God whose ways are far above our ways, whose thoughts are far beyond our thoughts, and whose love is far greater than our need for love, we wait before you as we begin a new week, admitting that we are totally dependent on your grace, mercy, and forgiveness. We humbly surrender our wills to you so we might find our greatest joy and truest satisfaction in doing your will. In your abiding Presence, may we find our deepest peace and happiest moments. Fill us with the Holy Spirit that we will reflect in our words and our work your holy character. Help us to prefer one another, holding each other in the highest regard, honoring each other as children you love. And above all, let your name be uppermost in our minds and your praise be constantly on our lips. For the sake of your kingdom and all that you love, we pray, in Jesus' name. Amen.

DAY 3

Freely you have received; freely give. (Matthew 10:8b)

Lord Jesus, I have asked for your mercy; help me to be merciful. I have sought your forgiveness; may I be willing to forgive. I have received your love; may others know I am your disciple by the way I love. I have experienced your joy; may I look for ways to celebrate life with others. I have known your peace; as your child, may I be a peacemaker. I have worshipped you here in this moment; may I give you praise in every place, throughout this day. I have trusted you as I have prayed; now, may I fully obey the leading of your Spirit, moment by moment, so that at the end of the day I may enjoy contemplations of time well-spent. Let it be, Lord Jesus. Let it be. Amen.

DAY 4

I no longer call you servants, because a servant does not know his master's business. Instead, I have called you friends, for everything I learned from my Father I have made known to you. (John 15:15)

Lord Jesus, you taught your disciples that there is no greater love than being willing to lay down one's life for a friend. And then you called your followers "friends" because you confided in them and revealed to them the very heart of God. You dared to love all who felt unlovely and unlovable. You took the risk of loving them even when that love was not returned. You gave your life for the eternal salvation of your friends. Sometimes we feel that we do not deserve to be your friends, to receive such love, to be worthy of your sacrifice. We are not so likeable or dependable, and we are ashamed of our foolishness. We are not such good friends. Yet, as we ponder the depth of your love, affection, and respect for us, we come back to this: You first loved us and laid down your life for us, your friends. You unilaterally chose us to be your friends. Lord, I can give you no less than my love and respect, devotion, and obedience. I want to be more like you, a friend who is willing to love unconditionally and risk being mocked for being friends with sinners. What a friend you are, and such a friend I want to be to you and for the sake of all your friends. Amen.

DAY 5

I lift up my eyes to the mountains—where does my help come from? My help comes from the LORD, the Maker of heaven and earth. (Psalm 121:1–2)

Our Heavenly Father, too many of your children are living in fear day after day—fear of what we know; fear of what we do not know; fear of what has been; fear of what might be; fear of what may change; fear of what may not change; fear of unseen devils, and even fear of you. Hear us as we pray, O Lord, for these and for ourselves. Convince us that you are Lord, Almighty God, and your kingdom will surely come, and your will surely shall be done. Convict us when we assume more responsibility than we are meant to handle and when we are indifferent about the things of the greatest importance, things that break your heart. Whenever fear tries to smother faith and doubt preoccupies our minds, help us to lift up our heads and look above and beyond the shadows, putting the full weight of our trust in you, the One who has given us not a spirit of slavish fear but the Spirit of power, love, and self-control. Reassure us with your Presence whenever fear threatens to disturb our souls and disrupt our peace. Because our hope is in you, through the merits of our Lord Jesus Christ, we choose to live this day not in fear but in anticipation, for yours is the kingdom and the power and the glory today and forever and ever. Amen.

Day 6

Many are the plans in a person's heart, but it is the
Lord's purpose that prevails. (Proverbs 19:21)

Lord Jesus, we need you to set our hearts and minds right at the beginning of this not-so-ordinary day. Just a few days ago life seemed so normal—or at least ordinary. We were organizing our calendars, making plans for special occasions, and anticipating the usual experiences in this season of the year. How quickly life can change, and how suddenly we are confronted with the reality of our mortality. We need you, O Lord, to do for us what we could never do for ourselves. Help us to learn to be content in any and every circumstance: our lives in your hands, our loved ones to your care, our hopes to your eternal plan, our unanswered prayers to your perfect timing. This we believe: No eye has seen nor ear heard nor has anyone imagined what you are preparing for all who love you. Help us set our hearts and minds on you, Jesus, that your peace may rule our hearts in this not-so-ordinary day and in every kind of day. Amen.

Day 7

Your path led through the sea, your way through the mighty waters,
though your footprints were not seen. You led your people like
a flock by the hand of Moses and Aaron. (Psalm 77:19–20)

Jesus, we profess with our lips and believe in our hearts that one day, every knee will bow and every tongue will confess that you are Lord. Between this ordinary day and that glorious day, assure us that there is divine purpose unfolding and holy power at work beyond our understanding. Forgive our doubts that limit our confidence in you, the Good Shepherd who cares and provides for his flock. Help us trust you day by day, step by step, moment by moment, to unfold what is right and true and good in your perfect timing. May we leave all the burdens of tomorrow with you today, our Savior and Lord. We can bear only what you expect of us each day, and we thank you, for that is enough and all you ask of us. Our prayer, Lord Jesus, is simply that you will show us the way that we may embrace Truth and walk the path with you. For your sake and for the sake of all you love, we pray in your most holy name. Amen.

WEEK THIRTY–SIX

DAY 1

I thank God, whom I serve, as my ancestors did, with a clear conscience, as night and day I constantly remember you in my prayers. Recalling your tears, I long to see you, so that I may be filled with joy. (2 Timothy 1:3–4)

God of grace and glory, I want to thank you today for the people who are responsible for so much that is good in my life. Thank you for parents who did not insist that I succeed where they failed but who allowed me to love myself. Thank you for pastors and Sunday School teachers whose skill in sharing your Word was matched by their warmth, humor, and grace. Thank you for friends who grew up with us and who, by their patience and love, kept us growing as persons in your image. Thank you for husbands and wives with whom we share our lives and our hopes of eternal life. Thank you for children who share, enrich, and bless our lives; thank you for these special people you have given us to enjoy and to love. Accept my praise and thanks for these, your special servants who have blessed my life. In Jesus' name. Amen.

DAY 2

Teach us to number our days, that we may gain a heart of wisdom. (Psalm 90:12)

O Lord, on days when the sun does not shine, the clouds are dark overhead, the flowers are hidden, and the cold rains fall, how difficult it is to rejoice and be glad. There are times when life seems so good and rich, and there are days when life seems so uncertain and disappointing. There are days when my heart is so full and overflowing with praise, and there are days when I feel chilled to the bone and anxious about everything. I need this reminder that every day is a gift to be embraced, explored, and enjoyed. In every kind of day I must learn to say with the psalmist, "This is the day the Lord has made. Let us rejoice and be glad in it!" As it was in the beginning, it is now and ever shall be, world without end. Amen and amen.

DAY 3

The LORD came and stood there, calling as at the other
times, "Samuel! Samuel!" Then Samuel said, "Speak,
for your servant is listening." (1 Samuel 3:10)

I do not want to miss this moment, O Lord. It is not what I want you to reveal to me so much as I long for the presence of your Spirit to be with me and to work through me. As I seek to understand your call on my life, I ask for discernment to recognize your voice. I pray for courage to embrace your will and strength to set it all in motion. And I ask you to help me continue to do the one thing necessary: remain in a posture of prayer whereby I will live and move and have my being in the power of your Spirit. Then and only then will I be set free from my self-will and ready to experience and express what you have been waiting and wanting to do in and through me. And so, I wait quietly on you, believing that you alone are able to do far above all that I can ask or think or imagine, because yours is the unshakable kingdom that has no end and the immeasurable love that will never be exhausted. Amen.

DAY 4

But when he, the Spirit of truth, comes, he will guide you into all the truth.
He will not speak on his own; he will speak only what he hears, and he
will tell you what is yet to come. He will glorify me because it is from me
that he will receive what he will make known to you. (John 16:13–14)

Holy Spirit, fill my heart this morning and stay with me throughout this day. Consume all my thoughts. Inspire all that I imagine. Guide all my decisions. Occupy the center of my will and order all I that I do. Be with me in the silence today and in every word I speak. As I rush about and when I relax, when I am with others and when I am alone, in the freshness of a new day and in the weariness of the evening, give me grace at all times to enjoy your friendship. In moments I am able to worship and pray today, may you be honored and praised, for you alone are worthy. I offer this prayer, as I offer myself to you, in Jesus' name. Amen.

DAY 5

This, then, is how you ought to regard us: as servants of Christ and as those entrusted with the mysteries God has revealed. Now it is required that those who have been given a trust must prove faithful. (1 Corinthians 4:1–2)

Jesus, as disciples who profess you as Lord, our devotion is not simply to do what we think is right or what is our duty. In our own strength we can do only what is proper or required of us. You desire something more—the full devotion of our undivided hearts: "If you love me, keep my commands" (John 14:15). Paul exhorted us to be renewed in the spirit of our minds that we may know and approve what your will is. The true happiness we seek is not success or satisfaction with our accomplishments. Our reward is your pleasure. Your joy is our joy. Your glory is our passion. To love you supremely is our desire and our prayer. In our lives, Lord, be glorified today. Amen.

DAY 6

We wait in hope for the LORD; he is our help and our shield. In him our hearts rejoice, for we trust in his holy name. May your unfailing love be with us, LORD, even as we put our hope in you. (Psalm 33:20–22)

Lord Jesus, you encouraged your disciples to continue to pray and not lose heart. Desiring your Presence brings hope. Experiencing your Presence brings joy. Resting in your Presence brings peace. Even when our best efforts seem fruitless and our words seem so shallow, you restore our souls as we pray. Bless our hearts. Calm our nerves. Forgive our sins, and free us from sin. Renew our strength as we wait and remember that you are God, and we are not. May your Peace that passes all understanding keep our hearts and minds set on you, praying without ceasing, always rejoicing, and giving thanks in everything. This is your will, and this we pray in your name and for the sake of all you love. Amen.

DAY 7

Such confidence we have through Christ before God. Not that we are competent in ourselves to claim anything for ourselves, but our competence comes from God. He has made us competent as ministers of a new covenant—not of the letter but of the Spirit; for the letter kills, but the Spirit gives life. (2 Corinthians 3:4–6)

O God, our help in ages past, our hope for years to come, you have spoken in the past and have guided us through the years by faithful witnesses to your Word. You are as present with us in this moment as you were with them. You are the God of tomorrow who holds the destiny of all nations in your hands. You are shaping the future for the sake of your kingdom that will surely come. In the meantime—right now—you invite us to do kingdom work. For this reason, O Lord, I bow before you today in the name of Jesus who offered himself as the atoning sacrifice that we might have peace with you and be reconciled to one another. I renew my pledge of allegiance to the Church, the Body of Christ, the community of the faithful, which keeps alive the ministry of the Word for the salvation of all people and the healing of the nations. Through your Spirit, I renew my commitment to love those whom you love and to forgive those whom you have forgiven. I will do my best today to live responsibly, love faithfully, and give generously, believing that this is one day closer to the consummation of your divine will throughout the earth. This I pray with great hope, because of Jesus. Amen.

WEEK THIRTY-SEVEN

DAY 1

Great and marvelous are your deeds, Lord God Almighty. Just
and true are your ways, King of the nations. Who will not fear
you, Lord, and bring glory to your name? For you alone are
holy. All nations will come and worship before you, for your
righteous acts have been revealed. (Revelation 15:3–4)

We worship and honor you today, O God, for your extravagant love and your life-transforming grace; for the beauty of your holiness and the utter perfection of all that you are and everything that you do. There is nowhere we can go to find you, yet in your mercy you continually seek us out. There is nothing we can say or do that will make us worthy of your love, yet you claim us as your children. There is nothing about our lives or our accomplishments, our loyalty, or our devotion that makes us more acceptable, yet you choose to fill us with the Holy Spirit. You transcend our highest thoughts and exceed our deepest meditations, yet you call us to be witnesses of the gospel story and instruments of your peace throughout the world. We praise and bless you, O God, that because of Calvary we can know and live with such love, acceptance, forgiveness, freedom, assurance, and hope. Your Presence fills our lives, completes our joy, and satisfies our longing to belong. May the words of our mouths and the meditations of our hearts throughout this day bring glory and honor to you for the sake of your kingdom and all you love. In Jesus' name we pray. Amen.

DAY 2

You, God, are my God, earnestly I seek you. I thirst for
you, my whole being longs for you, in a dry and parched
land where there is no water. (Psalm 63:1)

I cherish these moments alone with you each day, O God, when we commune as Friend with friend. Before I am troubled with the burdens of the day, I feel your strength. As I am tempted to fear the unknown, I am comforted by your Presence. When I think of opportunities yet to be explored, I am tentative but willing. Knowing that nothing could ever separate me from your eternal love, I am at peace. Giving what I cannot keep to gain what I cannot lose, I am content. May the joy of this moment fill every moment of this day as I offer you the only gift you did not first give me: my praise. How good and loving and holy you are, Father, Son, and Holy Spirit! Amen.

DAY 3

And when he had taken it, the four living creatures and the
twenty-four elders fell down before the Lamb. Each one had
a harp and they were holding golden bowls full of incense,
which are the prayers of God's people. (Revelation 5:8)

O God, we are humbled by the privilege of the high and holy calling of prayer. Here we actively participate in what we believe, not simply stating what we believe, in the beauty of holiness. How easily we are tempted to stop praying when our prayers are seemingly unfruitful and unanswered. When all is well, we pray and profess how good and loving you are, but in the face of unexplained grief and suffering, we often are at a loss of words. But then we observe the saints among us, those who have devoted their lives to this high and holy calling, breaking up the silence of heaven as they intercede for family and friends, sinners and saints. May we add to their prayers, O Lord, though the fig tree does not bud and there are no grapes on the vines. Let us pray, and we will honor you and bless others for your sake and for the sake of your kingdom. In Jesus' name. Amen.

DAY 4

For God was pleased to have all his fullness dwell in him,
and through him to reconcile to himself all things, whether
things on earth or things in heaven, by making peace through
his blood, shed on the cross. (Colossians 1:19–20)

Your Word teaches, O God, that each of us is marvelously and wonderfully made. You created us of the earth, yet we are made for heaven and are restless until we make peace with you. We have heard your name since we were small children, yet we only know you as you make yourself known. Only in Jesus have you revealed yourself in a way we can understand. Only in his life do we begin to know who you are and the depth of your love for the world. Only in his words do we perceive who we are and how we are to live and love one another. Only in his death do we see the truth of our sorrow and our sin and the reality of your healing and redeeming grace. Only in his Resurrection do we glimpse the unshakable kingdom that has no end and the immeasurable love that will never be exhausted. Only in such hope can we live above circumstances, be set free from regret, and find renewed courage for today and every kind of day. This we pray, believing and rejoicing in the strong name of Jesus Christ, our Savior and Lord. Amen.

DAY 5

As they talked and discussed these things with each other, Jesus himself came up and walked along with them. (Luke 24:15)

Lord Jesus, you touched the fevered brows of the ill, held the trembling hands of the fearful, comforted the brokenhearted, and gave hope to the grieving. Walk with us today and touch us in our need. In our suffering, may we feel the excitement of your Presence and experience your healing touch. Set us free from slavish fear and paralyzing anxiety. Let your peace wash over us like a mighty river, carrying us into the ocean depths of your love. May the reality of Resurrection life come upon us all, pilgrims walking the Emmaus Road with you, feeling our hearts strangely and wonderfully warmed on this journey to spiritual wholeness. O Lord, like little children, we often shy away from those things that frighten or upset us. Remind us of your faithfulness all along the way so we will never be unaware of you as our Companion, Savior, and Lord. This we pray with joy, for yours is the kingdom and the power and the glory and the life forever. Amen.

Day 6

And why do you worry about clothes? See how the flowers of the field
grow. They do not labor or spin. Yet I tell you that not even Solomon
in all his splendor was dressed like one of these. (Matthew 6:28–29)

Thank you, Lord, for the many ways you are at work on our behalf
even when we do not see or understand. Life is hard, and often we
simply are overwhelmed by the lack of answers, resources, direction,
hope, and inspiration. In such moments, help us to pause and "consider
the lilies of the field, how they grow." We are inspired by the beauty
of creation when all is in full bloom, radiant in sunshine, abounding
in fruitfulness. How easily we forget that for most of the year, seeds
of the lily that are full of life lie dormant, buried under ground, out of
sight and ignored. Jesus, we often feel the stress that we should always
be at our best, on display and admired by all. How easily we forget that
like lilies, you cannot nurture and prepare us for your glory unless
we have spent time in the dark, waiting and preparing. Your desire is
for us to hide our lives in you so that, in your perfect will and perfect
timing, we will be ready for your purposes. O Lord, help us to let go of
the stress and the toil and the spinning and believe that our Heavenly
Father knows best. We wait and we pray in your holy name. Amen.

Day 7

Surely goodness and mercy will follow me all the days of my life,
and I will dwell in the house of the LORD forever. (Psalm 23:6)

Lord, I praise you for your abiding Presence. You are near, and
I praise you that there is not a moment of my life when you are
not. Sometimes my heart is bursting with joy, and at other times my
heart feels like it is breaking in two. Sometimes my heart sings, and
sometimes it sighs. Yet, I praise you that your Spirit is with me in
those times when I pray and in those moments when I least expect
you. I look back on yesterday and see how you were with me—in the
strength I needed to resist temptation, the comfort I needed in a dark
moment, the joy I felt when a burden was lifted. That was you, faithful

and unexpected and perhaps even unsolicited. Forgive me, Lord, when I have been too busy or preoccupied that I did not sense you were near. As I continue through this day, help me to pause and be aware that you are near—very, very near. May I acknowledge, feel, and enjoy your Presence. Always. Everywhere. Thank you. Because of Jesus. Amen.

WEEK THIRTY–EIGHT

DAY 1

Grace and peace be yours in abundance through the knowledge of God and of Jesus our Lord. His divine power has given us everything we need for a godly life through our knowledge of him who called us by his glory and goodness. (2 Peter 1:2–3)

O Lord, our God, we are absolutely delighted in you. Before we recognized your glory or appreciated your goodness, you were at work in our lives, preparing us to believe and receive and be filled with your love. We praise you, Jesus, for coming into our world of space and time, taking on our flesh, and shedding your blood for our salvation, and we are full of hope every day and in every kind of day until you come again. We praise you, Holy Spirit, for opening our eyes not only to see the world as it is but also as you intend for it to be. We praise you for your Presence in all the world and your power that transforms us into the covenant people who bear witness to you in the world. Your attendance to what matters to us brings meaning to all that we do, for we know that no matter what we are doing or facing today, we will be comforted by your Presence and sustained by your power. May our lives echo your glory and the wonder of your holy name. For the sake of your kingdom and all that you love, we pray in Jesus' name. Amen.

DAY 2

Therefore, brothers and sisters, since we have confidence to enter the Most Holy Place by the blood of Jesus, by a new and living way opened for us through the curtain, that is, his body, and since we have a great priest over the house of God, let us draw near to God with a sincere heart and with the full assurance that faith brings.... (Hebrews 10:19–22a)

I come to you today, Lord, just as I am, that I may be changed by your grace. I come with emptiness, that I might be filled with the Holy Spirit. I come with darkness, seeking your light onto my pathway. I come with my weakness, needing your strength. I come with my brokenness, that you may make me whole. I come with my ordinary life, that I may embrace the extraordinary life of the Spirit. I come with questions, fears, and doubts, that I may have your Peace that passes understanding. I come with my worship and praise, that you may know how much I love you. I come with prayers, that your glory may fill the earth. I come to you, O Lord, just as I am, that I may be changed by your grace. O Lamb of God, I come, I come. Amen.

DAY 3

Yet he did not waver through unbelief regarding the promise of God, but was strengthened in his faith and gave glory to God, being fully persuaded that God had power to do what he had promised. (Romans 4:20–21)

Lord Jesus, you are our Redeemer and Friend. You bring life out of dead ends. You give hope in the midst of despair. You are at work in the darkest hour, even in our most painful moments. Forgive me, Lord, for delayed obedience, my cautious compassion, and my timid reluctance to advance what is right, true, and good. Teach me confidence that leads to intentional acts of kindness and clarity of vision. Give me a trust that inspires a faithful, bold witness and generous, unfettered compassion. Make me a captive of Perfect Love that frees me from worry and releases fear. Create in me a clean heart, O God, and renew a right spirit of love, hope, joy, and peace. For your sake and for the sake of all you love, I pray in your holy name. Amen.

Day 4

But while he was still a long way off, his father saw him and
was filled with compassion for him; he ran to his son, threw
his arms around him and kissed him. (Luke 15:20)

Heavenly Father, you watch over me even when I journey into the far countries of the spirit and waste my spiritual inheritance in self-indulging ways. Thank you for your patience and faithfulness. As I begin this day, help me to see what my life is in the eternal scheme of things. I am so prone to follow my own path and miss the path of goodness, mercy, and righteousness. I am tempted to seize a momentary pleasure rather than striving for what is eternally significant and fruit that remains. As I wait on you in the quiet of this moment, prepare my soul for all before me. Help me to choose the better way, the way that ultimately will lead me home where life is loving, generous, and at peace. As I feel your loving and forgiving arms around me, may my outlook be filled with joy, excitement, and anticipation of the better things to come. I am your child, Lord, humbled by my need and sin, yet ready again to celebrate life with the family that bears your name. Through Jesus Christ, my Lord, I pray. Amen.

Day 5

The Lord is not slow in keeping his promise, as some understand
slowness. Instead he is patient with you, not wanting anyone to
perish, but everyone to come to repentance. (2 Peter 3:9)

O Lord, our Lord, how majestic is your name above all the earth! Your love extends far beyond the comfortable borders in which we nestle our souls. You are forever reaching out and beyond to include others while we prefer to draw the circle so small. You continually remind us that we all are in need of healing grace, lavish forgiveness, and unconditional love. You are no respecter of persons, loving each of us as if there is only one of us. Forgive us, Lord Jesus, when our pride and arrogance block the flow of your blessing through us to others. Forgive us when we fail to look into the eyes of others and not see children who are the objects of your love, longing to be loved, forgiven, and made whole. Enlarge our hearts and enable us to extend our arms as your friends to all who need a Friend. For your sake and for the sake of all you love. Amen.

DAY 6

I am the LORD your God who takes hold of your right hand and says to you, Do not fear; I will help you. (Isaiah 41:13)

O Lord, our Lord, how majestic is your name in all the earth! You have ordained the seasons of the year and the seasons of our lives. We praise you for your steadfast love and mercy which support us every day and throughout every kind of day. Help us to embrace your Presence in this moment, that our lives today will be occasions of the Holy Spirit. Where we are afraid, give us courage. Where we are anxious, give us peace. Where we are confused, give us discernment. Where we are lonely, give us friends. Wherever we are today, let the mind of Jesus become our mind as well, drawing us into true worship, intentional growth, and loving service. Thank you for leading us on this journey to spiritual wholeness and the sense of purpose that comes with the dawn of each new day. O Lord, our Lord, how majestic is your name in all the earth! Amen.

DAY 7

God made him who had no sin to be sin for us, so that in him we might become the righteousness of God. (2 Corinthians 5:21)

Holy God, I am so thankful that I can come to you this morning knowing not only that I am loved but that there is no one who will love me more. My heart is full and overflows with unalloyed joy. Thank you that I do not need to persuade you that I am worthy of such love. Because of Jesus, I am forgiven, accepted, and welcomed into your Presence. O God, I thank you that you are willing and able to set us free from anything and everything that enslaves us and dissuades us from loving and serving you. I thank you for life in the Spirit that frees us from negative attitudes, broken promises, roots of bitterness, hurtful words, the burden of guilt, the agony of regret, and the power of sin that make us ashamed. I praise you that we can live every day in the confidence that we are your children, not by right or responsibility but by grace alone, freely offered and forever enjoyed because of the atoning death of our Savior and Lord Jesus Christ for our sakes. With a thankful heart, I offer this prayer in his name and for the sake of all you love. Amen.

WEEK THIRTY–NINE

DAY 1

Jesus performed many other signs in the presence of his disciples, which are not recorded in this book. But these are written that you may believe that Jesus is the Messiah, the Son of God, and that by believing you may have life in his name. (John 20:30–31)

O Lord Jesus, thank you for the gospel, the message of all that you have done and the victory you have won for us. How wonder-filled is the story of your birth, your life, your ministry of teaching and healing, your touch of those hurting, and your reaching out to those who were rejected. We thank you for caring for those in great need and for forgiving even those who crucified you. And we thank you that you are with us still. Even now it is your desire to continue your ministry to us and to the entire world in the power and presence of the Holy Spirit. We have only begun to imagine what you are seeking to do for us and through us. There is more truth to be discovered, more light to be revealed, more hope to be shared, and more love to flow from the empty cross, the empty tomb, and the outpouring of the Holy Spirit. O Lord, how we thank you for the privilege of being partakers and partners of the gospel for our sake and for the sake of the world you love. Praise your holy name! Amen.

Day 2

We remember before our God and Father your work produced by faith, your labor prompted by love, and your endurance inspired by hope in our Lord Jesus Christ. (1 Thessalonians 1:3)

O Lord Jesus, I turn once more to you today. Early in the morning, I set out with your blessing, and throughout the day I pray that you will uphold me by your amazing grace. I pray that you will grant me peace. I cast all my cares upon you, knowing how much you care for all that concerns us all. What good I do this day, may that good be multiplied. Forgive whatever harm I do in ignorance, easing the hurt I may cause someone unknowingly. Lord Jesus, have mercy on all who are heavy laden, all whose work is beyond their strength, and all whose bodies and spirits need your divine, healing touch. May your will be done in us and through us as it is in heaven. With you, the Father, and the Holy Spirit be glory and praise forever. Amen.

Day 3

Then a great and powerful wind tore the mountains apart and shattered the rocks before the LORD, but the LORD was not in the wind. After the wind there was an earthquake, but the LORD was not in the earthquake. After the earthquake came a fire, but the LORD was not in the fire. And after the fire came a gentle whisper. (1 Kings 19:11–12)

I wake in the morning, O God, open my eyes, and there you are. You neither slumber nor sleep. You watch over us throughout the night and are with us throughout the day. Even when we are preoccupied with lesser things and are unaware of your Presence, you constantly are speaking into our lives in the words of Scripture, the stirring of our hearts, the unexpected opening of a door, the dawning of a dream, the counsel of a friend, the gentle whisper of the Holy Spirit. How great are your gifts, O God, and we hardly know how to thank you. Save us from the dullness of what is beautiful, good, and holy. Open our hearts to truth; your Word is truth. Make us sensitive to the sanctity of others created in your image and to the wonderful ways you are moving in and speaking through their lives. Show us how to embrace life and love, to celebrate the forgiveness and freedom so graciously given us in Jesus our Lord, in whose name we pray. Amen.

DAY 4

Does the LORD delight in burnt offerings and sacrifices as much as in obeying the LORD? To obey is better than sacrifice, and to heed is better than the fat of rams." (1 Samuel 15:22)

How easily I fall into the trap, O Lord, of trying to prove my love and loyalty to you. Like Peter, I want to affirm myself and impress others with my strong convictions, with how willing I am to do anything, sacrifice everything, to demonstrate the depth of my devotion. I want to pass the test that I am worthy of your love. But you do not want my offerings, sacrifices, or evidence of my loyalty. You desire my obedience, plain and simple. It is not about my worthiness or what I must give up to earn your approval. It is about you and full surrender to your divine purposes. I trust you for salvation, the fullness of your Spirit, and the assurance of eternal life. Help me now to trust you with all the details of my life. O Lord, may I concentrate on one line every moment of every day—single-minded obedience to your will. In Jesus' name. Amen.

DAY 5

Therefore, he is able to save completely those who come to God through him, because he always lives to intercede for them. (Hebrews 7:25)

Almighty God, I pray today for all of your children who are prayer-less. Many simply do not or cannot pray. For many, life has been very cruel, and they do not believe that you care or are even there. Many have been misled, are confused, and have wandered away. Others are ashamed and are overcome by guilt and regret. Through the power of the Holy Spirit, speak to their hearts, draw them close, and help them try again. We pray with them and for them, believing that you hear us even when doubts overwhelm and faith is such a struggle. From our own aching, humiliating, firsthand experiences, we understand the doubts of all doubters, the loneliness of loners, and the sadness of being ignored. As we pray for others to pray, hear our prayers. Draw us closer. Fill us with the Holy Spirit, our Comforter and Teacher, who will help us learn the honesty and the quiet, the intimacy and the awe, the joy and the release of simply being in your Presence. Especially curb our pride so we dare to confide in and share with others the lessons we are learning in this school of prayer. Through Jesus Christ our Lord, who ever lives and intercedes for us. Amen.

DAY 6

Jesus answered, "Everyone who drinks this water will be thirsty again, but whoever drinks the water I give them will never thirst. Indeed, the water I give them will become in them a spring of water welling up to eternal life." (John 4:13–14)

We long to feel your Presence, O Lord. With the psalmist we cry out, "As the deer pants for streams of water, so my soul pants for you, my God" (Psalm 42:1). May the unalloyed joy of such companionship and the serenity of your abiding Presence become our witness to others who long for you in their lives. Draw near, Lord, especially to those of us who are suffering in our bodies, minds, and spirits, that we may be healed; who are separated from family and friends or have lost loved ones to death, that we may be comforted; who have lost jobs, struggle with school, or grieve over broken relationships, that through the pain we may find new purpose and direction in life. May the fellowship of our communities of faith become a home to the wounded and a shelter to all who feel forgotten. We need you, O Lord. We long for you. May we sense that you are near today—very, very near. For your sake and for the sake of all you love, we pray in the holy name of Jesus, our Savior and Friend. Amen.

DAY 7

There remains, then, a Sabbath-rest for the people of God; for anyone who enters God's rest also rests from their works, just as God did from his. Let us, therefore, make every effort to enter that rest, so that no one will perish by following their example of disobedience. (Hebrews 4:9–11)

L ord Jesus, you know how hard it is for me to stop and be still, to let go and rest in your Presence. All day long I rush from one thing to another, whipping up the hours of the day into some sort of accomplishment. Night comes, and I can't relax. I am still troubled by the tyranny of the urgent, feeling I have left too much undone. Actually, I too often accomplish too little in all this busyness, failing to stop long enough to hear the cries of my loved ones, friends, neighbors, and strangers. Forgive me for being so preoccupied with the next thing on my "to do" list that I have not listened to the words, felt the pain, and shared the tears of your loved ones. Calm me down, Lord. Help me to stop, listen, and learn that if I care for the depth of my love for you, you will take care of the breadth of the impact of my life for your sake and others. May it be so, Lord Jesus. Let it be so. Amen.

WEEK FORTY

DAY 1

As you sent me into the world, I have sent them into the world. For them I sanctify myself, that they too may be truly sanctified. (John 17:18–19)

L ord Jesus, we pray for the Church as you prayed for all believers in every generation to be the unmistakable witness of who you are and why you came into our world of space and time. You and you alone have revealed through your life, ministry, suffering, death, resurrection, and ascension the eternal glory of the one, true God. Even now you are interceding for us to be kept, sanctified, and unified by your Spirit. Our life together is the new life we experience through repentance and faith, and then express in your name by offering mercy and giving testimony to your saving grace. And so we pray that the world may clearly see in our lives that the primary work of the Church is incarnational ministry rather than institutional preservation; that the guiding passion of the Church is to be sanctified by the Word of truth rather than seeking to be relevant, popular, and powerful; that the holy aspiration of the Church is to prepare the world for the coming of your kingdom rather than striving to maintain the status quo; that the risk-taking mission of the Church is to proclaim the gospel across the street and around the world, making disciples who will make disciples; that the distinctive witness of the Church in the world are hearts fully devoted to God, Spirit-filled believers who are willing to give what cannot be kept to gain what could never be lost. This we pray, O Lord, in your holy name and for the sake of the Bride, your Church. Amen.

DAY 2

Carry each other's burdens, and in this way you
will fulfill the law of Christ. (Galatians 6:2)

With the dawn of a new day, I lift my heart to you, O God. Thank you for the beauty of the morning that refreshes my soul and renewed mercies that give me hope. Throughout this day, help me be a means of your grace, a witness of your righteousness, and an instrument of your peace. Help me as I share burdens and pray with all whose hearts are breaking and aching today. In the strong name of Jesus and in the power of the Holy Spirit, assure us of your abiding Presence and the forever fellowship of the community of faith as we feel our spirits are lifted and our hope restored. This I pray for the sake of your kingdom and for all that you love. Amen.

DAY 3

But because of his great love for us, God, who is rich in mercy, made us alive with Christ even when we were dead in transgressions—it is by grace you have been saved. And God raised us up with Christ and seated us with him in the heavenly realms in Christ Jesus, in order that in the coming ages he might show the incomparable riches of his grace expressed in his kindness to us in Christ Jesus. (Ephesians 2:4–7)

Jesus, you walk with us through the valley of the shadow of death every day: the death of innocence, of hope, of ambition, of civility, of manners, of institutions, of relationships, of dreams, of loved ones, and the death that is at work in these mortal bodies. Therefore, we choose to praise you at the break of this new day for the gospel, the message of Life, abundant and eternal, that you preached, lived, and still invite us to embrace: the life of the Spirit, of faith, of love, of hope, of peace, the life for broken lives, for diseased and afflicted lives, the life of loved ones, the life for myself, and life forever with you! Furthermore, we ask you to help us die to self, sin, and small ambitions so that we may live for you, for all you love, for all we love, and for your kingdom—to live life to the utmost. Jesus, you are our risen Lord and forever Friend. Help us to embrace every moment of life every day, knowing that our life is in you and your life is in us. To that end we say, Hallelujah! For yours is the unshakable kingdom that has no end and the immeasurable love that will never be exhausted. Amen.

DAY 4

"Where, O death, is your victory? Where, O death, is your sting?" The sting of death is sin, and the power of sin is the law. But thanks be to God! He gives us the victory through our Lord Jesus Christ. (1 Corinthians 15:55–57)

There can be some very lonely days on this spiritual journey, Jesus. The isolation, confusion, discouragement, and grief can feel overwhelming at times. But you felt all that and more on the lonely road you walked. How often did you feel misunderstood, unappreciated, and abandoned? You were tempted in every way that we are tempted.

In the end, everyone deserted you. You were put to death as a common criminal, mocked, tortured, abused, and left to suffer alone. Ah, but what many thought was the end was only the beginning. You assumed our full humanity—our broken hearts, minds, souls, and bodies—to make us fully human, no longer slaves to sin or the fear of death but alive in the Spirit. Now, we can go through every day and every kind of day with assurance, hearing your voice above the noise of the crowd, even when this journey feels terribly lonely, difficult, and uncertain. May the Spirit who raised you in power and glory be with us today so that we may be your willing, obedient servants as you lead us where you need us to help other wandering, lonely pilgrims find you as their faithful Companion on the Way. Amen.

DAY 5

All the believers were one in heart and mind. No one claimed that any of their possessions were their own, but they shared everything they had. With great power the apostles continued to testify to the resurrection of the Lord Jesus. And God's grace was so powerfully at work in them all that there were no needy persons among them. (Acts 4:32–34a)

Holy God, you made us in love and for love. Every one of us is created in your image and at the center of our existence is the capability and the desire to form holy and lasting relationships. Such holy love extends beyond comfortable boundaries, making the circle bigger and the table longer. We may think we need only a few people in our lives, that we relate only to our own "kind," and that we should keep strangers at arm's length. Yet every word you speak reminds us that we all are in need of redeeming love, boundless mercy, and healing grace. We all need to be reminded continually that Jesus died for all sinners to make us one in your Spirit and one with each other. And we need to discover how capable we are of experiencing and expressing such love, being more willing to serve than to be served, to understand than to be understood. Refashion us in love and for love so our witness for Christ is marked by authentic relationships, unalloyed joy, and uncommon peace. In the strong of our Savior we pray. Amen.

DAY 6

By this we know love, that he laid down his life for us, and we ought to lay down our lives for the brothers. (1 John 3:16 ESV)

Holy and loving God, when the storms of life are at their worst for so many families, friends, fellow citizens, and people of other nations, help us who are called by your name to be at our best. When forces beyond our control have done what is feared the most, help us to seize that moment to do what we do best. Let us rejoice with those who rejoice, weep with those who weep, grieve with all who mourn, and bear the burdens of others as we pray without ceasing. Let us be generous in our giving, gracious in our serving, and genuine in our compassion. Let us be witnesses of hope to the weary, messengers of peace to the conflicted, and mediators of faith to the discouraged. May we be your ears and voice as we lovingly listen, understand, and respond to their suffering, pain, and loss. In the power and by the leadership of the Holy Spirit, may we be your hands and feet, doing all the good we can, wherever we can, as often as we can, as long as we can for the sake of all you love. This we pray in the strong name of Jesus. Amen.

DAY 7

The LORD is gracious and righteous; our God is full of compassion. The LORD protects the unwary; when I was brought low, he saved me. Return to your rest, my soul, for the LORD has been good to you. (Psalm 116:5–7)

Lord, in the quietness of this moment, assure me of your Presence. In the stillness of this hour, remind me that I am not alone. In my weakness, give me strength to do your will. In the darkness, help me to hold fast to hope. In my doubt, give me patience to press on. In my need, help me to learn to be content. In my work, give me glimpses of your kingdom. In my serving, let me see your smile. In my life, Lord, be glorified. Amen.

WEEK FORTY-ONE

DAY 1

Therefore, since we are surrounded by such a great cloud of witnesses, let us throw off everything that hinders and the sin that so easily entangles. And let us run with perseverance the race marked out for us, fixing our eyes on Jesus, the pioneer and perfecter of our faith. (Hebrews 12:1–2a)

Lord Jesus, thank you for the joy of knowing you as our Savior and Lord and for the life we share with others on our spiritual journeys; for all the faithful servants who throughout the centuries have known you and made you known; for those who led us to trust you and showed us the path to life that is new and abundant and forever; for those who have been patient with us in our ignorance, prayed for us when we were struggling, understanding us when we were broken, listened to us in our deep distress, held us when we were hurting, and offered healing grace when we were in deep need. Thank you for the fellowship, joy, and hope we share because of the life we share in you. May we be the friends who help others follow you closely on the Way as your friends have helped us. How we thank you that we are not alone on this journey. For the sake of your kingdom and all you love, we pray in your holy name. Amen.

DAY 2

I am the LORD your God; consecrate yourselves and be holy, because I am holy. Do not make yourselves unclean by any creature that moves along the ground. I am the LORD, who brought you up out of Egypt to be your God; therefore, be holy, because I am holy. (Leviticus 11:44–45)

Heavenly Father, I praise you today that you love us perfectly in the beauty of holiness. I praise you that you have promised always to be with us, and you have never broken that promise. I praise you that no matter what we do, where we go, or what we are facing, you will never, ever forsake us. I praise you that wherever we look around on earth or into the heavens, we see your fingerprints. I praise you that

Jesus is the Good Shepherd who knows each of us by name, guides us every day along the journey, and walks with us through the shadows. I praise you that for our sake, Jesus was obedient unto death, the Lamb of God who takes away the sin of the world. And I praise you for the Holy Spirit who comes with cleansing fire and fills my heart so that I love you and all that you love. Amen.

DAY 3

LORD, you alone are my portion and my cup; you make my lot secure. The boundary lines have fallen for me in pleasant places; surely I have a delightful inheritance. (Psalm 16:5–6)

Good and gracious Lord, I praise you for the gift of this day and the chance to make a new start. There will be moments to learn new things and opportunities to serve the needs of others. Perhaps I will make a new friend or two today as well as be reminded to give thanks for those with whom I have shared so much over the years. There will be reasons to thank you for all you have done, divine moments when I realize with awe how holy and good you are. There will be experiences to receive and give a deeper measure of your love. I have the wonderful privilege of living in this world, on this day, for such a time as this. And so, I pray that you will open my eyes that I may see, prepare my ears that I may hear, and free my heart that I may be ready for the occasions of the Holy Spirit today. For the sake of your kingdom and all that you love, I pray in the strong name of Jesus. Amen.

DAY 4

This is what the Sovereign LORD, the Holy One of Israel says, "In repentance and rest is your salvation, in quietness and trust is your strength, but you would have none of it." Yet the LORD longs to be gracious to you; therefore he will rise up to show you compassion. For the LORD is a God of justice. Blessed are all who wait for him! (Isaiah 30:15, 18)

Honestly, Lord, waiting may be the most difficult spiritual discipline for me. To "rest in the Lord" is not to "rust in the Lord." You want me actively to wait on you, not do nothing. To wait on you and rest in you is to maintain the patience and confidence that you do all things well. I am so tempted to take the initiative, put things in my proper order, stay in control, or "ride off on swift horses" to guarantee my preferred outcome. But then, I am putting my wits on the throne of my life, not resting, waiting, trusting, abiding in your peace. O Lord, help me to unclench my fists, open my hands, release that which is not my responsibility, and receive your strength in the quietness and confidence of your faithfulness. You are good and your love endures forever; your faithfulness continues through all generations. And your timing is perfect. Praise your holy name. Amen.

Day 5

Blessed are the poor in spirit, for theirs is the
kingdom of heaven. (Matthew 5:3)

We bless you, O Lord, for you are good and your mercy endures forever. But our souls are troubled as we pray. Some of our loved ones carry heavy loads today. Some are anxious about health problems, their own and the illness of loved ones. Some are deeply concerned about finances, how to make ends meet in an expensive and uncertain world. Others are upset about their children who are spiritually indifferent, spouses who are emotionally distant, and friends who are less than reliable. And some are angry with you and confused that their prayers go unanswered. We can neither fix their problems nor answer their questions. But we can pray for them, with them, and for ourselves to be adequate witnesses of your mercy and grace. We choose to share their heavy loads as they trust us and as we trust you to give us wisdom, strength, and compassion for the poor in spirit and body. And in the meantime, we dare to believe that all the great questions of life ultimately are satisfied in the atoning death of Jesus and in the power of his resurrection. Have mercy on us, Lord, and give us peace, for yours is the mystery and the glory forever. Amen.

DAY 6

The thief comes only to steal and kill and destroy; I have come
that they may have life, and have it to the full. (John 10:10)

Our Heavenly Father, we thank you for the miracle of life and the joy of sharing this faith journey with loved ones and others who make life better for all. We thank you for all who have responded to your call to serve, protect, provide, and care for the needs of others. We thank you for the witness of those who choose life and stand firm against all that intend to steal, kill, and destroy the abundant life you intend for all your children. We thank you for Jesus who came into our space and time, took on our flesh and blood, suffered our sorrows and death, and then was raised in power to give us hope and the promise of eternal life. We thank you for every sign that the Holy Spirit is at work in the world, healing bodies, transforming lives, and renewing our life together. Help us throughout this day to affirm life in the conversations we have with friends, family, and strangers; in the burdens of others we will gladly share; and in the wonder we observe all around us in matters great and small. Accept our sacrifices of praise, O Lord, to your honor and glory as we lift this prayer to you with thankful hearts in the precious name of Jesus. Amen.

DAY 7

I am the vine; you are the branches. If you remain in me and I in you, you
will bear much fruit; apart from me you can do nothing. (John 15:5)

Our Heavenly Father, will we ever learn? Will we ever understand that so much of the darkness that shrouds our souls is of our own making, that much of the pain we feel and the trouble we face is due to our own foolishness? We harden our hearts, wander away from you, ignore your Word, neglect worship, avoid fellowship, snub neighbors, and then act surprised when we are filled with despair and find ourselves alone and afraid. Our foolish attempts at self-reliance do not fool you. Yet, our disappointments can become your appointments. There is a better way, and may we learn that way—that apart from you, there is no real peace, no steadfast hope, no authentic contentment, no lasting fruitfulness to our labors. May we learn to confess that you are God, and we are not. May we learn to prefer the grace of Jesus and yield to the power of the Holy Spirit. May we learn to deny ourselves, embrace the cross daily, and enjoy the journey with you. O Lord, renew a good and right spirit within us that we may abide and walk in the light of your love today. For the sake of your kingdom and all that you love, we pray in Jesus' name. Amen.

WEEK FORTY–TWO

DAY 1

Instead, speaking the truth in love, we will grow to become in every respect the mature body of him who is the head, that is, Christ. From him the whole body, joined and held together by every supporting ligament, grows and builds itself up in love, as each part does its work. (Ephesians 4:15–16)

We come before you this morning, O Lord, from a variety of experiences. Some of us are half-asleep. Some of us are wide-awake. Some of us are worn thin with weariness. Others of us are ready to take on bold, new challenges. Some of us are hurting and carry heavy hearts. Some of us are filled with such joy we can hardly sit still. Some of us are confused and terribly uncertain. Others of us are at peace. We are different, unique, and we come into your Presence openly and honestly, just as we are. We are glad that you are looking at our hearts, not our appearances or our past experiences. We share this journey to spiritual wholeness with others unlike ourselves. With tender hearts and compassionate spirits, help us to see one another as you see us. Give us your mind so we can better understand as well as patience to be understood. Above all, may the fellowship of the Holy Spirit become our new normal and the ways of your kingdom be our preferred future, our hearts' desire. This we pray in your name and for our sakes, Lord Jesus. Amen.

Day 2

And hope does not put us to shame, because God's love
has been poured out into our hearts through the Holy
Spirit who has been given to us. (Romans 5:5)

Almighty God, we offer you our praise as we hope in you today. We
praise you because you alone are worthy of our praise. We have
hope today because you proved to be faithful, true, and good yesterday.
We praise you because you first reached out to us while we were yet
sinners, freely offering grace and forgiveness through our Lord and
Savior Jesus Christ. We have hope for a glorious future because all we
have learned on this journey thus far convinces us that you will not
disappoint. We praise you that you are the Author and the Perfecter
of our faith, and our hope is that what you have begun in us you will
complete far beyond what our hearts can imagine and our minds can
conceive. O Lord, we praise you as we place the full weight of our hope
in you again this morning. Because of Jesus, in whom we have found
the Way, the Truth, and the Life. Amen.

Day 3

As they were walking along the road, a man said to him, "I will follow you
wherever you go." ...Jesus replied, "No one who puts a hand to the plow
and looks back is fit for service in the kingdom of God." (Luke 9:57, 62)

O Lord, save me from the false notion that sentimentality is devotion.
How easily I can be swept up in high and devout emotions through
inspiring words, glorious music, and delightful fellowship. Such
experiences thrill my soul for a moment but too seldom translate into
action. Consequently, I crave the next stirring of my soul that blesses
me but costs me nothing. I disregard other experiences that are more
real but less sentimental, and then I wonder why spiritual wholeness
seems impossible, unreachable. Being your disciple is a choice—an act
of my will—followed by immediate obedience. For the joy set before
you, Jesus, you obeyed, endured the cross, scorning its shame. Let me
not grow weary or lose heart when my long obedience in the same

direction is less than enjoyable. For your sake and for the sake of your kingdom, I pray. Amen.

DAY 4

The LORD your God is with you, the Mighty Warrior who saves. He will take great delight in you; in his love he will no longer rebuke you, but will rejoice over you with singing. (Zephaniah 3:17)

Heavenly Father, your goodness exceeds the limits of my mind. Your mercy is marvelous, and at times, your grace leaves me speechless. Your glory is beyond my imagination, yet your goodness sustains the universe every day. I cannot describe your majesty, yet your sovereignty gives me courage for every kind of day. I worship you as the one, true, living, and loving God, the only One who deserves my heart and soul. Before the first thought came to my mind, before I inhaled my first breath or made a sound, you claimed me as your own. Before I sinned, your Son was given as the Lamb of God who takes away the sin of the world, even mine. Before I believed in you, you believed in me and delighted in me. My tiny, finite mind cannot comprehend such holy, amazing love, yet you desire to make your home in my heart. Let it be so, Lord. Come, and may your joy be my strength. Amen.

DAY 5

Therefore, do not let what you know is good be spoken of as evil. For the kingdom of God is not a matter of eating and drinking, but of righteousness, peace and joy in the Holy Spirit, because anyone who serves Christ in this way is pleasing to God and receives human approval. (Romans 14:16–18)

Today, Lord, I pray for the de-churched, those persons who no longer feel that they belong or want to belong to the fellowship of God's people. While I pray for them, help me search my own heart and ask myself if I in any way hindered rather than helped my brothers or sisters absent from our faith community. Have I not heard a cry, felt a hurt, or seen a tear? Have I failed in some measure to be a messenger of your peace and presence? Holy Spirit, stir our hearts to bow humbly at the foot of the Cross, and then let us rise, reach out, and commit to love one another as you love us. Help us, as your servants, to forgive as we have been forgiven, to bless as we have been blessed, and to live together in such a manner that others will give glory to you as they say, *Behold! How they love one another!* May it be so, Lord. May it be so for your sake and for the sake of your forever family. Amen.

DAY 6

Can a mother forget the baby at her breast and have no compassion on the child she has borne? Though she may forget, I will not forget you! See, I have engraved you on the palms of my hands.... (Isaiah 49:15–16a)

Jesus, my heart is heavy this morning as I think of friends and family who have longed for a life of joy and contentment but whose hopes are unrealized, whose dreams have been broken, and whose expectations are tattered to shreds. I am thinking of others who planned for nothing, and it seems that is what they have achieved. They are frustrated by the emptiness of their lives, the wasted opportunities of yesterday, and the foolishness that damaged the lives of others as well as their own. I pray for all who have never enjoyed the life you died to give nor embraced the love that others have offered, nor experienced the pleasure of being responsible for the wellbeing of others. Lord, have mercy! You know the hurts and pain, the fears and regrets, the tears poured out, and the sin that enslaves. Fill the emptiness of these hearts with perfect love, Lover of our souls, that they may overflow with the joy of living, loving, and being loved. Hear the deepest longings of all our hearts. In our weakness, give us your strength. In our brokenness, pour out your healing grace. In our desperation, may we cling to hope, believing and asking these things in your name, Lord Jesus, for the sake of all you love. Amen.

DAY 7

What then, shall we say in response to these things? If God is for us, who can be against us? He who did not spare his own Son, but gave him up for us all—how will he not also, along with him, graciously give us all things? (Romans 8:31–32)

I thank you, O Lord, that I can trust you every day and in every kind of day and not simply when life is good and wholesome. I thank you for the deep assurance that there is no darkness your love cannot penetrate, no burden that you will not carry. There is no pain you will not bear and no joy that your Presence cannot make richer. I thank you that you came into our world with its brokenness, fear, and pain, walking where we walk, facing what we face, and were tempted as we are tempted. Ah, how I thank you, Lord Jesus, for being obedient, even to the point of death, for my sake and for the sake of all you love. I thank you that there is no limit to what you will do to find anyone who is lost, no enemy of our souls or bodies greater than your resurrection power. As I rise to face the uncertainties of this day, my heart is glad and filled with hope, for nothing—absolutely nothing!—in all creation will be able to separate me from your love. Thanks be to God for this gift too wonderful for words! Amen and amen.

WEEK FORTY-THREE

DAY 1

But you, dear friends, by building yourselves up in your most holy faith and praying in the Holy Spirit, keep yourselves in God's love as you wait for the mercy of our Lord Jesus Christ to bring you to eternal life. (Jude 20–21)

God of grace and glory, we did not choose you, but you chose us and have made yourself known to us in such a way that we may understand your will and purpose for our lives, and we are thankful. Because of Jesus, we now know that there is nothing in heaven or on earth, not even death itself, that can separate us from your love, and for that we praise your holy name. Through the power of the Holy Spirit you convict us of our sin, convince us of grace, and call us to be instruments of your peace across the street and witnesses of your love around the world. For this honor we humbly thank you. As we gather around tables today with loved ones or perhaps share a meal with strangers, make yourself known to us in the breaking of bread so that the deepest longing of our souls will be satisfied and every heart will be warmed with the pure joy of your Presence. To you, O God, Father, Son, and Holy Spirit, be all honor, glory, praise, and thanksgiving forever and ever. Amen.

DAY 2

And my God will meet all your needs according to the
riches of his glory in Christ Jesus. (Philippians 4:19)

O God, you are perfect in all your ways. You are gracious beyond our imagination. Your unfailing love sustains us every day. Our humble prayer today is that you will give us what we need to honor you faithfully to the end of our lives. Give us all we need so our love and joy may never fail. Give us all we need so we can be channels of your peace, mercy, grace, and forgiveness to the lonely and the lost. O Lord, our God, our Savior, and our Friend, give us what we need most: undivided hearts filled with holy love, bearing witness of the glorious hope that no eye has seen, nor has any ear heard, nor has any heart imagined the things that you have prepared for all who love you. How great and good and gracious you are, Father, Son, and Holy Spirit. Praise your holy name. Amen.

DAY 3

Do everything without grumbling or arguing, so that you may become blameless and pure, "children of God without fault in a warped and crooked generation." Then you will shine among them like stars in the sky as you hold firmly to the word of life. (Philippians 2:14–16a)

Honestly Lord, I would prefer life to be less complicated, less confusing, less controversial. If only things were well-ordered, signed, sealed, and delivered on time with no margin for error. That is how I often think, but in reality, you love us too much to manipulate us, to make us independent of grace, mercy, and love. So, I dare not pray to be fearless, for only a fool could be unafraid. I do not ask to have a guarantee of how things should go, for no one should dare be so presumptuous. I will not pray even to be exempt from trials and temptation, for life is full of pressure and tension, unexpected conflicts, and problems of our own making. My prayer this morning is simply this: to be steady and hang on to hope in spite of my fears; to be open, ready to listen, learn, and grow in spite of my ignorance; to make the effort to love others as I have been loved by you; to be devoted to you, the Author and Perfecter of my faith, affirming you in the face of confusion and complications. This I choose, believing you are pleased with my intent even more than my performance. And so, I am content to choose to be dependent on your grace, mercy, and love in this not-so-well-ordered life I live. Because of Jesus. Amen.

DAY 4

They reeled and staggered like drunkards; they were at their wits' end. Then they cried to the LORD in their trouble, and he brought them out of their distress. (Psalm 107:27–28)

O God, in you and you alone we find mercy we do not deserve and grace that is greater than our need. There is no god like you, and there is no other God than you. You alone are the Creator and Sustainer of the whole universe. You alone are the center and Source of Life. You alone are the center and source of all that is good, true, holy, and wholesome. You alone are the center and source of Hope, Peace, Joy, and Love. Why then are we surprised when we feel so helpless, hopeless, alone, and afraid after our attempts at self-reliance and self-satisfaction? We fail to see that our disappointments can become divine appointments. You did not create us to struggle on our own nor to figure it all out without help. You came into our world of space and time, taking on our flesh and blood that we might be healed and have hope and a future. Forgive and free us from self-pity when things go wrong. Hear our cries for help and hope. We lift up our hearts to you,

O God, for in you and you alone we find mercy we do not deserve and grace that is greater than our need. In Jesus' name. Amen.

DAY 5

Be strong and courageous. Do not be afraid or terrified because of them, for the LORD your God goes with you; he will never leave you nor forsake you. (Deuteronomy 31:6)

As we pause before we engage in other demands and activities of the day, we seize this moment with you, O Lord, to look beyond the challenges, pains, and fears, and to remember that we are not alone on this journey. We hold fast to your promise that you would never leave us or forsake us. We believe the promise that you are the God of all comfort, the Wonderful Counselor who hears and understands, the Good Shepherd who knows his sheep, the Resurrection and the Life who has preempted all our fears. That is why we keep showing up, drawing near, and trusting you to do for us what we could never do for ourselves. In these moments, we are learning to wait on you. You are faithful and, in your way and good time, every tear will be wiped away and every hurt will be healed. And so, before we leave this space and resume other places in our lives, we deliberately cast our every care upon you, knowing that in the face of Jesus we have seen Perfect Love. That is enough, and so we pray with all our wonder, love, and praise in his holy name. Amen.

DAY 6

Therefore, since we have these promises, dear friends, let us purify ourselves from everything that contaminates body and spirit, perfecting holiness out of reverence to God. (2 Corinthians 7:1)

Holy God, you are gracious, good, faithful, and true throughout all generations, yet we confess that as a community of faith we have grieved your Spirit. We have wasted so-called moments of holy conferencing and have not been good stewards of the resources the saints before us gave sacrificially for the work of your kingdom. You have given us sound minds, but we have been careless about what we have pondered. We have abused our bodies with harmful habits and poor choices. We have starved our spirits by neglecting your Word. Although you equipped us with talents and abilities and provided opportunities to share these generously with those in need, we have hoarded and satisfied only ourselves. We have forfeited holy manna for a pot of porridge. Forgive us for the disrespect we have shown you in simply ignoring you. Forgive us for discouraging others by our lack of empathy. Forgive us for being so careful that we are afraid to speak your name. Rekindle the passion of our first love so we may be the devoted servants you need us to be for such a time as this. For the sake of your kingdom we pray in Jesus' name. Amen.

DAY 7

Only be careful, and watch yourselves closely so that you do
not forget the things your eyes have seen or let them fade from
your heart as long as you live. Teach them to your children
and to their children after them. (Deuteronomy 4:9)

Thank you, most patient God, for keeping faith with me in spite of my lack of faith. Thank you for providing such wonderful witnesses to remind me of hope, faith, and love: the old man who is planting trees in the neighborhood even though he knows he will not live to enjoy them; the young woman who suffers from a terminal disease, yet exudes a holy presence of unalloyed joy and steadfast hope; the spiritual leaders of our community who day after day demonstrate authentic faith with their heartfelt prayers, clear words of witness, and tireless work for the sake of your kingdom; husbands and wives who agree that, in spite of current affairs, this world is still a fit place for having and raising children. Forgive me for the unbelief that causes my doubts, fears, and anxiety. Remind me that you have been our help in ages past, and you are our hope for years to come, even today. This I pray in the strong name of Jesus, who gives us hope and a future. Amen.

WEEK FORTY–FOUR

DAY 1

Give thanks to the LORD, for he is good. *His love endures forever.*
Give thanks to the God of gods. *His love endures forever.* Give thanks
to the Lord of lords: *His love endures forever.* (Psalm 136:1–3)

I choose to live this day, O God, not with fear, frustration, doubt, despair, anger, or angst but with praise and thanksgiving. I praise you that you made this world and each one of us. I thank you that you hold this world in your hands, and you care for all you have made. I praise you for the joy of living in this wonderful world, because it is filled with so many wonderful people, places, and things. I thank you for eyes to see, ears to hear, a mind to understand, and the desire to learn more about you and this place we call home. I praise you for Jesus, for his self-giving love and the power of his resurrection; for the gift of the Holy Spirit, whose peace and presence is your promise to be with us always. I thank you that even when our hearts break, when it is hard for us to trust you, when it is difficult for us to love each other, and when we are ready to give up and give in, your giving has only begun. I praise and thank you, O God, through the amazing grace of our Savior Jesus Christ, who lives and reigns with you and the Holy Spirit, world without end. Amen.

DAY 2

Tremble and do not sin; when you are on your beds,
search your hearts and be silent. Offer the sacrifices of
the righteous and trust in the LORD. (Psalm 4:4–5)

You restore my soul, Lord, when I am still. I have a sense that I am centered in eternity when I simply let go, relax, rest, and wait on you. Teach me how to be still more often, to set apart and treasure such moments when the day is hectic, when I am stressed, when others have lost their calm, when the news is bad, and when life seems to be out of control. In the stillness, I sense your Presence, and

I am healed. In the stillness, you search my heart, I confess my sin, and joy returns. In the stillness, I am renewed, hope is reborn, and I begin again. And so, in the stillness of this moment, I ask you, Lord Jesus, to draw near. Be my Guide, my Savior, my Healer, my Friend. Cleanse my heart from all that is unhealthy and unholy. Correct my attitude. Restore my faith. Renew my energy. In this stillness, prepare me for the opportunities of this day that will have eternal significance in the lives of others. This I pray, Jesus, for yours is the unshakable kingdom that will never end and the immeasurable love that will never be exhausted. Amen.

DAY 3

I will give them a heart to know me, that I am the LORD.
They will be my people, and I will be their God, for they
will return to me with all their heart. (Jeremiah 24:7)

O Lord, all that we have seen that is right, true, and good affirms that we can trust you whom we have not seen. You have cared for us even before we were born. You have watched over us all our days, through every kind of day, in the most difficult days, including this day. Help me, Lover of my soul, to relax in that love with the assurance that as you have been you will continue to be with me all along my journey. May I try not to be smarter than I am, nor more religious than I am, nor more important than I am. Rather, I humbly ask for a heart full of your Spirit so that I can fully experience and express your love. Engraft your Word to my soul that I may passionately pursue and embrace Truth. Help me release my greatest fears to the power of the Spirit so I can obey unconditionally. This I pray, Lord Jesus, in your name and for the sake of your kingdom and all that you love. Amen.

DAY 4

Truly I tell you, if you have faith as small as a mustard seed, you can say to this mountain, "Move from here to there," and it will move. Nothing will be impossible for you. (Matthew 17:20)

O Lord, I pray this morning for authentic faith. How easily I confuse faith with a long list of things to believe. I confess my faith in creeds, reciting the words perfectly and regularly, but these are only my feeble attempts to assent to traditional beliefs of our community of faith. To be a faith-filled, Spirit-led disciple, I need more than a once-a-week recitation of an historic statement. I need a powerful faith that lifts me out of the valley of fear wherein I sometimes walk, out of the dark of despair where I sometimes grope, out of the gloom of circumstances that often are beyond my control. I need a courageous faith that turns me toward life, untethered by your strength and passion, unafraid to love, give, and serve. O Lord, I need a deeper faith today to act out my strongest convictions and remain loyal to my deepest beliefs. I do not need more faith but authentic faith, complete trust in you as the Faithful One that keeps me humble enough to be teachable yet bold enough to be courageous, so you can do through me what you have been waiting and wanting to do. Let it be so, in the name of Jesus, the pioneer and perfecter of faith, I pray. Amen.

DAY 5

So in everything, do to others what you would have them do to you, for this sums up the Law and the Prophets. (Matthew 7:12)

O ur Heavenly Father, we desperately need your help in living out the Golden Rule. What seems so easy to understand and so simple to memorize is neither the conventional wisdom nor the common practice of the day, even among those who claim your name. As children, we were taught to do for others what we would like them to do for us. As adults, too often we expect others to do for us what we are unwilling to do for them. We wonder why others do not appreciate or respect us, but then we choose to be narrow-minded, defend our prejudices, liking only those with whom we agree. We want to be heard and understood, but then we stubbornly clamor for the last word, resisting others who think differently, and are unwilling to be enriched by their insights. Jesus said that unless we become like children we would never participate in your kingdom. O Lord, have mercy on us. Somehow along the way, we have lost your preferred future of our living, playing, and praying together as your children. May we humble ourselves and prefer to pray for the glorious freedom, the transforming power, and the pure, unalloyed joy that is found in the simplicity of childlike trust and self-giving love. Again, we ask your kingdom to come on earth into our communities, homes, and hearts, as it is in heaven. For the sake of Jesus and for the sake of all you love we pray. Amen.

Day 6

All the nations you have made will come and worship before you, Lord; they will bring glory to your name. For you are great and do marvelous deeds; you alone are God. (Psalm 86:9–10)

Holy God, the span of this amazing universe cannot contain your glory, and yet you desire to make your home in our hearts. You deserve the praise of every person that has ever been born and every child yet to be born, and you even delight in my feeble attempts to honor and worship you. Your glory cannot be limited to one time and place, yet you come to each of us in the Spirit as Comforter and Counselor. You promise peace for our troubled hearts, power to do above and beyond what we can imagine, and joy that this world does not give and cannot take away. To the glory of your holy name and for the healing of the nations, pour out your Spirit upon us in Pentecostal Power. Come and do in us that which you have been waiting and wanting to do so you can do through us what we have been created to do. Help us to fully love you and freely share with our neighbors across the street and strangers around the world so they, too, may embrace genuine hope, deep peace, great joy, and eternal life through Jesus Christ, our Savior and Lord. We pray in his name and for the sake of all you love. Amen.

DAY 7

Because your love is better than life, my lips will glorify
you. I will praise you as long as I live, and in your
name I will lift up my hands. (Psalm 63:3–4)

O Lord, my God, I come just as I am in the quiet of this day to
worship you and give you honor, glory, and praise. I worship
you not because it changes your mind but because the worship of you
changes me. I worship you because I catch a glimpse of heaven and the
way things could be on earth. I worship you because I can hear a still,
small voice that lets me know that I am loved with everlasting love. I
worship you because you desire to meet me face to face in spite of my
fears, insecurities, limitations, and inadequacies. O Lord, I come with
an open heart and open hands to worship and adore you. I ask that
you honor my worship today by making your face shine upon me and
giving me kingdom work to do so that I may gladly serve all whom you
love. This I pray in the blessed name of Jesus, whose kingdom has no
end and whose love can never be exhausted. Amen.

WEEK FORTY–FIVE

DAY 1

Blessed are the meek, for they will inherit the earth. (Matthew 5:5)

Today, Lord, I want to thank you for the beautiful feet of those
believers who have walked faithfully with you and trusted you
in the shadows of life. I thank you for the encouragement they have
been to many others who were inspired and lifted above their pain,
suffering, disappointment, and heartaches because of their gospel
witness. These humble servants have continued to honor you and
bless others day by day with gentleness, hope, grace, peace, joy, and
love. Their testimonies of radical obedience and unconditional love
transcend their personal circumstances and concerns, reminding all
others that our lives are more than health and strength. Their prayers

are a source of divine power released across streets and around the world. "For our light and momentary troubles are achieving for us an eternal glory that far outweighs them all" (2 Corinthians 4:17). We hold fast to this promise because of all we have heard and seen in you and the lives of your faithful servants whom we bless this day. With grateful hearts we offer this prayer in your name. Amen.

Day 2

Therefore, my dear friends, as you have always obeyed—not only in my presence, but now much more in my absence—continue to work out your salvation with fear and trembling, for it is God who works in you to will and to act in order to fulfill his good purpose. (Philippians 2:12–13)

Lord Jesus, I am humbled by the fact that you chose me to be your disciple and have sent me to make disciples of others you are calling. This is not something I can do on my own or can expect others to do. I confess that I am powerless to produce fruit that will last—transformed lives who will influence this and many generations to come with the gospel of peace. I am utterly weak to stay the course, to continue on the journey day after day without your strength working in me and through me for your good pleasure. This call is not how righteous, good, or holy I am; your Story is my story, for you are the Faithful One who calls us to yourself and then is able to make us what you call us to be. In my life, Lord, be glorified for your sake and for the sake of all you love. Amen.

Day 3

I thank my God every time I remember you. In all my prayers for all of you, I always pray with joy because of your partnership in the gospel from the first day until now, being confident of this, that he who began a good work in you will carry it on to completion until the day of Christ Jesus. (Philippians 1:3–6)

Thank you, Lord, for all the companions with whom I have had the privilege of sharing my spiritual journey thus far. Many dear friends have helped me discover how to love and be loved, trust and be faithful, give and receive. Lovingly they have been a refiner's fire to my soul, not disregarding those immature areas of my life that needed to be addressed. They have been your messengers to make me more aware that I need you, that I need others, and that I need others to need me. We are finding that because of Jesus, lives can be radically changed, walls of division can be torn down, and broken relationships can be reconciled. We also have found genuine joy through healing words and the redeeming love of Jesus. This is the heart of the gospel that others have shared with me and I love to share. And so, I pray, O Lord, that you would keep my heart tender, my soul vulnerable, and my life transparent so that you can complete the good work you began in me many years ago. I pray that the fellowship I share with my fellow pilgrims along our daily walk will bring honor and glory to you and demonstrate the faith, hope, and love of the community of Jesus to others. For his sake and in his holy name I pray. Amen.

DAY 4

Do not conform to the pattern of this world, but be transformed by the renewing of your mind. Then you will be able to test and approve what God's will is—his good, pleasing and perfect will. (Romans 12:2)

O Lord, there is so much every day that clamors for my attention: headlines and deadlines, schedules and agendas, calendars and memos, texts and tweets, talking heads and robocalls. I fall into bed at night, exhausted from all the noise and the frenetic pace of this hectic routine. How easily I allow this world to squeeze me into its own mold as if this is all that matters. How quickly I forget to re-open the window of my soul to be refreshed by the wind of your Spirit. How desperately I need to pause and think on things beyond this world and to be transformed by the renewing of my mind. In such moments, I can hear heavenly whispers of hope and assurance that there is something more than all this, something better if only I will wait and watch for the Eternal. Lord, restore my tired, spent, and frazzled soul with the comfort of your Presence and renew my spirit with the joy of your salvation. This I ask in the name of Jesus. Amen.

DAY 5

May the peoples praise you, God; may all the peoples praise you.
May the nations be glad and sing for joy, for you rule the peoples
with equity and guide the nations of the earth. (Psalm 67:3–4)

Almighty God, at no time have you left yourself without a witness on earth. In every generation you raised up saints who proclaimed the gospel and led the faithful in the way of truth and love. We praise you for those who inspired, blessed, taught, and prayed for us. These are your servants who carried the light of the gospel and shined it before our dark souls. Today, we pray for those who, following in their footsteps, are now laboring to bring that light to others across our streets and around the world. We especially pray today for pastors and missionaries who are reaching out and serving the least, the loneliest, and the lost in very difficult and demanding circumstances. Give them passion, conviction, courage, hope, and the deep assurance of your Presence as your witnesses in this moment. Provide the encouragement and resources they need to do all they are called to do. May they be assured that you will never lead them where your grace cannot keep them. This we pray in Jesus' name not only for our sake but also for the sake of all who come after us. Amen.

DAY 6

When evening came, many who were demon-possessed were brought
to him, and he drove out the spirits with a word and healed all the sick.
This was to fulfill what was spoken through the prophet Isaiah: "He
took up our infirmities and bore our diseases." (Matthew 8:16–17)

This morning, God of all mercy and love, we share your burden for those who are suffering physically, emotionally, mentally, and spiritually. We pray for all whose lives have been damaged over the years by the words and deeds of others; all who are filled with resentment because of what they have suffered; all who have been taught to hate others who do not look like themselves; all the little ones who are led away from faith and family; all who have been dominated by others and made to feel as if their lives do not matter; all who feel unworthy, unloved, and unvalued; all who once were so hopeful their joy was contagious but now feel rejected, unwanted, unnecessary, and afraid; all who are facing physical and mental illness and all who are caring for these loved ones; all whose past continues to haunt them, unable to think of a future or even face today; all whose suffering is unknown and whose tears are unseen. Most merciful and loving God, in the strong name of Jesus Christ, our Savior who bore our sin and carried our sorrow, we pray for healing and peace for these loved ones whom we name before you. Amen.

DAY 7

How good and pleasant it is when God's people live together in unity! It is like precious oil running down on the beard, running down on Aaron's beard, down on the collar of his robe. It is as if the dew of Hermon were falling on Mount Zion. For there the LORD bestows his blessing, even life forevermore. (Psalm 133)

Today, O God, I want to thank you for the joy of sharing life together. Thank you that every day is an adventure in learning how to love one another. Thank you for making each of us in your image, enabling us to experience covenant relationships as you, Father, Son, and Holy Spirit, are One in Perfect Love. Thank you that because of Jesus we have seen what life together means: to live for the good of others, to walk in love with one another, and that we are not alone in our pain, loneliness, fears, and failures. Thank you that in the deep fellowship in the Holy Spirit we share in suffering and joy, disappointment and hope, death and resurrection. I am poorer when I disregard such covenant relationships. And so, I pray that today, O God, you would help me experience the riches of your glory through others with whom I live in this world. May I be genuinely pleased and even surprised by the joy of our life together, and may all others find in me a faithful and loving friend. For the sake of all you love, I pray and offer my praise in your holy name, Father, Son, and Holy Spirit. Amen.

WEEK FORTY–SIX

DAY 1

Among the gods there is none like you, Lord; no deeds can compare
with yours. All the nations you have made will come and worship
before you, Lord; they will bring glory to your name. For you are great
and do marvelous deeds; you alone are God. (Psalm 86:8–10)

How do I describe you, Lord? No thought can hold you. No
actions explain you. No picture reveals you. You are utterly and
completely beyond us. Your greatness and sovereignty simply cannot
be imagined. I humbly bow before you and praise you for the beauty of
holiness that leaves me in complete awe. Everything I see, touch, hear,
taste, and smell—all that I experience—is because you have made it so.
I can think, plan, and choose because you have made it so. I can love,
praise, and worship you because you have made it so. Everywhere I
look today affirms your glory, and everything I hear declares that you
and you alone are worthy. I praise you, O God, not simply for what
you have done in creation but especially for what you have done in
our re-creation. You are the Eternal Word made flesh. You make all
things new, and I praise you for life, death, and resurrection. I worship
beyond my capacity to understand but fully in my desire to honor you.
There is no other. You alone are Lord, my Lord, and I give you my
heart, lost in wonder, love, and praise. Amen.

DAY 2

It is for freedom that Christ has set us free. Stand firm, then, and do not
let yourselves be burdened again by a yoke of slavery. (Galatians 5:1)

Praise your holy name, God of grace and God of glory! You alone are
the source of all that is right, true, and good. It is your desire, so
much more than anything we could ever imagine, to fill our lives with
goodness, truth, and love. You long for us to be free not simply to please
ourselves to do as we wish or to gain personal liberty at the expense of
others but to be the persons you created us to be, the persons we long

to become, and the persons others need us to be for the sake of your kingdom. Because of Jesus, your offer of freedom begins at an empty cross, an empty tomb, and the emptying out of the Holy Spirit upon the world. In his life, death, and resurrection, you have demonstrated your power to set all things free. And so, we praise you this morning that you have made all the resources of heaven available for every person on Planet Earth to live freely and fully the life you intend for all your children and every generation. May we bring glory to your holy name in the way we experience and express this glorious freedom today, in Jesus' name. Amen.

DAY 3

Jesus answered, "My teaching is not my own. It comes from the one who sent me. Anyone who chooses to do the will of God will find out whether my teaching comes from God or whether I speak on my own. (John 7:16–17)

What a joy it is, Heavenly Father, that you created so much good, so much beauty, in this world for us to experience! Every day is a gift to open and discover the wonders of life above us, around us, and within us. You have given us the ability to learn, think, plan, and choose. Jesus called disciples to be with him, to open their minds to learn of him, and their hearts to receive the kingdom. Thank you for those who helped me hear his call and choose to follow him as his disciple. The more I learn, the more I want to learn about the possibilities of your amazing grace working in and through my life. Forgive me for wasted opportunities when I have been unwilling to listen and learn. Forgive me for not using my mind to consider your ways, especially at those times when I closed my heart to the Message and your messengers. Inspire me today to be more teachable, more ready, and more willing to learn about you, this world, and my calling as a true disciple of Jesus Christ. In his name and for the sake of your kingdom I pray. Amen.

Day 4

So Jacob was left alone, and a man wrestled
with him till daybreak. (Genesis 32:24)

O Lord, how often in my obstinacy do I, like Jacob, try to strangle an answer to my own prayer? I may think this is a struggle with others or circumstances or evil forces, but actually this wrestling match is spiritual; I am fighting with you. I find myself in that lonely place trying to prevail because constantly striving to take care of myself is what I do. And so, I refuse to yield to you and your control of my life. I fight for myself, but I know that I cannot prevail. All I can do is cling to you and refuse to let go until you do for me what I cannot do for myself. Like Jacob, I discover that it is in full surrender to you, I win; your strength is made perfect in my weakness; when I am most vulnerable, I am most approachable and no longer alone. As Jacob was reminded by the limp from his crippled hip for the rest of his life, O Lord, let me lean on you all along the journey. Amen.

Day 5

The person with the Spirit makes judgments about all things, but
such a person is not subject merely to human judgments, for
"Who has known the mind of the LORD so as to instruct him?"
But we have the mind of Christ. (1 Corinthians 2:15–16)

J esus, you are faithful, loving, and worthy of all our trust and praise. You are our Rock and Redeemer, the true source of our confidence and help in our time of need. Yet, too often we lean upon our own understanding and fail miserably because we simply have neglected your help. Forgive us for depending solely on human wisdom rather than bowing in prayer. Forgive us for relying on the security of what is perishable rather than trusting and obeying your eternal Word. Forgive us for thinking too highly of ourselves and too lowly of you. May our first thoughts turn toward you, seeking your mind and asking for the Helper to guide us in the better way. This journey is too difficult for us to make in our own wisdom, strength, and confidence. With hearts and minds centered on you, we can rest in the promises that you are faithful, loving, and worthy of all our trust and praise. Let us be mindful of you and your mind be in us for your sake and for the sake of your kingdom. Amen.

DAY 6

Praise be to the God and Father of our Lord Jesus Christ, who has blessed us in the heavenly realms with every spiritual blessing in Christ. For he chose us in him before the creation of the world to be holy and blameless in his sight. (Ephesians 1:3–4)

You are the God of wonder and love. For the beauty of this earth, the relationships of friends and family, and, above all, the promise of Life abundant and eternal, we thank you. We pray for all who are troubled this morning because they are not aware that you are the Source of such wonders and love. Their ambitions are unfulfilled, their desires unrequited. They see only this world, want only what this world can give, and, honestly, we often are tempted to join them. Help them and help us, Lord, to embrace the joy of little things, the pleasure of being content, and the satisfaction of sharing. Above all, help us throughout this day to ponder the riches of your grace that Jesus Christ has lavished on us. Help us remember that it was in the giving of himself for our sakes that our Savior satisfied the deepest longing of our souls. This is the power for salvation to all who believe. In him we live and move and find our true selves. Praise your holy name! Amen.

DAY 7

Now have come the salvation and the power and the kingdom of our God and the authority of his Messiah. For the accuser of our brothers and sisters, who accuses them before our God day and night, has been hurled down. They triumphed over him by the blood of the Lamb and by the word of their testimony; they did not love their lives so much as to shrink from death. (Revelation 12:10–11)

I thank you, Lord, for all your faithful witnesses who have come with words of hope, faith, and love; who have acted with courage, patience, and sacrifice to set people free; whose words and deeds have revealed the love of Jesus; for those who challenged our way of life, our prejudices, and our unrighteous notions and drawn us closer to the One who makes all things new; for those devoted servants who down through the centuries have changed history; for those who, through the power of the Holy Spirit, have preached and taught the Word, setting people free from sin, injustice, and all that spoils life as you intend for all. I praise you, Almighty God, that through Jesus and the power of the Spirit we can be free to worship you in truth, to serve you in love, and to witness of your glory to those across the street and around the world. O Lord, use our words, thoughts, and deeds to set captives free into the glorious liberty of your kingdom. For the sake of Christ and the sake of all for whom he laid down his life we pray. Amen.

WEEK FORTY–SEVEN

DAY 1

One thing I ask from the LORD, this only do I seek: that I may dwell in the house of the LORD all the days of my life, to gaze on the beauty of the LORD and to seek him in his temple. (Psalm 27:4)

Come, Lord Jesus. Be near us here and now. As we gather to sing and pray and hear your Word, rekindle in us an abiding hope, a passionate love, an abundance of joy, and a deep, satisfying peace. You were long expected and so greatly needed when you first came into our world of space and time. Help us to live everyday confessing our need and expecting you to show up in our lives, to comfort our troubled hearts, to help us in our weakness, to forgive and free us of our sins, to heal our broken bodies, and to restore our weary souls. Help us to pray with absolute hope and radical obedience to your good and perfect will. Our Savior and Friend, be near us here and now. Renew our spirits and restore our joy. Come, Lord Jesus. Amen.

PRAYERS FOR THE JOURNEY

DAY 2

Very early in the morning, while it was still dark, Jesus got up, left the house and went off to a solitary place, where he prayed. (Mark 1:35)

O Lord, my God, I come to you out of the darkness of the night into the light of this new day. There will be many experiences today that will tempt and try me, moments that can steal my joy and frustrate the possibilities of your grace. Already, I am tempted to roll over, close my eyes and my mind to all of that, and let others bear the burdens of the day. But I hear your gentle voice once again inviting me to embrace your companionship and continue with you on the journey wherever it may lead. By your Spirit, you are re-creating me and through me making possibilities of grace available to others. I am a Christ-follower, and so I gladly rise and resolve that, *This is the day the Lord has made. I will rejoice and be glad in it!* In the name of Jesus, the One who makes all things new, I pray. Amen.

DAY 3

It is right for me to feel this way about all of you, since I have you in my heart and, whether I am in chains or defending and confirming the gospel, all of you share in God's grace with me. God can testify how I long for all of you with the affection of Christ Jesus. (Philippians 1:7–8)

Today, O Lord, I am thinking of those whom you have given me the privilege of sharing this life journey: colleagues with whom I have served near and around the world; friends in my local church and throughout the community; those who walked the path with me for a season and are no longer among us; those who shared only a moment in my life yet were there when I needed them; those who guided my path with their passion, wisdom, and love. I thank you for all the laughter and the tears; for the joys and the sorrows we have shared; for things we discovered together which we would not have found by ourselves; for thinking, doing, listening, and learning. Good and gracious God, I thank you for the words and deeds of those who have been life-changers for others, bringing the gospel of hope to those who are broken, the message of love to those who are lonely, the message of forgiveness to those who were wrong, and the message of encouragement to those without joy. I love this journey with Jesus and his friends. The joy we share as we sojourn together is like no other. Praise your holy name. Amen.

DAY 4

Christ loved the church and gave himself up for her to make her holy, cleansing her by the washing with water through the word, and to present her to himself as a radiant church, without stain or wrinkle or any other blemish, but holy and blameless. (Ephesians 5:25–27)

Lord Jesus, you have done for us, the body of believers, what we could never do for ourselves. We are your witnesses of that finished work through our faith and service. You called us out to proclaim to every generation throughout the world what you have done and can do for our salvation and sanctification. You have not called us to success but to obedience as we deliver this gospel message for the redemption of the world and to the glory of God. As your Bride, we pray to be radiant in love, holy in devotion, and blameless in character. Only through the riches of your infinite grace are we made worthy of your holy name. Only in the power of the Spirit can we do the works of God. May it be so in my life, Lord Jesus, and through your Church across the street and around the world, we pray for your sake and for the sake of all you love. Amen.

DAY 5

And God is able to bless you abundantly, so that in all things at all times, having all that you need, you will abound in every good work. (2 Corinthians 9:8)

Lord Jesus, I want to thank you today for the difficulties in my life that reveal the limits of my ability and my need to trust in your complete availability. This is where you want me to be and where I find you, along with the sufficient grace to do what is needed according to your will. Along this journey I am learning that when I walk ahead of you out of arrogance or lag behind you out of disappointment, I tire and conclude there is no way. But when I walk closely with you, regardless of the circumstances, you make a way forward even when there seems to be no way. And so, I ask that you help me remember the riches of your grace you have lavished upon us that I may get back on my feet and share in the joy of the journey with you. Thank you, Jesus, for guiding and keeping me on the Way. Amen.

DAY 6

In the same way, let your light shine before others, that they may see your good deeds and glorify your Father in heaven. (Matthew 5:16)

O God, as those who repent of our sins and believe the gospel that Jesus delivers us from the power of sin, we pray that our lives will produce fruit that is a witness of your redeeming grace. Save us, we pray, from the tyranny of the urgent and the drudgery of the routine that overshadow the reality of your good and perfect will. Reveal to us amazing and exciting possibilities to give witness to the power of the gospel: filling our cups with cool water and reaching out to thirsty persons; giving both our shirts and our coats to those who have none; sharing our bread with those who are hungry; walking not only the mile required of us but in the strength of love, going the second mile. O Lord, make us worthy as your witnesses, eager and ready to welcome others under the canopy of your steadfast love and saving grace into the fellowship of the Spirit. In word and deed, may we truly be the Body of Christ in whom others will recognize and welcome the Savior who loves them. For your name's sake and for the sake of all you love, we pray. Amen.

DAY 7

For God so loved the world that he gave his one and only Son, that whoever believes in him should not perish but have eternal life. For God did not send his Son into the world to condemn the world, but to save the world through him. (John 3:16–17)

I thank you, O Lord, that there are no boundaries to your love. Whether we do good things or whenever we do wrong, you never stop loving us. You care about us when we are unkind, selfish, hurtful, and angry. Your eyes are continually on each of us when we go our own way, get lost, and look for excuses to blame others. You don't quit on us; rather, you grieve as we reject and resist your love. You always want the best for us—and you are the best for us. How amazing that it is your grace, not our grit, that changes us; it is the power of your love, not the performance of our lives, that brings us deep peace, real joy, and abiding hope. It is because you have done for us on the Cross what we could never do for ourselves that none of us is hopeless. Defeat is not the final word. Endings become beginnings, and regrets are redeemed. O Lord, our Savior and Friend, do not let us take this wonderful gift of life for granted and refuse to change and be changed. Create in us clean hearts that we may see you more clearly. Renew a right spirit in us that we may follow you more nearly. Restore the joy of your salvation in our souls that we may love you and each other more dearly. Convince us to embrace the unlimited possibilities of your grace. Come, Lord Jesus. Fill us with your love. Amen.

WEEK FORTY–EIGHT

DAY 1

Blessed are you, Simon son of Jonah, for this was not revealed to you by flesh and blood, but by my Father in heaven. And I tell you that you are Peter, and on this rock I will build my church, and the gates of Hades will not overcome it. (Matthew 16:17–18)

At the beginning of a new week, O Lord, I praise your holy name for all things bright and beautiful, all creatures great and small, all things wise and wonderful—all that you looked upon at the end of that first week and called "good." I praise you for the crown of your creation, humankind, whom you called "very good." I especially thank you for your people, the Church, who lovingly have included me in their lives with compassion, patience, forgiveness, encouragement, mercy, and justice. Help me to recognize their brightness and beauty at all times and to value our life together for the wonderful gift it is, has been, and will be forever as the family of God. As we continue on this journey to spiritual wholeness, speak to my heart that I may have the courage to do what is right and true, the passion to pursue what is good and holy, the joy of re-creation, and the power of the Resurrection. This is the day you have made, O Lord, a day for the people of God to worship, grow, and serve. I will rejoice and be glad in it! Through Christ our Lord I pray. Amen.

DAY 2

Because your love is better than life, my lips will glorify you. (Psalm 63:3)

Bless the Lord, O my soul, and all that is within me, bless his holy name! I bless you, Lord, for all the reasons I have to praise you today: for life shared with family and friends; for the memory of loved ones whom I no longer see; for the promise of a day well spent. I bless you for prodding me and pushing me into joy and celebration with spoken words and silent gestures; with laughter and hugs and pats on the back; with unexpected gifts and pleasant surprises. I bless you, Lord, for this living Word that explains my heart this morning: "For the LORD is good and his love endures forever; his faithfulness continues through all generations" (Psalm 100:5). I bless you, Lord, for the breath I have with which I praise your Holy name. I will magnify you with thanksgiving today and every day, in the name of Jesus, the name above every name and the only name by which we are saved. Amen.

DAY 3

Whoever wants to be my disciple must deny themselves and take up their cross daily and follow me. (Luke 9:23)

Jesus, you call us to follow you before a watching world that thinks so little of you. We prefer to assume that the world is appreciative, accommodating, and accepting of your values and priorities. However, we inevitably come to a crossroads where we must decide if we are willing to follow you whatever the cost. You expect us to make a hard and radical choice that divides rather than unites, offends rather than affirms. "Those of you who do not give up everything you have cannot be my disciples," you said (Luke 14:33). As your disciples, we continually live with the clash of values of this world system and your call on our lives. We are either all in or not in at all. Our decision to love, trust, and follow you shapes all the other decisions of our lives. Only by your grace and through the power of your Spirit can I prove to be your disciple. This is my choice, every day. I am on this journey with you, and there is no turning back, so help me, Lord Jesus. Amen.

Day 4

For this reason I remind you to fan into flame the gift of
God, which is in you through the laying on of my hands. For
the Spirit God gave us does not make us timid, but gives
us power, love and self-discipline. (2 Timothy 1:6–7)

L ord, I am sorry for those times when I have let fear rule my life instead of you. I am sorry for the times when my fears have led me to sin—thinking that you cannot provide for my needs and therefore assuming to satisfy them myself—often in destructive ways. I am sorry for the times I try to control and manipulate people and situations because of my fear and lack of trust that you already are at work. I am sorry for avoiding people and worse because of my fear of loving others and being loved by them. I am sorry that in seasons of change I have allowed fear in the unknown to arrest my soul rather than firmly, confidently holding on to you to inspire me to a glorious future. For these sins of commission and omission, I ask for your grace and forgiveness and a fresh outpouring of your Spirit over my soul. In your mercy, displace my fears with the overwhelming peace, love, and joy of your Presence. Thank you, Jesus, that even when I am faithless, you are faithful. Amen.

Day 5

The path of the righteous is like the morning sun, shining
ever brighter till the full light of day. (Proverbs 4:18)

Holy God, you breathe life into every day. You fill our days with hope lest we live in fear and despair. You renew mercies lest we be slaves to guilt and regret. You promise joy in the morning lest we become overwhelmed by sorrow in the night. We admit, Lord, that we are more often inclined to focus on the dark clouds and disappointments than to look for silver linings and possibilities. We let gray skies cover our souls and block out the rays of your grace. We let rain dampen our spirits and spoil the showers of your blessings. So often we allow the forecast to order our spirits rather than allowing your Spirit to order our day. You opened the eyes of the blind to see what they had never seen. Open ours eyes to see you in the beauty of holiness. Open our hearts to experience and express the fullness of your love. Open our ears to hear words of eternal life, hope, and peace. Open our minds to the mind of Christ that we may learn how to order our days and bask in the sunshine of your amazing, sanctifying grace. In the name of Jesus, the Bright and Morning Star. Amen.

Day 6

"Love the Lord your God with all your heart and with all your soul and
with all your mind." This is the first and greatest commandment. And the
second is like it: "Love your neighbor as yourself." (Matthew 22:37–39)

Holy God, we rejoice that you have made us in love and for love. We are made in your image, and you placed within us a desire for companionship and trusted us to form holy and lasting covenant relationships. You are worthy of all our love, yet we confess that we have not loved you with all our hearts, minds, souls, and strength. We have not loved our neighbors and have avoided the stranger. Forgive us, Lord, when we have sought to remake others to fit our needs rather than seeking to be and love like Jesus, serving their needs. In your mercy, forgive what we have been, amend what we are, and help us to become what we may be, that we may honor you and bless others in your name. May we delight to do your will and walk in your ways, we pray, in Jesus' name. Amen.

DAY 7

Praise be to the God and Father of our Lord Jesus Christ, the Father of compassion and the God of all comfort, who comforts us in all our troubles, so that we can comfort those in any trouble with the comfort we ourselves receive from God. For just as we share abundantly in the sufferings of Christ, so also our comfort abounds through Christ. (2 Corinthians 1:3–5)

You have called us, God of all comfort, to service as grace-bearers, helpers to help others along the journey. This is a high and holy privilege to share in the sufferings of Christ, bearing the burdens of others crushed by the sorrows and weight of the world. But we are of little or no use if we only show empathy and compassion, perhaps even shedding a sympathetic tear. May we become wounded healers who have found your comfort in our pain, your strength in our weakness, your healing in our brokenness, your saving grace in our sinful hearts. "As a mother comforts her child, so will I comfort you" (Isaiah 66:13). This is your promise, this is who you are, and this is what you have done and will do for all who draw near. Out of our brokenness and in the power of your healing grace, let us be comforters who bring the broken-hearted to Jesus, the One who surely has borne our griefs and carried our sorrows. Praise your holy name. Amen.

WEEK FORTY-NINE

DAY 1

In him we were also chosen, having been predestined according to
the plan of him who works out everything in conformity with the
purpose of his will, in order that we, who were the first to put our hope
in Christ, might be for the praise of his glory. (Ephesians 1:11–12)

Dear God, I want to thank you for the close, personal relationships I enjoy in the community of faith, my church family. Thank you for the joy I share with new and old friends, the delight on the faces of children in worship and play, the grace of our elderly friends as they fold their hands in prayer, and the devotion of our leaders to fulfill our mission to make disciples of Jesus Christ across the street and around the world. I pray for the Church to be faithful in maintaining worship that rightly honors you; in edifying believers to be formed in the image of Christ; and in sending disciples beyond the walls to share the gospel in word and deed. I pray for every one of us who is known by your name to be Spirit-filled and Spirit-led as we continue on this journey together. For the sake of your kingdom and all you love, I pray in Jesus' name. Amen.

DAY 2

But I trust in your unfailing love, my heart rejoices in your salvation. I
will sing the LORD's praise, for he has been good to me. (Psalm 13:5–6)

I praise you, Creator God, for this beautiful and amazing world you created and are still creating. I praise you for the gift of time that allows me to grow in grace, love, and understanding. I praise you for the diversity of the human family that forces me to open my heart and mind more broadly every day. I praise you for the daily struggles that reveal my need of more grace. I praise you that my need of more grace creates an intense desire for more of your grace which you are willing to give. I praise you for the opportunities I will have today to be more gracious especially toward those with whom I disagree. And

I praise you that you are patient, willing to wait on us and work in us until you complete that which you began. My Lord, if you are willing to give such time for me, I must make more time for you. Let it be so. In Jesus' name. Amen.

Day 3

And I heard a loud voice from the throne saying, "Look! God's dwelling place is now among the people, and he will dwell with them. They will be his people, and God himself will be with them and be their God. He will wipe every tear from their eyes. There will be no more death or mourning or crying or pain, for the old order of things has passed away." (Revelation 21:3–4)

Almighty God, Creator of the heavens and the earth, I thank you that you are near to me in this place, at this time. I do not need to pray as though you are far away from me. You have taken the initiative to come to us—walking in the garden in the cool of the day with the first man and woman; entering our space and time, born of a woman, taking on our flesh and blood, living and moving among us; coming as another presence, the Spirit, poured out upon all flesh. There have been times when I have felt your Presence more than my own. I have been troubled and confused, broken and bruised, and you were there as the Comforter who is beyond my understanding. You have not left me to my own devices when I have wronged another and betrayed love. You have come to me in moments of great desperation to help me make it through another day. You have come to me in singing and sighing, praising and praying. This is who you are. You desire to be near to each of us as if there was only one of us. Thank you that you come to us so we may know you are near at this very moment and forever. Because of Jesus. Amen.

DAY 4

From everyone who has been given much, much will be
demanded; and from the one who has been entrusted
with much, much more will be asked. (Luke 12:48b)

I praise you and thank you, most gracious and loving Lord, for the
blessings of today: the freshness of the dawn, the contentment of
good health, the freedom of making choices. All these good gifts, and
so much more, have come from you. They are yours to give and yours
to withhold. They are not mine to keep. I hold them in trust, and so
I pray, do not let these deceive me into a false reliance on my own
strength, worthiness, or entitlement. Only as I continue to depend on
you for all things and learn the secret of contentment in all conditions
can I rightly enjoy and generously share these blessings. Today, with
all the abilities of my mind, body, and soul, and with these gifts at
my disposal, may I honor you and bless others in your name. Use my
words, shape my thoughts, guide my hands, and open my heart to do
your will. I pray this for the sake of your kingdom and all you love, in
Jesus' name. Amen

DAY 5

The voice of the LORD is over the waters; the God of glory thunders,
the LORD thunders over the mighty waters. The voice of the LORD
is powerful; the voice of the LORD is majestic. (Psalm 29:3–4)

With your voice, O God, you spoke the universe into existence.
With your voice, you communed with the man and woman in
the garden as Friend with friends. With your voice, you called Abraham
to begin the journey to spiritual wholeness for all people and Moses to
lead your chosen people to possess their inheritance. With your voice,
you spoke through the prophets to the people to repent of their sin,
trust in your faithfulness, and obey your Word. The Word became
flesh, and when Jesus spoke, cripples were healed, fig trees withered,
water was turned into wine, the blind received their sight, the dead
were raised, sinners were forgiven, disciples were called, and the poor
in body and spirit believed the gospel. O Lord, there is nothing we can

imagine that your voice cannot say and cannot do. You have spoken through burning bushes, Balaam's donkey, and Bethlehem's star. You can write messages on walls, shut the mouths of lions, quench the flames of a fiery furnace, and stop a sudden storm on the Sea of Galilee. We love the sound of your voice. You speak over us words of love, hope, faith, joy, and life in the language we understand. You speak and set all things right. Forgive us, O Lord, for living a week, a day, or even an hour without hearing your voice, assuring us that you are near and guiding us all along the journey. Speak, Lord, for your servants are listening. Amen.

DAY 6

And his commands are not burdensome, for everyone born of God overcomes the world. This is the victory that has overcome the world, even our faith. (1 John 5:3b–4)

We cannot travel this road with you, Jesus, without confronting hope-extinguishers that try to rob us of the victory and peace of mind you promise. The enemy of our souls is relentless in deluding and discouraging us at every turn. We are tempted to accept such setbacks as the typical experience of a Christian pilgrim, conceding that defeat, disappointment, and discouragement are to be expected and tolerated. However, such a concession says more about us than about you; that is an admission of unbelief rather than a confession of faith. It is in such moments that faith in the One who is faithful can change everything. No matter how dark it is, no matter how troubling the situation, no matter how hopeless we feel, you can change the narrative as we open our hearts to you, fully believing that you are able to alter the story according to your divine purpose. We stand on the promise that greater is your Presence in our lives than the evil one who is in the world, lurking at every turn to kill, steal, and destroy. And so, we will sing and believe with the saints that faith is the victory that overcomes the world. Thank you, Jesus. In your strong name we pray. Amen.

DAY 7

I waited patiently for the LORD; he turned to me and heard my
cry. He lifted me out of the slimy pit, out of the mud and mire; he
set my feet on a rock and gave me a firm place to stand. He put a
new song in my mouth, a hymn of praise to our God. Many will see
and fear the LORD and put their trust in him. (Psalm 40:1–3)

There are some songs, Lord Jesus, we learn only in the valley. Oh,
we love to sing and shout your praises from the mountaintops. We
practice and perfect them so others will be blessed by their sound. But
the songs of the heart are born out of yesterday's personal experiences.
Some are our painful memories of heartache and heartbreak, some
are our testimonies of redeeming and sanctifying grace, and others
are songs of hope, faith-believing after experiencing the shadows. No
angel could ever write or sing these songs, for they have never been
where we have been nor felt what we have felt. There is a depth to these
songs where we met you, Jesus, in our deepest need and our greatest
joy. We have learned to sing songs of praise and lament, prayer and
celebration, hope and comfort. We bless and honor you, our blessed
Savior and Lord, as you teach us to sing songs of the unshakable
kingdom that has no end and the immeasurable love that will never
be exhausted. Amen.

WEEK FIFTY

DAY 1

Therefore go and make disciples of all nations, baptizing them in the
name of the Father and of the Son and of the Holy Spirit, and teaching
them to obey everything I have commanded you. And surely I am
with you always, to the very end of the age. (Matthew 28:19–20)

We rejoice with the angels today, O Lord, as people from diverse
cultures, languages, and communities across this globe make
public professions of faith, trusting Jesus Christ as Savior and choosing
to follow him as Lord. Hallelujah! Thank you for the renewal that will

come to the church through their devotion to Christ, their faithfulness in the face of adversity, the opportunities to share their story, their hope that inspires our faith, and the impact of their giving, serving, and loving others in your name. We pray for their sanctification as Spirit-filled, Spirit-led disciples. Establish them firmly in your Word. Give them a strong sense of your Presence as they pray. Help them engage and enjoy authentic community where they can worship, grow, and be sent to serve. Save them from the temptation to surrender purity of heart for popularity and goodness of spirit for cheap thrills. When they fail, let them not be ashamed to ask for help and when they seek help, let them find generous and graceful friends of Jesus. Thank you for calling these disciples, for the sake of your kingdom and for all you love. In Jesus' name. Amen.

DAY 2

Now when Daniel learned that the decree had been published, he went home to his upstairs room where the windows opened toward Jerusalem. Three times a day he got down on his knees and prayed, giving thanks to his God, just as he had done before. (Daniel 6:10)

My Lord, I come to this hour and place, in this posture, not because I must but because I long to feel you near. I come not because I am worthy or have anything of value to offer but to give you the glory and honor that is rightfully yours and yours alone. I come not even for my own benefit or to receive a blessing or affirmation but because you are worthy of all my praise and thanksgiving for all that you are, all you have done, and all that you promise. This is time well-spent day after day, this private moment when all that matters is between your heart and mine. The joy we share as we tarry here I pray, O Lord, may many more of my loved ones come to know. For the sake of your kingdom and all that you love, I pray in your most holy name. Amen.

Day 3

For you know that it was not with perishable things such as silver or gold that you were redeemed from the empty way of life handed down to you from your ancestors, but with the precious blood of Christ, a lamb without blemish or defect.... Through him you believe in God, who raised him from the dead and glorified him, and so your faith and hope are in God. (1 Peter 1:18–19, 21)

O Lord, my Lord, how majestic is your name in all the earth! I bow my head and lift my heart in praise and honor of your holy name. I pray that my thoughts today should not be focused upon anything that displeases you, the One who has given me the power to contemplate on things beyond this world of space and time. I pray that I should be satisfied with the things that meet my immediate wants and needs. I ask that you grant me the privilege to do something that demonstrates that my heart is set on things that are eternally significant. May I grow more content every day with the gift of eternal life freely given through Christ Jesus our Lord, and may I gladly share with others the hope that lies in my heart. May the answers to this prayer today exceed whatever I expect, to your honor and the glory of your name. Amen.

Day 4

I will repay you for the years the locusts have eaten—the great locust and the young locust, the other locusts and the locust swarm—my great army that I sent among you. You will have plenty to eat, until you are full, and you will praise the name of the LORD your God, who has worked wonders for you; never again will my people be shamed. (Joel 2:25–26)

There are times, O Lord, when I hear the voices of blame and shame, stirring up those memories of past regrets and failures. I am reminded of poor choices, lost opportunities, costly mistakes, and damaged emotions. I journeyed into the far country and lost my way. I hear the whisper of my accuser: *You can't undo the past*, and that much is true. Such experiences could lead me to be more clever, cunning and crafty, but then your voice breaks in: "Behold, I make all things new!" (Revelation 21:5 NKJV). When I shut out every other voice but yours and my own testimony of your saving and sanctifying grace, my life is neither confined nor defined by disappointment but hope, not regret but anticipation that the best is yet to come. You can make the past in my spiritual history as if it had never been, redeeming even the worst of those moments for your glory and eternal purposes. Thank you, Lord, that because of Calvary you have saved us to the uttermost. In your name we pray. Amen.

Day 5

For this reason I remind you to fan into flame the gift of God, which is in you through the laying on of my hands. (2 Timothy 1:6)

We pray today for all the young people who recently have opened their hearts to Jesus and have committed to follow him as their Lord. We rejoice with the angels in these new disciples who have made peace with Christ and now belong in the forever family of God. As pilgrims and sojourners on the journey, they will be challenged to walk daily with Jesus along the Way, letting go of every weight that impedes their progress yet taking up their own cross in self-giving service to others in his name. Their faith will be tested and tried, doubted and dismissed, resisted and rejected, but they also will learn how to love the Lord and others more deeply as they share in the sufferings of Christ. We pray, O Lord, for these precious children of God to be surrounded by the steadfast love of authentic Christian community, supported by Spirit-filled mentors and friends, and sealed by the Holy Spirit, that they may be safe and secure from the fiery darts of the evil one. Thank you for the hope and inspiration they bring to believers across the world, that you are calling, equipping, and sending a new generation of disciples to make disciples across our streets and around the world. May they have no reserve, no retreat, and no regrets on their journey to spiritual wholeness, for the sake of your kingdom and all you love. In Jesus' name. Amen.

Day 6

I desire to do your will, my God; your law is within my heart. (Psalm 40:8)

Thy will be done. Jesus, this is how you prayed in the garden and how you taught your disciples to pray. These four words truly are the deepest desire of our hearts, yet we can pray them too carelessly, simply reciting them by memory, or very carefully, fearful that "Thy will" is something obscure and so different from what we prefer. Help us believe that at the heart of "Thy will" is your promise of freedom and joy, fulfillment, and peace. Help us understand that "Thy will" is the only experience you desire for every one of us. Help us feel your pleasure as we humble ourselves, pray, and seek your face and embrace "Thy will." In those dark moments when we are troubled and uncertain, frustrated and fearful, help us find that your grace is sufficient as we dare to believe that ultimately "Thy will" shall be prevail on earth and in our lives as it is in heaven. Jesus, hear us as we pray these four words with the full surrender and devotion of our hearts as you showed us and taught us how to pray: *Thy will be done.* Amen.

Day 7

The Word became flesh and made his dwelling among us. We
have seen his glory, the glory of the one and only Son, who
came from the Father, full of grace and truth. (John 1:14)

Come, Lord Jesus, into a world that is twisted and broken by sin, that lives in fear, hate, and self-despising. Convict us of our hard hearts, of all that deeply grieves you and causes us to harm others. Convince us of the possibilities of grace so that we may be healed, hopeful, and compassionate. Come, Lord Jesus, give us your strength and fill us with passion for what is holy and true. Teach us as we follow you and let us speak freely of our faith, boldly out of hope and generously with love. Come, Lord Jesus, renew your Spirit in our spirits as we worship you in the beauty of holiness. Give us unalloyed joy in your Presence and genuine love for our brothers and sisters. Come, Lord Jesus, and let the truth of your incarnation fill our souls again. Help us in this moment to see you in your glory, the One humbly born in a stable and crucified on a cross. Open our ears to words of hope, songs of praise, and testimonies of grace—sounds that obscure the din of a raucous world. Come, Lord Jesus, for we are your people, who pray in your name and for the sake of all you love. Amen.

WEEK FIFTY–ONE

DAY 1

For where two or three gather in my name, there
I am with them. (Matthew 18:20)

Lord Jesus, how often have you cared for the details in our lives that we have not appreciated—turning confusion into order, condemnation into acceptance, isolation into fellowship, fear into confidence, apathy into faith. Thank you for all the ways and all the times you show up. We especially thank you for taking the initiative to come to us where we are, in our space and time, our flesh and blood, our sin and guilt. You love us even when we have not loved you. Forgive us for failing to see that we cannot go it alone without going astray. Help us to realize that our way forward is in community, for wherever and whenever we gather in your name, you are faithful to be with us. Thank you as we begin this day together. Amen.

DAY 2

Come to me, all you who are weary and burdened,
and I will give you rest. (Matthew 11:28)

Lord Jesus, we come as we are today to become what you mean for us to be. We come as we are—broken, afraid, and full of disappointment—to be made whole and to be set free. We come as we are, with all our plans, dreams, joys, and sorrows, to be touched by your grace and held in your love. We come as we are because you invite us and welcome us to come. There is no other way for us to come. We come as we are to praise you, the One who is worthy to receive all honor and glory and praise forever and ever, even today. We come as we are, Jesus, because you came to us. Praise your holy name. Amen.

DAY 3

I eagerly expect and hope that I will in no way be ashamed, but will have sufficient courage so that now as always Christ will be exalted in my body, whether by life or by death. For to me, to live is Christ and to die is gain. (Philippians 1:20–21)

O God, let me never lose the eagerness to seek the best you desire nor the humility to trust you in the worst I can imagine. Let me never lose the willingness to examine my own heart and test the spirits. Let me always have a tender heart and an ability to weep. Renew my faith every day that I may believe and obey you with boldness. Let me see life as it is, not oblivious of its pain, suffering, betrayal, and loss. Rather, give me courage to pray, work, love, and serve you and all you love, fully engaged and fully confident that you will work all things together for the good for all who love you. And so, I will hope for your best today because you are good and faithful and your mercies endure forever. This I pray, with an eager, trusting heart, in Jesus' name. Amen.

DAY 4

Worthy is the Lamb, who was slain, to receive power and wealth and wisdom and strength and honor and glory and praise! (Revelation 5:12)

O Lord, our God, we come this morning in awe of your holiness, yet ushered into your Presence with your steadfast love. We come because we are in need of your mercy as we confess that we have not loved you or one another as you have loved us. We come in the confidence of your faithfulness, even though we have had our doubts, fears, and other moments of spiritual weakness. We come declaring your majesty and glory, for you alone are worthy to receive our worship, thanksgiving, and praise. We come because you called us and in you and only you we find abiding hope, unconditional love, unalloyed joy, and peace that passes understanding. We come before you in the wonderful name of Jesus, the Lamb of God, who came to us to take away the sins of the world, including ours. Hallelujah and amen!

DAY 5

How beautiful on the mountains are the feet of those who bring good news, who proclaim peace, who bring good tidings, who proclaim salvation, who say to Zion, "Your God reigns!" (Isaiah 52:7)

Eternal God, in every age you have raised up men and women who have heard your Word, responded to your voice, believed the gospel, trusted you as Savior, and followed you as Lord. They have joined other followers in proclaiming your name unashamedly, unapologetically doing what is right, liberally loving mercy, lovingly living in community, and humbly walking with you. We do not know fully how to pray as these servants need us to pray, but this we ask: that they will be strong friends to those who are weary and suffering because they name you as Lord; that they will encourage all who lack hope as they stand in danger at this hour because of their faith; and that they will be an occasion of the Holy Spirit to proclaim good news to the poor, bind up the brokenhearted, comfort those who mourn, and offer crowns of beauty, garments of praise, and anointings of gladness. May your faithful servants feel the love, support, hope, and joy of the community of faith that sends them with great joy and deep appreciation for their single-minded obedience to your will. And Lord, we pray for ourselves, that joined with those from ages past and those who serve you with full devotion today, we may inherit the kingdom you promised and rejoice before your throne forever with all the saints from every nation, tribe, people, and language. Come, Lord Jesus. Amen.

DAY 6

Do not deceive yourselves. If any of you think you are wise
by the standards of this age, you should become "fools" so
that you may become wise. For the wisdom of this world is
foolishness in God's sight. (1 Corinthians 3:18–19a)

We dare to pray a bolder prayer today, O God. We ask that you bless us with a restless dissatisfaction with easy answers, half-truths, and shallow relationships so that we may seek the truth bravely and love you and one another more fully. We ask that you bless us with holy anger at injustice, persecution, and prejudice so that we may work tirelessly for justice, freedom, and peace among all people. We ask that you bless us with broken hearts so we can weep with those who suffer from pain, rejection, hunger, or the loss of what they cherish. Help us as we reach out and comfort them with the comfort we have received. May their grief be transformed into joy. We ask that you bless us with enough foolishness to believe that in the face of doubt, unbelief, and cynicism, we, by your saving and sanctifying grace, are able to do what others claim cannot be done. This we humbly ask in your holy name, for your sake, and for the sake of all you love, Father, Son, and Holy Spirit. Amen.

DAY 7

Pray then like this: "Our Father in heaven, hallowed be
your name. Your kingdom come, your will be done, on
earth as it is in heaven." (Matthew 6:9–10 ESV)

We thank you, Lord, for slower days when we can reflect casually, be renewed spiritually, and be refreshed physically. May the peace of Christ and the stillness of your kingdom life, which is so different from the chaos and madness in this world, restore our souls. Help us to step aside and be quiet that we may hear you speak of what matters most. Help us to invest ourselves, our time, and our resources in that which has eternal significance, things that future generations will appreciate, preserve, and share with their children. And then, O Lord, help us to see as you see, that we may live into the vision of your kingdom for which we pray to come on earth as it is in Heaven. This we pray in Jesus' name, believing your kingdom is very near. Amen.

WEEK FIFTY–TWO

DAY 1

And the things you have heard me say in the presence of many witnesses entrust to reliable people who will also be qualified to teach others. (2 Timothy 2:2)

O Lord, we never come before you alone. We first heard your name through a member of the faith community. We have learned your Story as we listened to their stories, and we have come to believe because someone shared the spoken or written Word with us. Throughout our lives we have been surrounded by a great cloud of witnesses and supported by the faithful prayers of saints. Many of us heard your name from the moment of our birth. Others have learned your Story sitting at the feet of godly parents and grandparents. Through the faithful witness of your Word, teachers and preachers led many of us to trust you, love you, and follow you on the journey. Thank you for this long line of faith that creates our fellowship with the saints whose lives and witness have made disciples of Jesus across the years and around the world. We believe because others believed and lived faithfully. We pray because others have prayed for us and with us. Help us now as we make that journey of long obedience in the same direction as these faithful servants, telling your Story so others across our streets and around the world may trust in Christ, and Christ alone, for salvation. This we humbly pray, with thanksgiving, for yours is the unshakable kingdom that has no end and the immeasurable love that will never be exhausted. Amen.

DAY 2

I can do all this through him who gives me strength. (Philippians 4:13)

O Lord my God, I begin this day with a profession of my faith and hope. I will not be discouraged, for I know I am not alone. I will not fear, for I am loved with perfect love. I will not lose heart, for Christ in me is greater than every enemy of my soul. I will not lose my way, for your Word is my lamp and my light. I will not quit, for I am filled with the power of the Holy Spirit. I will not stay put, for you have called, I have answered, and I am now ready to go across the street and around the world to make a difference for the sake of your kingdom and all those you love. In the strong name of Jesus I pray. Amen.

DAY 3

Then they came to Elim, where there were twelve springs and seventy palm trees, and they camped there near the water. (Exodus 15:27)

This has been a very busy season in my life, Lord, and my soul is uneasy. There is business yet to be done, responsibilities unfulfilled, conversations unspoken, challenges to be faced, and needs to be met. I worry about too much, so I pray that you will help me now as I pause, return to the center of everything, and truly worship and adore you. In the joy of your consolations, may I realign my hopes and desires, my plans and my passions, my questions and my understandings, my confidence and my convictions. I tune my spirit to turn in your direction so that with faith restored, dreams amended, and hope renewed, I may serve you well today, for Jesus' sake and for the sake of the kingdom. Amen.

DAY 4

The LORD said to Moses, "Speak to the entire assembly of Israel and say to them: 'Be holy because I, the LORD your God, am holy.'" (Leviticus 19:1–2)

Lord, you call me to yourself, and you call me to be holy. I can only come to you as you draw me to yourself, and I can only become holy as you impart to me your holiness. You have not called me simply to do holy things. You call me to be holy, and only by your grace can I become something I am not. It is in the full, unconditional surrender of my right to myself that you can claim my whole heart and begin that process of making me the person I was created to be. And so, I do not ask for more power to imitate your holiness but for more grace to love you and all that you love. Convict me of my need of a holy heart, O Lord, and then convince me that you are willing right now to satisfy the deepest longings in my soul. This I ask in Jesus' name, the only name by which we are saved. Amen.

DAY 5

Jesus Christ is the same yesterday and today and forever. (Hebrews 13:8)

Lord Jesus, you promised that you would be with us always, even to the end of the age, yet we are discovering that life on this journey is not easy. There are times, even when we are surrounded by many others, that we are more aware of our distance than our closeness. Loneliness is part of our human condition, and we often feel its power. We cannot expect anyone fully to understand us; we do not even understand ourselves. Yet, your promise remains—You do not forsake us. You understand who we are, why we are, and what there is in each of us that you are creating. Jesus, be near those feeling the loneliness of being responsible and making decisions. Give them wisdom and peace. Stand with those who are standing alone in the face of enormous pressure to conform against your will. Give them courage and strength to endure. Through every season of loneliness, draw us into a more intimate relationship with you and the community of faith, where we can experience your redeeming grace, unconditional love, and the unalloyed joy that befits a child of God. This we pray for the sake of all you love. Amen.

DAY 6

Blessed is the one who does not walk in step with the wicked
or stand in the way that sinners take or sit in the company
of mockers, but whose delight is in the law of the LORD, and
who meditates on his law day and night. (Psalm 1:1–2)

You, O Lord, are the Redeemer of our yesterdays, the Strength of
our todays, and the Hope of our tomorrows. Show us how to move
beyond the limits of yesterday's dreams, to care beyond the boundaries
of what matters today, and believe beyond the scope of what we dare
to imagine. Refresh us, Holy Spirit, so we can pray large prayers. May
our troubled hearts find peace and our depressed minds find joy. In
our loneliness may we find friends, and in our grief let us find comfort.
In the face of difficulties beyond our control, may we find confidence
and courage to continue doing what is right and true and good. In our
wandering may we find mercy, and in our seeking, may we find saving
grace. Bless this fellowship of believers known by your name so that
as pilgrims on the journey to spiritual wholeness, we will honor you in
our prayers and songs and bless others in deeds of mercy and love. For
the sake of your kingdom on earth and to the glory of Jesus our Lord
we pray. Amen.

DAY 7

Benediction

Do not pray for easy lives; rather, pray to be strong men and
women, boys and girls. Do not ask for a task equal to your power;
rather, ask for power that is greater than any task. Then, the doing of
the work will be no miracle, but you will be the miracle, and you will
be constantly amazed at what you can do and what you become by
the grace of our Lord Jesus Christ living within you. It is to him that
we give all honor and blessing and praise, as we go forth in his name,
remain in his peace, celebrate his joy, and filled with his love, make a
difference in the world. Amen. (Adapted from Phillips Brooks)

SCRIPTURE REFERENCES

Old Testament

Genesis
12:1–4a	16
32:24	212

Exodus
3:17	16
14:14	17
15:27	237

Leviticus
11:44–45	188
19:1–2	237

Numbers
6:24–26	87

Deuteronomy
4:9	200
6:23	14, 19
7:9	63
29:29	153
31:6	199

Joshua
1:9	136

1 Samuel
3:10	168
15:22	181

1 Kings
19:11–12	180

1 Chronicles
28:9a	30

2 Chronicles
7:14	23
16:9a	24

Nehemiah
8:10b	138

Job
42:1–3	108

Psalm
1:1–2	239
4:1	139
4:4–5	201
5:3	33
8:3–4	89
13:5–6	223
16:5–6	189
16:7–8	129
16:11	119
18:6	153
19:14	90
23:4	22
23:6	174
25:4–5	94
27:4	214
27:14	123
29:1–2	141
29:3–4	225
32:1–2	117
32:8	126
33:20–22	169
36:7–9	116
40:1–3	227
40:8	67, 231
42:11	149
46:1–3	132
46:10	60, 98
51:10–12	49

New Testament

PRAYERS FOR THE JOURNEY

Made in the USA
Las Vegas, NV
26 November 2021